T0366086

I am a Standupster

A Second-Generation Holocaust Survivor's Account
by the Daughter of David Zauder

Karen Zauder Brass

authorHOUSE®

AuthorHouse™
1663 Liberty Drive
Bloomington, IN 47403
www.authorhouse.com
Phone: 1-800-839-8640

Published by AuthorHouse   11/30/2012

ISBN: 978-1-4772-7993-9 (sc)
ISBN: 978-1-4772-7992-2 (hc)
ISBN: 978-1-4772-7991-5 (e)

Library of Congress Control Number: 2012919714

Acknowledgments

Thank you, David Brass, my husband, who has huge belief in my many purposes for writing this book. He afforded me the amount of time away from my family responsibilities to concentrate on completing this endeavor. As well as gifting me by spending his time to edit my original first draft. I give him much kudos for holding the reins while I wrote. I offer sincere thanks to both of my children, Shannah and Adam, who understood the importance of giving me quiet time so I could complete this book.

David and Karen Z. Brass—est. 1996

Deep gratitude and appreciation is extended to Jim Floyd of Altitude Media Productions, www.ampvid.com, for his support and unyielding belief in my vision. Jim made me hundreds of DVD's for my website, and has supported my speaking engagements for years. Sometimes, while not even being asked to be there, he was there to document the legacy.

Special thanks to Demond Jefferson, who put up with my energy, antics, and unstoppable questions. Believing that I had an important story to tell, he also understood that I am writing about civil rights and human rights for all, and this message spoke to him as well.

A huge debt of gratitude is owed to Greg McBoat, www.gregmcboatphotography.com, a great photographer who turned a moment in time into a lifetime of memories. His photos are found both on the cover of this book and throughout its pages.

Sincere thanks to Royce Williams, who has heard me speak, knows my family and me well, and who was my first chapter editor. Thanks to my special friends who cheered me on: Doug Hahn who believed my secrets needed to be shared for the greater good, Audrey G. Friedman who always reminds me to slow down and breath, Susie {Webb} Garner who has known me since we were three years old, Jodie Goldstein who feeds my soul, Darcy Yates who is always supportive in all I endeavor, Audrey Friedman Marcus who gave of her valuable time in the early stages to share valuable editing suggestions, KatieJoe McDonough who is also a cancer survivor and a believer, and deep thanks to Nancy Mack, a graphic goddess, who helped me to develop my Standupster logo, among other things! To Eva Metzger Brown, for her insightful comments, validation of my childhood self and her unwavering support and investment in me, as well as in all of our Second-Generational issues through her professional work.

A giant thank you to Lisa Jefferson, my kind and insightful "book doctor" from A Book Nerd Company, for helping me to complete this important book in record time, and in time for my father to hold it in his hands.

Thank you to each and every one who read and endorsed my book. I could not have been more supported.

Those who know me well know that I am willing to do everything in my power to do my best. They also are acutely aware of how often I make mistakes, have difficulty speaking and writing and using the English language properly. My closest friends have witnessed and know of the extra work I must do to accomplish my best. I thank them for their continuous support and encouragement during this very personal project.

To contact me for a Standupster® Presentation, to provide funding to support programming or to learn more, or to order presentation materials go to:

www.standupsters.com or contactus@standupsters.com

Dedication

To David Seth Brass; my love, my beshert, my best friend and my husband; You are my hero!

To Shannah Rose Brass; for your big heart and your commitment to Tikkun Olam. Watching you grow, work harder than anyone I know, strategizing around your learning differences and difficulties and for being an advocate for yourself; you will be my joy forever!

To Adam Gabriel Brass; for proving nothing is impossible in this world, for your hard work ethic and perseverance, for your loving kindness, for being my growth catalyst, I am in awe of you and your journey and I am grateful to be bearing witness to your life. You are a gift of love in my life.

To my father, David Zauder; YOU KNOW I LOVE YOU!

Foreword

My daughter, Karen, has honored me in many ways, which have sustained my psyche of self-esteem, and given me personal validation that has helped me to maintain my sanity. She has undertaken to use my life experiences and their effect on her for addressing school students in their education of human values. Karen has created her project of Standupster®, using her Holocaust education to address the growing epidemic of bullying in our school systems. This epidemic of has caused countless traumas due to the lack of education and understanding of what actually causes bullying.

My life experiences as a Holocaust survivor can demonstrate the violence and tragedy that can result from bullying. Karen has honored me by using some of the details of my experiences being "bullied by professionals", as I have been known to state, during the Holocaust and World War II. Her Standupster® program, which she teaches in the schools as well as in other forums, has been completely effective and successful, proven to have very positive and long lasting results as demonstrated by the thousands of letters written by students and teachers, staff and parents.

To say that I am proud of her and of her efforts and appreciate her commitment to community service is a gross understatement! I am extremely lucky to have witnessed my daughter's growth to fruition, which has also brought me great personal satisfaction.

The events depicted and referred to in this book reflect what occurred during my life and within our family. Any other information is of such a private nature as to be inappropriate to disclose at this time due to the young age of my grandchildren. Karen Z. Brass is my "Memory Keeper" and Advocate. With the full awareness that she will use and share our experiences for the benefit of our and other Holocaust surviving families, and those who have witnessed or suffered genocide, individual persecution, ie: "bullying", I give her my permission and I hereby transfer all intellectual property and give her full rights in the use of my story now and in the future in any form; by book, media or for personal use in her public speaking and educational forums.

My daughter, Karen Z. Brass, is a college-educated teacher, a successful small business owner and community leader, an advocate and activist, as well as now president of her own company, Can I Count On You LLC. She turned her Standupster® program into a nonprofit organization as well. She is also the mother of two special-needs children, who would have become targets of bullies if it were not for her consistent advocating and teaching those around them how to make better choices. She has helped me to accept my past and I value our life together.

I love her.
David Zauder

David Zauder and Karen Zauder Brass

Contents

Chapter 1
My Inspiration for Sharing

I want my book to inspire others to be a Standupster®. I both purposefully and intentionally want everyone to feel that it is incumbent upon us all to take action. To understand the devastating impact of Holocaust history on personal lives is a large request, but I believe people today can use this information to better our future generations. From mothers and fathers to sisters, brothers, cousins, and children, knowing and understanding the complex consequences for the second and third-generation exposed to their parents' and grandparents' damaged and injured psyches, we must work together now and no longer ignore the atrocities of today that affect our society, our community, our families.

> *In spite of everything, I still believe people are really good at heart.* ~Anne Frank

I hope that what I share here testifies to the strength of spirit and to the courage, respect, understanding, compassion, humility, acceptance, and finally forgiveness that it took many of my second-generation brothers and sisters and me to confront the truth. That truth is what ultimately allowed me to forgive my father's weaknesses and vulnerabilities as well as bring personal enlightenment and the promise of serenity to me as a second-generation Holocaust survivor. Having him join my family and me in his final stage of life, living with us since 2007, has been a culmination of all the work I was willing to do—personally, emotionally, and spiritually. My work as a teacher of Holocaust awareness and my anti-bullying campaign has been both my passion and my focus. In addition to my wife and mother roles, as well as my career and volunteer activities, being in a position to share my home with my father was a choice my husband and I both made.

My father's willingness to grow, change, and accept responsibility for what he did and did not do during my life, made for easier amends between us. His personal decision to change his MO, his modus operandi, allowed for successful growth within him, which allowed him to rely on others during his final stage of life; a unique change from the majority of his life. He has been a loner since he was ten years old, missing serious developmental stages while fighting to remain alive during the Holocaust. This explains some of the reasons why he behaved in the ways he did, but ultimately, in his adulthood, he made choices; choices that created distance between us. He was not personally there for me when I needed him, repeatedly choosing work over my need for his physical presence and emotional support.

My father's life has been very difficult at times. Certainly, before and during the Holocaust it was extremely so.

Since moving in with my family, he has needed many in the health care industry to help facilitate changes to his personal routine, especially in the past four years as his health declines. This is a very difficult stage for all aging people, but for my father, there are additional emotional and psychological complications. He has had much loss in his life and now loses additional physical stamina and abilities to enjoy doing all that he likes to do. Losing physical capabilities reminds him that without being able to perform work, duties, and tasks important to him, it becomes more and more difficult to prove his life is being earned. David Zauder needs to earn daily being alive—due to both survivors' guilt and his personal need to contribute something daily. When he sees all of us working and he cannot help physically, he feels useless and unworthy of being here. Unworthy of being alive. Losing freedoms like driving an automobile due to the side effects from medications he is now on is almost too much to bear, since he fought so hard to earn his freedom.

I work daily to pass on to our children the benefits of the gifts and life lessons I share in this book, while I hold them to a high level of personal responsibility, as they are third-generation Holocaust survivors. I hope I can be a memorial candle for them to shine a light into the dark places of their world and their heart. A memorial is in the honoring of the memory of others. Taken from what they've learned from someone now gone. In this book, I am sharing deep personal scars reopened through the eyes of a second-generation Holocaust survivor. I hope to give my children hope and a feeling of deep gratitude and motivate them to take action.

The importance of life is not to be minimized. Life is not to be wasted. How incredibly tragic it is that so many were deprived of becoming their full potential and, many others their lives during the Holocaust. How much richer the world could have been had they been allowed to make their full contribution. May we, together, ensure that there never is another Holocaust. May we recognize the importance of teaching human and civil rights to today's youth. The amount of bullying occurring today is abhorrent, and the damage done lasts a lifetime. The loss of lives from suicides due to intolerance and hatred also begs the question, what contributions would have been made if not for the loss of their lives?

> *We live in a world in which we need to share responsibility.*
> *It's easy to say it's not my child not my community not my*
> *problem. Then there are those who see the need and respond,*
> *I consider those people my heroes.* ~Fred Rogers

From Hell to Heaven was a title my father dreamed up for the book he is never going to write: the story of his life as a world-renowned classical musician, master teacher, administrator, Big Brother, community volunteer, friend, husband, father, as well as Holocaust survivor, refugee, and immigrant to the United States of America.

4

Unlike my father, I received one of the greatest blessings this world has to offer—I was born an American. But as a child of a Holocaust survivor, I find myself living simultaneously in two worlds—one as a normal person, a happily married wife, dedicated mom, daughter to my parents, sister to my only sibling, sister-in-arms with other second-generation Holocaust survivors, invested and trusted friend, volunteer, and successful businesswoman. And in the other world, I am a second-generation Holocaust survivor, who deals with post-traumatic stress disorder passed down through what feels like DNA, transmitted by the effects of my father's influences.

Sometimes, I feel as if I am failing to be my best in both worlds. Yet, because of all my father has been through—and because I am his daughter—failure has never been a real option.

My father is a pragmatist, a realist, and my mother is a believer and an activist, among other things. Because I'm a dreamer who takes action and follows through, I have chosen to capture and emulate some of the best of each of them. This is a source of strength for me.

So while this book is in large part about *my* life experiences as a second-generation Holocaust survivor and my passions, it is riddled with my father's joy and pain, his agony and his victories, because our lives are inextricably woven together for all time.

I have never felt qualified to write my father's biography, but I have long held that because of how his life touched mine, I can speak and share his story to teach others the power of acceptance and tolerance, of growth and loving another, of the rewards of celebrating our diversity, and focus on the importance of a strong work ethic. When we come together, we can make a real difference in this world.

I accomplish this goal one step at a time, one listener at a time, through a vigorous public speaking schedule in Colorado, where I live, as well as across the country and around the world. I believe strongly in civil rights, human rights, and being an activist. When I see things that need to be changed, I get involved and help to change them; it is a passion of mine. As a mother of two special-needs children, it became eminently clear to me that I needed to continue to be strong in my passions while I learn the laws that exist and work to change the ones that need to be challenged and rewritten to positively affect as many people as possible. All the while, teach my children to be self-reliant, self-motivated, self-aware, and self-assured. They both are strong self-advocates and know who they are. They are their granddad's grandchildren—third-generation Holocaust survivors.

On more than a few occasions, friends and acquaintances who have heard me speak have suggested that I write a book about my family history and life experiences, as well as a book about my personal victories in overcoming my personal learning disabilities.

The thought of writing a book was daunting, not just because it's a huge endeavor, but because one of my many challenges is dyslexia. My husband and my closest friends and I share values of doing our best in every endeavor, and we help one another. That's what made this book possible.

By helping me to obtain the time and freedom required to accomplish this feat—not to mention reading, commenting on, and editing my earliest drafts for this book—my husband and a few close friends have brought to fruition the work you now hold in your hands. To me, it is a priceless gift and truly a manifestation of what I preach—that *together* we are stronger!

When we stand up for what we know is right, we live without regret. I value the importance of not allowing oneself to be victimized in any way—emotionally, physically, mentally, sexually, or spiritually. If you know you are not willing to play the victim role, you will be strong, you'll find your mentors, your support system, and you will make your life better. A system within which to live for yourself will sustain you through the difficult periods. In my opinion, this is not only a choice; it is imperative for our youth today that we support and protect them and not allow them the opportunity to accept the role of victim. To empower them with the knowledge that they are strong and capable, even when they are surrounded by technology that is making their lives easier than we've ever had it in the past. We need them to be empowered to make the hard choices and to speak out and change the world for the better.

The actions we take today and the choices we make today can give us the ability in the future to look back on what we accomplished and feel proud. Make the hard choices and be proud!

I thank God for the wonderful people who helped me to make good life choices. I sought them out, I searched for good role models, and I still have many in my life today who have remained close to me. I don't feel I can ever repay them, but it won't keep me from trying.

My father was little more than a child when he survived unspeakable atrocities inflicted by one human onto another. Because of his determination to survive, I feel I honor him by protecting and promoting the hope and expectations he had in mind when he survived and chose to come to America and make his personal contributions.

I was a young child myself when I first began to understand that I have life only because he overcame impossible odds to survive, experienced pain, suffered and survived great loss to become an American. Then to become a husband and father, and to pass on his values and work ethic, he chose to contribute even more. Most of my life, I have been aware of an unspoken truth, as though he were saying, "I survived, and now you're here. What will you do to make *your* life worth it, worth the suffering I went through?"

My answer is, "I am here for a reason," and this book and my public speaking comprise a great part of my purpose. I truly hope that every person who spends time with me will feel empowered for having spent that time. I feel strongly that this is one of my many gifts. I am honored and humbled to bestow it upon others. I believe each of us is here on Earth for a reason. Each of us is embellished with gifts to share with others.

When I speak to audiences, my goal is to create simultaneous Holocaust awareness and to promote my anti-bullying campaign, which I call Standupster. My website; www.standupsters.com explains and shares much more.

If my father could overcome impossible odds to survive, how can I do anything but my best to conquer my own challenges today, as well. This is the essence of who I am. This is what I am sharing with you now.

When I stand before an audience, I am my father's voice. I seek to share his strength, his perseverance, his morality, and his unflagging determination to contribute something to this world. He is a remarkable man who has shared the stage with some of the most respected artists in classical music. But the truth is that much of what this proud immigrant has achieved was accomplished because of an unquenchable desire to prove his life was worth saving.

In sharing my story as a second-generation Holocaust survivor, I want others to know that the Holocaust continues to have long-lasting generational effects. I hope to instill in others the value of recognizing our common humanity in one another. We do not have to live through a tragedy to learn these lessons, only to know of them intimately, then to draw upon their strength and use it as our own. I want those I speak with to know that each of us has within us the power to reach our highest selves, if only we will embrace that power. I want people to know that it's not possible to hurt another without hurting ourselves.

I believe being a bystander today should be considered a criminal act. I recently saw a bus stop advertisement for Heineken beer. It had a picture of two people, one at the bar, and one about to leave with car keys in hand. The caption in capital letters read, *THERE ARE NO INNOCENT BYSTANDERS.* This is *my* message in five words.

In this book, I tell my story as a second-generation Holocaust survivor, as well as my father's story of survival and success; including thoughts my father has chosen to share through me. I have also included letters I have received from people who have heard my Standupster presentations and chose to change from the inside.

I believe these letters serve to help them to connect with the fact that their actions affect others, and it is their choice whether those actions will be positive or negative. They learn that their actions will cause joy or pain to others around them. I believe words within these letters will touch you deeply, as they have touched me.

> *If I am not for myself, then who will be for me? And if*
> *I am only for myself, then what am I? And if not now,*
> *when?* ~Rabbi Hillel

We really are all in this together and we *are* responsible for one another . . . for what we *see* happen and what we *allow* to happen on our watch. We must be willing to take action. This is *your* life; this is your moment, right now, today, and for those who cross your path today, you *can* make a difference.

Are you willing? After reading my story and hearing how you can be a Standupster too, I pray that your answer will be a resounding *yes*!

Karen Z. Brass

Chapter 2

My Story Begins Here

Truth has no special time of its own. Its hour is now-always. ~Albert Schweitzer

I am the daughter of an immigrant father from Kraków, Poland. He proudly gained United States citizenship after enlisting in the army in 1952. He is a refugee who survived the Holocaust and wore a tattoo on his left forearm in blue ink, which he never hid, given him by the Nazis. The Nazis murdered his parents. My mother, an only child, was born in Detroit, Michigan. Her father, Benjamin Ribiat, emigrated from Poland in the earlier part of the twentieth century with both of his parents and his sister. He too, had enlisted, but he was in the navy. He married my grandmother, Jean Gelman Ribiat, before he went to sea.

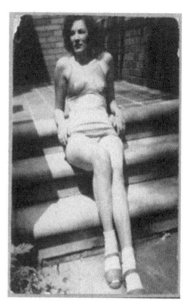

Ben Ribiat

Jean Gelman Ribiat

My earliest significant memory as a child growing up is how I was enrolled in Hebrew Sunday school. I was born in 1964 and lived in Cleveland Heights, Ohio, with my parents—my mother, Jeri Ardez Ribiat, and my father, David Zauder. After the Cleveland Orchestra hired my father, he moved to Cleveland, Ohio, from Detroit, Michigan, to continue his musical profession. After he settled in, he bought a house and invited my mother to join him, and they were married in 1960.

David Zauder and Jeri A. Ribiat's wedding

I became conscious of my family's special dynamics early on, and I felt I knew things at a deep level. I also felt I was to take action to prove I was worth being here on earth—living with a purpose. Because my father was a Holocaust survivor, he witnessed atrocities that no human should have had to endure. I felt strongly that I needed to make it worth it for him—prove to him that he survived for a good enough reason. I was here now because he survived. These thoughts entered my mind when I was six years old.

On a Sunday morning, while watching my favorite television shows, I announced to my mother that I wished to be a Catholic priest. I wanted to pray as my mother's best friend, Barbara Serr, did. I wanted to help people in the community like Bishop Sheen on *The Fulton Sheen Program (shown from 1961 to 1968)* television show. I also watched a Claymation cartoon called *Davey and Goliath*, a children's show, which I loved. That show was about a boy and his dog, and it taught moral lessons each week, which I yearned to learn.

Barbara Serr was Catholic, and I really enjoyed spending time with her and her family of five. They lived a few houses away from ours, and when I was with them, they prayed before eating at every meal, and I knew Barbara loved me. She treated me special, and I knew she understood my unique differences and supported me with respect and kindness every time I was at their house. I used to sneak over there, go upstairs, and slip under the heavy, quilted covers of her bed and feel hugged by her—safe and warm. Barb was one of my many angels.

At the time, I did not know which religion I was or what religion actually meant. I simply wanted my connection with God to be stronger. I knew God was in my life and in me, personally. I wanted to take action as a good person, and I wanted to do good work, much like the Catholic priest, Bishop Sheen.

I had no memories of being a Jew until the day I told my mother I wanted to be a Catholic priest. My father chose to keep secret from me his religion out of fear derived from his own issues as a Holocaust survivor. He had also apparently convinced my mother not to be religious in our home, even though she too had grown up as a practicing Jew. In fact, my mother told me that her grandfather was a founding father and a lifelong member of a synagogue. I had no memory of prayer. I believe my father didn't want to expose me, at my age of only six, to religion. He wanted to protect me from the hatred he had experienced as a child.

My announcement (to my mother's credit) was heard and taken seriously. She told me we were Jewish, so my desire to become a Catholic priest was not possible. She did inform me that we could pray, because Jews prayed too. Next, she told my father what I had said, and I thought I was going to die. Actually, I thought he was going to kill me right there. The look on his face was intense—anger and betrayal. I didn't understand his intensity and I was frightened. I knew my wishes had hurt him, but I didn't know why. I thought fearfully, why would my wanting to help others upset him so?

My mother strongly suggested that my Jewish education begin. She suggested that I enroll in Hebrew Sunday school at Park Synagogue, a conservative Jewish synagogue two blocks from the house. The house my father chose to buy was within two blocks of this conservative synagogue, and my father chose that house purposefully. After all, we did live in a Jewish neighborhood, and he had selected and purchased the home before he married my mother. He wasn't clear in deciding how to have a

Jewish identity in America when I began asking all these religious questions. He was rattled and full of fear. He wanted us assimilated!

I remember him saying at one time, ". . . going into a synagogue is just making it easier for 'them' to get us all in one place to blow us up." However, he did want me to have a Jewish education, as he believed education was paramount, and since I showed an interest in my culture, my heritage, my religion, they enrolled me the following week into the preschool program.

Park Synagogue, Cleveland Heights, Ohio

When I began attending the Hebrew school, I was shocked to learn that I belonged to a group of people with so many things in common who shared my way of life. We ate the same foods, sang the same songs, we had the same inflections of speech. So my family did live a Jewish life, we just didn't advertise it.

I was given Hebrew names upon entry into this new world of Park Synagogue. Seven days after a baby is born he or she receives Hebrew names; that is the custom, but my father had skipped this tradition when I was born. I had asked him why he did not give me any middle names. He told me that since all of his other family had been murdered and none lived in America, I did not need a middle name to be identified.

My Hebrew names given to me at seven years of age were Rosie, Etta, and Esther. Rosie; after my father's mother, Rose Lucks Zauder, who was murdered in the Holocaust. The second name was Etta; after my great-maternal grandmother, Etta Gelman. And finally I was given Esther; the name of my maternal grandfather, Ben Ribiat's mother's name.

My father was adamant that neither my brother nor I got an Americanized middle name. He told me on many occasions when I was older, that all the Zauders were killed in the Holocaust, therefore I did not need any additional names to determine who I was. The Hebrew names became special and additional to our actual American names. While at Park Synagogue, I was called Rosie.

I was named Karen because my mother had been an elementary school teacher, and her favorite student's name was Karen. She was a straight "A" student and very involved in Girl Scouts and had a Girl Scout sash filled with awards. I know this because my mother showed me a picture of this girl and told me I was named after her because she was perfect. I was okay with being named after such a wonderful girl, but in my heart, I knew I would never live up to my mother's expectations of being able to be anything like her. My father sometimes called me Kar-Kar, sounding like care-care. That was a strong message I didn't need to have repeated; I knew I was here to care for him.

My father was living in intense assimilation mode. He spoke five languages when he arrived in America: Polish, Yiddish, German, Czechoslovakian, and Russian, due to the training he had during the Holocaust to remain alive. He learned all those languages out of necessity; he needed to know what to do and where to go to stay out of the line of fire. Now he only speaks in English. He said he had to erase all the tapes of those five other languages in order to concentrate solely on English, to think in English—the language of America. Since America was in large part Christian, he wanted both of his children to fit in. I remember fondly attending multiple Christmastime parties through my parents' friends. However, I have no memories of celebrating Hanukkah or lighting a menorah until much later. In fact, to fit in, we had a Christmas tree.

I sat on Santa's lap, though not amused, I checked out.

Karl and I dressed for Christmas

The rules my father had for being an American were many. The top four were:

1. Assimilate.

2. Hide who you really are. Fit in. Do not advertise diversity.

3. Be quiet. Be good. Don't bring attention to yourself.

4. Suffer in silence.

I don't believe these rules were ever put in place so that they themselves were to be damaging to young children—emotionally or physically. I remember when I was in my thirties and someone asked my father, "What was it like raising Karen?" He answered without hesitation, "It was like she was never there."

My first thought was "Hurrah! I did it! I remained quiet, still, unemotional, and did not affect him in any harmful way! I had succeeded in not adding to his pain!" With as many disabilities as I had (dyslexia, nonverbal learning disorder, executive dysfunction, auditory processing disorder and a short working memory) this was a very difficult assignment, but I did it!

My next thought, was "How sad!" How sad for me to have been ignored and emotionally pushed aside purposefully to fuel his personal needs of maintaining control. I had to be silent. What if I said another thing that showed my slowness, my ignorance, or my naivety? If I did that, I would have proven to him that I would have never survived the Holocaust. How dare I not be a survivor like him! He never really knew who I was. It was so hard for him to connect with me.

Compton house with large pine tree planted
in my honor on right.

I knew he loved me; through his actions, I knew. He planted a tree at the corner of our house to honor my birth, which remains standing taller than the house today. Most loving communication was shown in silence—loving looks, gestures, and his inner emotions passed to me via our DNA, my intuitive understanding of my father's experiences, which he had yet to share with me directly.

A Zauder family portrait in Arizona.

My father selected my mother as his wife because she was a strong, beautiful, smart, and outspoken woman. Although she was not his best friend, he envisioned himself with a beautiful woman, a subordinate woman on his arm as he climbed the ladder of American success. She fit that role in the beginning. To be fair, to hear her side of the story, you would have to read her book. I'm certain it would be filled with explanations, insights, and deep thoughts. I always admired my mother for all that she accomplished. Despite her own disabilities and challenges, her perseverance and work ethic were stellar. However, this is not a book about her.

The American dream my father had envisioned included walking on streets paved in gold. That's what he was told when he lived in Poland, and he believed those stories. The idea that America had freedom and streets paved in gold were one of the many mistaken beliefs he encountered when he arrived in America. This was a disappointment, which served to be only the beginning of his personal journey, although he was extremely proud in becoming an American citizen.

I remember my father telling me a story about how beautiful his mother, Rose, was and how his father, Karl, required her to look perfect before leaving their one-room apartment. One day as she was leaving the apartment to go to town center for groceries, my grandfather yelled at my father to run after her and stop her in the courtyard and tell her that her stockings were not straight enough to be seen in public. Back then, stockings had a seam up the back. The expectation my grandfather had for his beautiful wife was that she look perfect.

On many occasions, my father has made similar comments to me about my hair, my lipstick shade, as well as my clothing. Because I knew the story from when I was a child, I knew his intent was not to insult or do harm, but rather to uphold a very high standard that had been passed down to him.

Sexist? Yes. Understandable while he was living between two worlds. Fair and appropriate? Not at all.

European standards didn't fit in with the culture of the United States of America. However, my father still had them, and they were drilled into him from his father. My father was in a constant state of realization that his reality, what he believed in, was often false. I felt protective of him from the beginning. Similarly to what I have read in the past decade by Eva Metzger Brown, PhD., in her Second-Generation care taking papers, which truly validated my early childhood memories.

My father's upbringing was seriously disturbed by anti-Semitism, the Nazi regime, World War II, the Holocaust, the murder of his father and his father's mother (his grandmother), his mother and her three sisters (his aunts whom he loved), and apparently two uncles and one aunt on his father's side he did not know until recently had even existed. It is unrealistic to expect him to have had the ability to understand and relate to my childhood. And for some unknown reason, I knew this about my father, and I accepted him for all that he was and was not able to give to me.

Due to the lack of parenting he experienced, finding himself an orphan during the Holocaust, my father was parentally deficient. Because of this deficit, he was not a good judge of character in choosing a woman who would make a good mother for his children. My mother relied upon both me and my younger brother to feed her needs and make her feel loved and appreciated.

While growing up, my mother often said, "If you loved me enough you would . . ." My mother's love was always conditional. To say I was feeling manipulated is an understatement. The guilt was massive and my failure rate for making her happy with my inabilities was a constant for me. My brother was better at communicating with my mother than I was. He didn't suffer from learning disabilities, and he fared far better because of his learned skills. My mother's parenting skills, or lack thereof regarding me, went unnoticed by my father. After all, I had a roof over my head, a dresser full of drawers with changes of clothing, three courses of food daily, and we were safe in America.

Me as a baby with steel braces on my feet

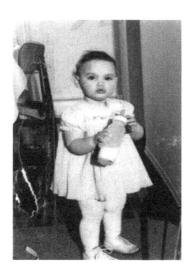

Standing finally at seventeen months old

Trying to run with pigeon-toed feet, falling often

My parents had a lot on their hands when I was born. I had some difficulties with my physical life. The doctor pulled my breached body out, breaking both of my thighbones, as well as my mother's pelvis. My father, as was customary at the time, was not allowed in the hospital room while I was being born. He could only pace outside and wait. He was full of fear, and he hoped that my mother and I would be cared for appropriately. They found out my legs had been broken, because the only times I cried was when they lifted me by my legs to change my diapers. So they did an x-ray and then casted my left leg, which was the worse of the two legs. Later, though I was still an infant, I wore steel braces, the ones that have a steel bar that runs between both shoes. After that, I needed corrective shoes, saddle shoes, to adjust to being badly pigeon-toed from the bones healing poorly.

My parents put me in ballet classes. The lessons were to help turn my feet out, which worked like physical therapy, but it put a lot of tension on my lower back, causing back pain and my pelvis to tilt internally, throwing off my body mechanics. I started ballet at the age of three with a referral from a doctor to help strengthen my legs and work with my pigeon-toed problem, which came following the braces and then the orthopedic saddle shoes.

During ballet lessons, I could not process the instructions fast enough to be doing the ballet activities without watching others first for nonverbal cues. Actually, this helped me with learning nonverbal cues because when

I got it wrong, my ballet teacher hit me swiftly with a long stick. I never told anyone. She also hit me when I bit my fingernails, so she cured me as a nail biter early. I took ballet for twelve years, and never once did I perform without having to look at my fellow classmates on both sides so I did not exit the stage in the wrong direction, which I did regularly early on.

Later, when I was twelve years old, after my parents' divorce, I received Rolfing, which is a deep tissue massage, initiated to move the muscle and tissue back to its correct position. Thanks to my mother and her insight, my severe pelvic tilt was corrected. I received this needed correction in lieu of her receiving a month's payment from a renter who was a Rolfer. He suggested he could help me. Painful, but it worked.

I was also provided with horseback riding, which served as hippotherapy for me. Hippotherapy is terrific for helping to build core muscle strength and stamina. In riding a horse correctly, the position a person's body is in affords correct alignment and it works core body muscles to develop stronger.

I was a horse enthusiast from the age of three. My father first put me on a pony to take photos, and every time he walked away from us to get distance for the photo, the pony walked right behind him. This sent me laughing hysterically to myself, because I would never laugh at my father while watching him in his frustration to take a photo. I have loved horses ever since.

When I took English horseback riding lessons, however, I could not understand the detailed oral directions. Often during those directional prompts, I was to steer my horse toward a lettered wall. I heard "B" when it was really "C" and "D" when it was "B." I quickly put coping mechanisms into place, strategies of following everyone else. I got proficient at reading the room.

Me riding on my white horse,
watching what others were doing.

Ballet class following my classmate to stay in step;
I'm on the right.

I also had many undiagnosed issues. Because of my auditory processing disorder—the inability to properly hear and process words and language and have my ears work simultaneously with each other to process the information heard—I had a short working memory. I also had executive dysfunction, which describes the missing skill set of goal setting, carrying out organized steps, and modifying a plan to complete a task successfully. These skills are important for learning from past experiences and applying this knowledge to new experiences. Attention, memory, impulse control, organization, planning, sensing time, and hierarchical thinking are the executive function-based skills that enable an individual to learn, generalize behaviors, and complete tasks.

On the couch sleeping and dressed wildly
with painted orthotic shoes

Another of my disabilities was a nonverbal learning disorder. "The NVLD syndrome reveals itself in impaired abilities to organize the visual-spatial field, adapt to new or novel situations, and/or accurately read nonverbal signals and cues. These are all social skills that are normally grasped intuitively through observation, not directly taught. If a child is constantly admonished with the words, 'I shouldn't have to tell you this,' something is awry. The child's verbal processing may be proficient, but it can be impossible for her to receive and comprehend nonverbal information. Such a child will cope by relying upon language as her principal means of social relating, information gathering, and relief from anxiety..." written by Sue Thompson, PhD. Being very literal becomes part of a strategy, as it did for me.

Since I also had dyslexia, even the verbal language was difficult for me to use and to hear, let alone to write. Dyslexia is a specific language-based learning disability. It refers to a variety of characteristics that result in people having difficulty in varying degrees with the language skills of reading, writing, spelling, and/or speaking. Research is showing that dyslexia is a neurological-based condition and that the brain of the dyslexic develops and functions differently from other brains. Not better, not worse, just differently.

I had to turn right from our house to walk the four blocks to school. To the left was the shopping mall. Finally, by the end of third grade, I had taught myself right from left. Going to the right was correct because that's where the school was; going to the left was wrong because that's where the shopping mall was located. I needed the kinesthetic learning to memorize right from left.

My relationship with my mother suffered due to these undiagnosed issues. She saw my actions as insubordinate and purposefully defiant. I simply could not retain information and use my short-term memory well enough or organize information given to me orally regarding instructions. I could not do what she asked of me daily. She would instruct me to go to a room upstairs and retrieve something for her. I would forget what it was that she asked for when I arrived in the room she sent me to. I felt stupid, unlovable, and perhaps unknowingly, she purposefully kept me feeling that way. She would say, "We can do this all day, Karen. I will tell you again, and until you choose to get it right, you will do it over again." Often, out of frustration, she would yell at me and not stop until shame overcame me.

I remember walking to Sunday school alone and wishing someone driving by would steal me and take me to live with them in their home. I felt as if I was a definite disappointment to my father. With all that was wrong with me, how could I ever have survived as he did? I wished I were with another family. It was a palatable wish.

I was always very emotionally close to my father. He was a serious, tall, talented, stoic man. I felt he needed me to be quiet and good. That was it; so I was. I was the best I could be around him. I felt pain emanating from him, I witnessed such deep sadness, and he often did not consciously know I saw. So I was good and quiet.

I remember our first cat. His name was Jonathan. I loved Jonathan so much, and he loved our whole family. He was a longhaired tabby cat who came when you called and purred all the time. I felt loved by him. One Saturday night, Jonathan was crossing the street and a car hit him. He was attempting to crawl his way home, and my mother found him after returning from an orchestra concert. He was an indoor-outdoor cat, so it was common that he had been outside while my parents were at the orchestra concert as they were every Saturday night. On Sunday morning, when I learned of his death, I was so sad and so distraught that I refused to watch television. I refused even to watch Bishop Sheen. I was quiet and very reflective that day. I remember it now as if it was a recent happening, and I remember thinking I wonder how my father was feeling with this loss. I was always thinking of him.

David Zauder, me, and Karl as a baby

Jonathan our cat with Karl and me

We had two cats when we were older, one named Lovey and one named Dovey. My mother said my brother was like Lovey, and I was not.

My father was a good man and though he may have been scared regarding being a father at times, he very rarely showed it outwardly. He was grateful to have a daughter and a son. He took us to both the Jewish Community Center and sometimes the YMCA for his workouts. He wanted to show us how he valued keeping his body strong, and of course, we tried to do the same because he was such a good role model. We were usually the only children present. I was good at running because of working out with him. In high school, I once ran a 5.38-minute mile, right alongside members of my gym class who played on the soccer team.

Due to my mother's expectations and my consistent failure at reaching them, I remember planning to run away. I planned it, I packed for it, and I thought I had it all figured out until I was walking out the side door of our home. I remembered my dog. This dog was a black Labrador mix of some kind and appropriately named Sweetie Pie. My father had given this nickname to my mother. Sweetie Pie loved me, and she knew she was my dog. My mother was jealous that this dog attached herself more to me than to her. When I was thinking of leaving, I could not abandon Sweetie Pie. So with bags packed, I began quietly calling my dog, unaware anyone could hear my child-like whispers. My father had been in our renovated basement and heard me.

He came up the stairs from the basement and asked me what I was doing. I told him I was moving out. I was going to the mall so another family could select me, and I would go and live with them. He was shocked that I had worked so many details out by myself, because at this time, I was only in the second grade and was seven years old. He did not understand the need I had to get away from my overbearing, highly-disappointed-in-me, mother. He also did not understand her jealousy or my learning disabilities. He chose not to see any of it until much later in my life.

I knew if I abandoned my family, I would be leaving him as well. I felt intrinsically that he knew *what* I was leaving. I did not feel sad about the idea of leaving this family, but

I did notice that my father needed me to remain with him. For me, remaining there with he and my brother, was a decision I made selflessly. Because at that time of my life, with all that I had going wrong, it would have been best for me to find another family where I could get my own needs met. It was my first memory of becoming selfless, and putting a man's needs ahead of mine, even though he was my father. I became an adult child that day. I put his needs before mine even though I was the child and he was the adult. It was not the last time I would do that—put a man's needs above mine. Can you say enmeshment issues?

Professional photo of family with Sweetie Pie

I felt I was like a memorial candle for him every time he looked at me. As I grew and lived another year, getting closer to the age he was in 1939 (the year his life turned upside down as he remembers being an almost nine-year-old boy), it was painful for him and he worried in silence. A memory of what he lived through, survived, and lost would hauntingly cross his face during normal daily living activities. I felt I was the only one who would notice his emotional disappearance. Even when things were good, it felt like we, together, were always looking over our shoulder waiting for the other shoe to drop.

Often, my father had to go to the Musician's Musical Arts Association Union in downtown Cleveland as part of his work responsibilities for the Cleveland Orchestra. He would often come home very upset. I never knew why, nor did I understand the complexities of what it must've felt like to him. He worked for the Cleveland Orchestra as their first-position cornet player, second-position trumpet player, and as their Assistant Personnel Manager-he had many responsibilities.

One day, in early 1968, I was four and a half years old, and I remember my father coming to the dining room table. He banged on it very excitedly and said to my mother, "It did *not* happen today . . . today was the first time!"

She smiled and acknowledged his happiness but did not discuss it in front of my brother and me. I had no idea what he was talking about, but you could not miss it; his enthusiasm was catching. I knew something big had happened to my father that day. Later, I walked into the kitchen and asked my mother why he was so excited and what specifically had "not happened" on this day?

She informed me that whenever my father went downtown, he would inevitably see mounted police officers. Police officers on horseback, dressed in uniform. Uniforms that mimicked Nazi soldier uniforms, with guns. She told me that every time he saw them, he felt such fear that he sometimes would freeze. Today was the first day he felt nothing when he saw them. He was forty years old. I knew this was big important news I would understand more clearly later in my life.

Years later, when I asked him about this incident, he remembered it because he recalled how he had felt when it happened. He told me it was at the corner of Mayfield and Coventry, and a mounted police officer was directing traffic. He stopped my father, and as my father looked at him and the gun the officer was wearing, the fight-or-flight response had left him for the first time since arriving in America.

He shared that was the first day he felt nothing when he saw the mounted police officer; he actually knew he was there for someone other than him this time. My father knew he was a law-abiding American, and had made no error to bring upon himself any difficulty or blame. He had caused no trouble and had not deserved an accusing law enforcement police officer. This was exceptionally important for him because of who he was and what he had lived through. He was finally a citizen of the United States of America in his heart, mind, and soul. He had accepted himself and felt truly free.

> *Freedom cannot be granted by another person. It cannot*
> *be bestowed. It is proclaimed and lived, or it doesn't exist.*
> *Don't wait for someone to grant you freedom. Seize it*
> *wherever you find it and don't let it go!*
> ~Rabbi Rami Shapiro

My father worked for the Cleveland Orchestra under the conductor, George Szell. My father was on probation during his first three years of employment. Others were told similar things, but for my father this meant no security. This was very stressful for him, as he knew he was doing the job correctly and often took severe criticism for musical notes he didn't even play. But the conductor knew my father could take it; he knew he was very strong, mentally strong, and so he continued to treat my father in this abusive way. My father realized his position with this amazing musician and conductor would remain the same. He was okay with it because he knew he was strong, he had survived the Holocaust, and he knew it was a mind game. For five years of incarceration during the Holocaust, my father dealt with mind games to stay alive. But this mind game was played with a level of musical brilliance that my father felt honored to be working for. He was taken off probation when he accepted the job assignment of assistant personnel manager as well as his musical position requirements, and he was given a contract, which made him feel secure.

My father had renovated the basement in our home and turned it into a practice room and office. I spent hundreds of hours sitting absolutely still in what I thought was a real leather chair while he practiced playing scales on his trumpet. You see, he allowed me to be there as long as I was quiet. It was a rule that could not be broken, and in the beginning, he sent me away until I was able to remain motionless. As a child, I found it difficult to sit in a plasticized fake leather chair and be quiet. I learned this chair was not made of real leather when I had arranged for it to join my father when he moved in with my family and me in June 2007. Imagine my disappointment when I realized that I had been set up to fail because *no one* can sit quietly in a chair made of that synthetic material! Yet I had remained motionless so that I could spend time with my father while I listened and he practiced, undisturbed.

Looking back now, I realize I gained personal control over my body movements, and I truly believe that my brain was fed by the classical music and perfectly played scales. I have a pretty good ear, too, as a result.

I may have had a number of things wrong with me at a very young age, but one thing I knew—I was special. I saw things from a different point of view, and I often felt lonely in my perspective. In the fourth grade, I began journaling and writing poetry. I did not make friends easily, as communication seemed so hard for me. I always felt awkward and did not often understand others' jokes nor was I included during social gatherings. I never made phone calls to invite others to play, so I was alone more often than not.

Always an outcast

Since I was not a fast or fluent reader, and my comprehension was well below par, I am grateful to share that the writings in this book are definitely originals. My fifth grade teacher, Mrs. Stern, supported me and made me feel gifted in writing my feelings and observations. I kept journals and wrote poems, stories, thoughts and feelings often. This one I call "Gypsies of Fantasy." I wrote it when I was nine years old. It tells of how I played alone in my backyard, up and down my neighborhood's backyards, and how I fantasized. I did this to escape my life, this very difficult, ever-changing life that was so hard for me to process and navigate through quickly. My writing was a way to feel honest with myself in an accepted and safe space.

~

Gypsies of Fantasy

The remnant sun is fast setting and the dinner bell has rung what seem to be many moons ago. As we run through the backyards of our neighbors lawns, we recognize the worn paths in the ground to be our warpaths. In our wildest imaginations, we are Indians coming home to eat from the hunt. At other times, we are masked clowns who have escaped from the circus to find new and more exciting adventures out from under the tents' camouflage. We travel light to get the farthest, and we travel quickly to win the races we perpetrate. We noticed that even the firefly is no longer a simple lightning bug rising and falling in the waves of the warm wind. It becomes a spaceship looking to land on a more substantial pad. We are gypsies of fantasy as we stretch our pretense to the most distant limits of our young minds.

~

In the mid-1970s, I remember hearing my parents fighting about money. After I was born in 1964, my father needed to take out a five hundred dollar loan from his union to pay the hospital bill. He was very scared when I had my legs broken and suffered so, as it had been a very difficult birth and out of his control. Both my mother and I had broken bones that needed time to heal. After that experience, I know my father had taken out one commercial insurance policy on his life, one insurance policy for the house, one for medical, one policy for both cars, and insurance on his instruments, making us over-insured and poor, according to my mother. He was so scared that something would happen to him that he would not be able to care for us. He felt inadequate and ill prepared as a father, and in his later years shared that with me. At some point, with those insurance policies, he gained some security, relaxed a bit, and began to release those fears. However, within fourteen years, he did pay off the mortgage on that first house on the corner of Compton and Euclid Heights Boulevard. He did not believe that being indebted to a bank was the American way. He was amazing.

Chapter 3

More Memories

When I was in the second grade, we took a field trip to the pond directly in front of the Natural History Museum and directly across from Severance Hall where my father worked. Everyone was running and having a good time, and I was alone and walking thoughtfully near the edge of the pond. A teacher always stayed near me, and I'll always be grateful to her for that. I bent down and reached out to touch a snail stuck to the side of the pond. Three children ran behind me, too close, and I fell in headfirst. I was soaking wet and smelled of snails. The field trip was over, and all the children got on the school bus except me. The teacher generously allowed me to ride home with her in her car, away from the laughter and the teasing. I don't remember being comforted upon arrival home.

I often felt like I didn't get it, *it* being whatever everyone else understood that I didn't understand. Sometimes I pretended. I pretended that I got *it* so no one would make fun of me or be the butt of a joke.

Late in elementary school, I rode my new bike to school every day. I didn't learn to ride a bike until I was in the fifth grade. I was uncoordinated. So I was very happy and so proud to ride my bike to school because I practiced all summer to get good at it. One day as I was locking up my bike, from the third-floor window, a fellow student leaned out and yelled down to me, "Hey Karen, now I know your bike combination. If you ride your bike to school tomorrow, I'll steal it!" I was horrified! He saw my bike combination, and I didn't want to lose my new bike, so I never rode it to school again. No one in my home asked me why. If they had, I may have told them what happened, and they could have told me that from three stories up, he could never have been able to see my bike combination. He had lied. Looking back, it hurts to know now what I didn't know then.

I was lucky to have two good friends very early on; Anne Marie and Susie {Webb} Garner. They are both still very good friends to me today. They know me and understand my many learning disabilities. The learning disabilities don't take away from who I am, and who I am is made up of many more gifts than just my deficits. One of those friends, Susie, moved away in the third grade, but we ended up keeping in touch and being roommates in our freshman and sophomore years in college. We are still very close today.

As David Zauder's daughter, people expected that I would have some musical talent. I began playing the piano at the age of six. The woman who taught me lived down the street from us and knew well who my father was. I knew what my father's expectations were for me.

To save my life, I could not figure out what my piano instructor was talking about while she was trying to teach me to read music. It occurred to me very early on in my lessons that I needed to forget what she was trying to teach me; I needed to learn the music and play the piano by ear. I played the piano for six years, and that includes holding regular recitals and performing in front of my peers and their parents. I never learned how to read the music. I was a survivor, and I knew my father would kill me if I could not learn to play the piano. So I learned to strategize around my disability.

I asked politely for the piano teacher to play the piece she wanted me to learn exactly the way she wanted me to play it for her the following week. Of course, I had memorized the scales; "Every Good Boy Does Fine" for the lines on the scale and "FACE" for the spaces. So I would go home and practice like a good girl every single day to try to make my music sound the same as the piano teacher's music did. When I couldn't remember, I used the strategy of reading the scale and figured out which note I was missing. Every week I returned, playing the piece not only perfectly, but the way she wanted to hear it—her way. I even learned to turn the page at the exact moment as if I were reading the music. I played in two recitals per year and I played perfectly, as expected. I had learned to play by ear.

Six years had gone by and when I asked her to play this first lesson for me she refused. She said she wanted me to put myself into the piece. I was horrified because I could not read music, and I had no idea how long it would take for me to play it note by note; FACE, Every Good Boy Does Fine. Try as I might, I failed her.

Upon my return the following week, I played the first part okay, but it was evident I was not the piano student she thought I was. Little did she know I practiced for more than an hour every day that past week just to get to that low level of playing and be proficient. I failed.

I failed her, and I definitely failed my father, for now she would tell him I could not read music. I was devastated. She quit teaching me. The teacher was so rightfully angry that I had not told her that her teaching methods were unclear to me. I had forged my way through six years of piano lessons without her knowing my weakness and the strategy I came up with on my own. I had lied to her, I felt horrible, and my hands began to peel. They peeled whenever I was highly anxious and felt that I was failing to do what was expected of me. They peeled when I believed I was shaming my father. They peeled when, despite my lack of awareness that I suffered from disabilities, I felt that I knew I should have been better than I was. They peeled a lot.

When my father found out, he was so angry he did not speak to me for two weeks. There had been an enormous sense of pride for him that I had performed perfectly for six years. He had played in a band with his father in

Kraków, Poland. He played the drums, and he played them well. He had anticipated that in time he and I would play together. The piano was the one instrument my father regretted not learning to play. He was playing through me, and I had lied.

When we would have dinner as a family, my father would arrive to the table in time to sit down, hear our prayer (Good bread, good meat, good gosh, let's eat), and then consume the meal. I perceived him to be stoic, businesslike, and focused on the food. My learning Hebrew prayers came later, as my father frowned upon them in the house. The prayers brought back too many bad memories, as he had been raised as an Orthodox Jew prior to the invasion of Nazi's into his home in Kraków, Poland, in 1939.

We did not spend a lot of time with family, as we didn't have any in Cleveland. Similarly, according to my father, he spent a large amount of time with his mother's sisters before the Holocaust, but he did not even know his father had siblings. I was closest to and felt most comfortable with my mother's best friend, Barbara Serr and her family down three houses. I knew I had family in Detroit, Michigan, on both my father's side—his first and second cousins and their children, and on my mother's side—her parents and her father's sister and her family whom my mother did not get along with well. My father had many close friends from his musical career, and we spent more time with them than anyone else.

When my brother and I were much younger, I vaguely remember seeing my great-aunt Anna, my father's aunt, his mother's sister, but only once. She looked a lot like my father's mother; after all, they were sisters. I was very aware how truly important she was to my father. She had been a beacon for him about coming to America. His aunt made certain that he was okay, educated, and she proudly attended his graduation from the New York Military Academy. She gave both Karl and me a silver dollar, and I knew how much that meant to her. It was more than a gesture; she was family.

There came a day when Anna Lucks Holtz passed away. It was an odd day. I remember feeling that something terribly bad had happened and my parents were not discussing the situation, but were packing for an unannounced trip to Detroit. It was July 10, 1970, and my mother thought that having my brother and me along was a good idea. She was right. Death is a part of life, and we deserved to see our aunt one last time, pay our respects, and support my father in yet another familial loss.

The casket was open for family viewing prior to the funeral. I remember having to step up on a stepstool and lean in to kiss the side of her cheek because my mother told me to. That is why this is etched in my memory. I had never kissed a dead human being before. Her cheek was cold and soft at the same time, and I missed her already. This was also the first time I saw my father cry. I knew my father had seen thousands of dead human beings during his Holocaust experience. Innately, I had known this. I also knew that my father was grieving a very deep loss, because by the way he saw it she was the last of his real family. He never cried during the Holocaust, over the loss of either of his parents, his aunts, or his freedom. There was no time for emotion. To this day, he still credits his aunt for raising the money for his voyage to America and arranging for him to live with her oldest of four children—Lillian and her husband, Harry Markle. He was crying for the first time, and I was quiet.

I'm on the left, Karl's on the right.
A visit to Lil and Harry with fourth cousins

I remember visiting the Markle family, their children, and their children's children infrequently. After my parents began fighting more, the visits became even less frequent, and because of this, Karl and I never did develop a strong bond with our fourth cousins.

I remember my father having the flu one day, and my mother answered the phone. A member of the orchestra was calling my father, who was then the personnel manager of the Cleveland Orchestra, at home, to say he was not going to be at work because he didn't feel well. My mother told the man that my father was throwing up in the bathroom, but he would be in the office later that afternoon, and she would have him return the call. My father's work ethic was so high that he never missed a day of work, even when legitimately ill.

My father forced himself into work day after day for forty years, rarely taking vacation or sick time. He sometimes referred to it as a "forced march," not so silently referencing his Auschwitz death march. "Work shall set you free" apparently was more than just a motto on an archway at Auschwitz for my father. My father's work ethic was the highest I have ever seen. It made me very conscious of my own work ethic and the reputation I was personally developing.

My father's ability to handle pain and difficulty was and is unique, and yet emotionally ill thought out.

We were all outside playing while my father was on top of a ladder leaned up against a plum tree in our backyard. He was getting plums down and handing them to my mother, Karl, and me. It was a jovial event until my father unknowingly bumped a wasp hive, and it fell to the ground. Apparently, he did not know what it was. The wasps streamed out of the nest and swarmed my father from head to toe. My mother screamed to both Karl and me to get inside the house immediately. Karl and I ran, and when I looked back, I saw my father fall out of the tree. My mother ran inside behind us. Bees stuck in her bouffant hairdo, and she screamed and swatted at them.

The rest is a blur, however, I have these memories; my father was stung thirteen times and began to have an anaphylactic shock reaction. He had crawled into the house and up to the bedroom to lie down. My mother was screaming at him to get up off the bed. I saw that he was white as a ghost and sweating. He said he would be just fine and that she should stop screaming. Next thing I know, my mother is dragging my father down the stairs by his hair, out of the house, and into her car. He was holding her hand with his against his head and wincing. He had such a nasty look on his face; it must have really hurt to have his hair pulled. I could tell that this was an emergency. The only way she could get him to move was to pull him by his hair. My mother saved my father's life that day because she drove directly to the emergency room so he could get a shot directly into his heart. Our neighbor, Barbara, called ahead to the emergency room staff to let them know that my mother was on her way with my father and he was in terrible condition. They didn't even wheel him into a room when they put the shot right into his heart, which saved his life. Barbara came and took care of us until my parents returned home. For my father not to know that his life was at stake, to not tune into his true physical condition, feel his feelings enough to recognize the severity of the situation, continues today as I care for him in my home with my family.

My father believes he is invincible. After all, he *has* been for seventy-three years from when he thought he should not still be alive. What makes him so special that he should live when those he loved were shot to death, often while standing on either side of him? Why should he repeatedly defy death throughout his five years of slavery?

I used to believe that either you are in my bunker, on my side, or you're not. If I didn't feel I could count on you to be there through thick and thin, then I didn't invest in you and our relationship. It seems a little harsh, but it was a survival-thought process that I was utilizing; one that I was taught and learned to use. I am lucky today looking back at my life and the relationships I've had with girlfriends, interpersonal relationships with others, and intimate ones with the opposite sex. I have always thought that I chose with deep thought, which of them I'd let get close to me.

I am grateful that I learned the art of detachment with love and discernment. Detachment with love is an art; it allows others their space to be themselves, ungrudgingly, while you mind your own business and love them from a distance. When you allow their issues to be theirs, and not yours to fix, you allow for detachment. "Do not judge others, lest you be judged." I learned to maintain loving them while not trying to fix them. Most importantly, I learned forgiveness.

My father, I feel, did the same. He had those who he was exceptionally close with, and then the rest of us were on the outside—his periphery. It hurts less when you care about people from a distance, and I believe my father was emotionally protecting himself when he did this. All my life I've experienced this feeling, this quietness, this necessary distance—the silence from him to me.

When my father first arrived at Markle's house, he shared with me that he was uncomfortable, scared, and fearful of what was next, and he wondered how he was supposed to survive. Every night, upon his arrival to the Markle family household, he slept with a hunting knife under his pillow. Every morning his cousin Lil would find the knife, take it, and hide it. Every night my father would not stop looking until he found it so he could sleep safely. This was a matter of no discussion. He needed the knife to feel safe, and she needed it put away from her toddlers. How he kept finding it baffled her. When the family moved from that house into the next, my father had pretty much moved out, but they always had room for him when he visited. On some weekends, the kids would often find him on the couch when he had taken a leave from the New York Military Academy.

My father valued what Lil and Harry Markle were doing for him, but he did not intend to be a burden on them. Upon his arrival in May of 1946, they had their eldest daughter—Sheila, their son—Alan, and baby Diane due in the fall. He shared with me that his goal was to be independent as soon as possible, just as he had been in Germany the year following the ending of the war. His experiences made his expectations different from the average teenager, different from the European or the American teenager then, and in today's society. The Markle family enjoyed his return on vacations and breaks from school, and later from work, but my father's view was that he was not to lean on them. Although he may have ended furloughs on their couch, sharing beautifully cooked meals together, he was very proud of what he was accomplishing on his own.

My cousin, Sheila (Markle) Gursky, recently shared with me how on his dresser in the old house, my father always kept a large bullet—hollowed out and painted silver. When she had asked him about it, he said it killed his best friend on the death march. This best friend was like family to him during the Holocaust, which he survived. Cousin Sheila too feels like she is a sister to my father; however, she was saved from the Holocaust by virtue of living in Detroit. It still affects her deeply as it does her siblings that her brother, her foster brother, her second cousin, went through so much.My father made close relationships with a number of New York Military Academy cadets, friends also stationed with him at West Point, as well as in the musical industry with which he threw all his energy into to succeed. Much of his experiences during these wide-ranging years were spent with friends he is still close with today. He had an amazing musical career working on Broadway, playing for churches, with the Boston Pops for two seasons, touring America and other countries, and in more venues than one could imagine. He never turned down a job.

When I was young, he was a Big Brother to David Harris, a boy from the inner city, for more than ten years. My father valued sharing what we had with the boy. I knew this was extremely important to him, but my mother didn't share his value in this area. She complained often that he was spending private time with David Harris and not with Karl and me. I thought he felt more comfortable giving to another fatherless boy. He related with the boy.

Sadly, David Harris was shot and killed getting off a city bus while attending school. This was the second time I bore witness to my father's pain in our current life. It was a horrible loss for him; so tragic and so unnecessary.

I missed having grandparents nearby. Even though my mother's parents were alive, we only saw them once a year for a while, and then not so much after they moved from Detroit to Florida. My father's parents had been murdered in the Holocaust, but I felt them close to me always. I wrote this poem in their honor during one of my lonely nights as a sophomore in college.

Yahrzeit

The candles burned
for the lost years we yearned
as the light flickered brightly
I secretly squeezed my hands tightly

For you I never knew
not even the dimmest color or hue
my vacant memory bleeds my heart
as my eyes searched his for where to start

I'll never know the pain you felt
nor the thrashing of the whipping belt
I'll never see your musician's hands
or your lovely tailorship worn o're the lands

I'll never know the work you did
nor the bread and butter you must have bid
I'll never see the home you kept
nor the blessing of the candles while you wept

I'll never see these things for which I yearn
I'll never feel those feelings though now they burn
I've never been with you in body or soul
but I live with you now in memory of your toil.

I felt a deep connection to my roots because I was so uprooted personally.

Because of my father's position with the Cleveland Orchestra, I often attended Saturday night concerts with my mother and brother. In fact, I believe that from the age of ten through high school, I spent most Saturday nights at a concert. It was a thrill to have such great seats in the balcony and watch my father on the back right side of the stage. While he played his instrument, he turned bright red with each blow. He was incredible to watch in the orchestra, and they had a familial way with which they congratulated and supported one another after a musician played well. They would silently rub their feet on the stage floor. From my perch in the balcony, I always looked for their congratulations toward one another and made it my business to discern whom they were congratulating, and I felt pride.

What a wonderful way of life my father had carved out for himself with The Cleveland Orchestra. To be a part of such an amazing musical family who loved and supported one another throughout all technical difficulties.

Often after a concert, there would be a special party for VIPs. I was taught to come to these parties on my best behavior. I was to smile, thank the amazing hostess, not eat too much, and bring my father bourbon, no ice. I never thought of myself as pretty or even beautiful, because my mother had told me specifically what was wrong with my face and body many times. So when I saw people gazing at me, I believed it was because I was David Zauder's daughter, and they were watching me to make certain I was well-behaved and deserved to be in the party room. I did my best, had short polite conversations, and made friends with people like Elsa Posell. Her husband was a bass player, and she later became one of my mentors and angels. She had shared with me at one of the VIP parties that she was very impressed that I was both beautiful and kind. I shared with her that I had been gifted both characteristics from my parents. She replied that I was wise for taking their good characteristics. She had me to her home for tea and taught me what a loving, respectful marriage looked like. I am eternally grateful for her mentorship and friendship; she was one of my angels.

My mother's parents were involved in charity work, and my grandfather was a Mason.

Jean and Ben Ribiat dressed up
for a Mason ball fundraiser

I was nine years old when I first visited my grandparents in Florida. After I got off the airplane and was in the car, a Cadillac, I stared in amazement at the palm trees. My grandfather pulled the car over, despite my grandmother's yelling, and he climbed a thirty-foot palm tree to get a coconut just for me. Both he and my grandmother, Jean Ribiat, made me feel like a million dollars. My grandmother always said that I was her favorite granddaughter. It wasn't until I was twelve years old that I figured out I was her only granddaughter; I was always so literal. My grandfather, Ben, would clean windows for businesses in the early morning light, fish the ocean in the afternoon, and bring home his catch. My grandmother would turn it into her style of gefilte fish in the afternoon. At that time, he also was the main custodian for the condominium building they lived in. I had an amazing time visiting them.

My grandmother, more than my grandfather, was verbally racist and it embarrassed me. Even at nine years old, I was acutely aware of what discrimination meant, and I was not going to participate. She was raised that way, but so was my grandfather, and he didn't choose to behave that way.

My grandmother moved to California when I was a senior in high school because she liked the weather there better. My grandfather was seventy-eight years old, dying of cancer and in a wheelchair, and he still came to my high school graduation. After that, I cared for him day and night. He passed away the week after I left for college. My mother held no funeral for him, and I did not come home from college to mourn.

Grandpa Ben at my high school graduation

Me and my Cleveland Heights High School diploma—I
always knew I would do what I had to do to graduate.

My memories of that time of my life are varied and detailed. I learned so much the hard way, mostly due to my learning disabilities. I thought my responsibility was to keep in touch with everyone who I believed were my friends by writing letters. This was before the Internet, e-mail, and cell phones.

One day my father was talking with me about my schedule, and I was complaining about how I did not have much time. First, there was the homework. I could not hear the professor speaking and write everything down fast enough, so I would go back to my room or to the library after each class and fill in the blanks with my notes. Then I'd reread them and highlight the important information, and then I'd read the chapters and do the same. This took me approximately forty hours per week for a fifteen credit hour semester. I always had at least two jobs, which equaled approximately twenty-five hours a week. I was having a hard time keeping up with my letter writing with my educational schedule. My father explained that it was not expected that I keep in touch through constant letter writing with old friends, comrades, and school acquaintances. I didn't have a real family, and I treated my friends as if they were.

On one of his first visits to see me in my freshman dorm, I was proud that I could take him out to lunch with the money I had earned at one of my two jobs. My father said he would take me by a bank so I could deposit my check, and then make my withdrawal for lunch. I quickly corrected him and stated that I didn't trust the banks in this small town; I had kept my money in a small bag under my mattress. My father, a very smart businessman, was shocked to learn that I had made such a strange and paranoid decision.

Before we went to lunch he took me to a bank, and I deposited my $923.00 into a savings account. I had earned $600.00 from being a camp counselor and the rest from my odd jobs that past summer. At the time of his visit, I was a waitress as well as a babysitter.

My father never called me to find out what I was doing on school breaks, or for the holidays, nor did he ask me why I was working so hard. I found out years later, he thought his paying child support to my mother was adequately meeting my nutritional needs and personal expenses, like the electric bill, the phone bill, long-distance charges, or gas money for the car while at school. She knew I was working all those jobs to pay for my expenses because I told her that I was.

While attending five years of college, plus summer school, and multiple jobs, I took notes in class, came back from each class, and rewrote every single class note to include all the words I had missed. Toward the end of my first semester, I got smart and bought a tape recorder. Doing double work was the only way I got through college.

One semester I had to retake an English class, which focused on writing, and it brought my credit hours up to twenty-one that semester. I had a very difficult time organizing my thoughts and keeping my writing fluid and clear. I didn't have a computer, just a typewriter, a gift from my father. I remember one professor who wrote on my paper, "If I didn't know what this assignment was about, I would have no idea what you are trying to talk about here."

Attending college was an interesting proposition, because I believe we all worried whether I would graduate. My father was very proud to be able to pay for the college courses I needed to take to graduate with a BSE, Bachelors of Science in Education. He knew my passion was working with children and that I wanted to be a great teacher. I also wanted to be the kind of teacher who helped students who suffered with special needs and learning disabilities as I did. Therefore, the bills were sent to him directly for the education I received, and that was all. I knew this going on, because my parents did not discuss anything calmly or rationally at this point in my life. I was again an adult child, on my own.

Looking back now, I do not regret the workforce experience I received or the pressure I was constantly under, working two to three jobs and carrying a full college course load. Apparently, I'm a workaholic like my father, but I'm attempting to be in recovery. As I write this, I currently have four jobs, but I'm passionate and driven!

Through my father's determination to survive, I feel I must protect the image, the expectation he had in his mind when he chose to survive. He admits freely that luck also played a key role in his survival. When he chose to start a family and pass on his work ethic and values, there became an unspoken sense of accountability. "I survived; now that you are here, what are you going to do to make your life worth it? Worth my suffering, worth my sacrifices, worth my losses? Make life have more significance; contribute something worthwhile to the world."

I definitely worked harder than anyone else I knew because of my learning disabilities, but one thing I remember very distinctly was my attitude of "I dare you." I would walk across campus alone with a huge chip on my shoulder, knowing I was a survivor not yet truly tested. I was also alone, no emotional family support of any kind. So I wanted to prove to myself I could survive.

Late at night on my way home from the library, I was not cautious, not requesting an escort. I knew I could physically hold my own should I be attacked, and I knew my attacker would be regretful. This stubbornness, this willingness to be in harm's way to prove myself, was an error in judgment and stemmed from a lack of communication between parent and child. I had not had anyone talk to me about street smarts. I felt alone, and yet I knew I would survive because I was a second-generation survivor. I knew education came hard for me, and learning what I needed to learn to be a great teacher was difficult for me, but *I chose to succeed*.

I remember a story my father shared with me that when on tour, during down time, he would walk the city. Sometimes he would jog early in the morning, as he was an avid runner and it released his stress. One night, after my father had just finished playing a concert in Boston, he was on his way back to the hotel when a large man came out from a side street, grabbed him from behind and under his neck, and demanded all his money. David Zauder had been so startled that he dropped the can of soda, and he became infuriated that his soda was now shaken. He broke the hold, spun around, and while screaming at the attacker, kicked the man in his jaw out of self-defense. Just then, a taxicab pulled up alongside acting as the attacker's accomplice, and the man jumped in the taxi and they sped away. My father was most upset about a shaken soda, which was now going to explode when he opened it, and he was thirsty after his concert. When he returned to the hotel, he informed the police. They knew who the culprits were, and they wanted my father to press charges and remain in the city an extra week and go to court. But that would not be possible for David Zauder, as he was leaving the next day with the orchestra. The police said that with his eyewitness account they had enough to charge the guys who had been accosting people. They called them the "taxi men". The police officer told my father, that with his testimony, the officer would no longer make any more bad Cleveland jokes as a way of providing thanks.

On another occasion, my father shared with me that he was wearing a long winter coat and walking down a snowy street at night after a concert. An attacker jumped out at him from between two loose boards in a fence and said, "Give me all your money!" With his hands in his pockets, David took a step directly toward the attacker, pointed one finger inside his pocket at the man, and said in a forceful, mafia-like way, "I've got a gun . . . you better run." The attacker ran. David Zauder is six foot tall with a Godfather-like aura. I think I was trying to imitate him on my college campus and in other times of my life as well.

When I missed my father the most, I would imagine him playing beautiful classical music on stage and having the musicians rubbing their feet on the floor complimenting one another in silence.

I arrived early by twenty minutes for a class one day carrying my mail that I had collected earlier. There was a package from my father, so I opened it up and inside was a small transistor radio with earplugs. It was already set to the station WCLV, the radio station that played classical music and many of the Cleveland Orchestra recordings. I wrote this poem after this experience.

~

Thank You for the Radio

I just heard you play a minute ago. I felt my stomach jump as the sound of your trumpet quaked over the surrounding music from the orchestra.

I felt you had spoken your piece.

I didn't know it had been the Cleveland Orchestra playing, nor did I know it had been Lorin Maazel conducting.

But when the short yet expressive trumpet solo arrived,

I knew it was you.

It almost brought tears to my eyes, as I suddenly felt closer to you. It almost brought me clear back to our basement of years hence when I used to sit in your large leather chair and quietly hum the scales you repeated so diligently.

As I listened, practically straining my ears so as not to miss a single note, I didn't feel so lost.

I had been waiting for my class to start, as I had arrived early as usual, and put on my new earphones to escape and relax a bit. I just wanted to forget I was at college and sink into my desk and disappear.

But when I heard you play, I wanted to shout, "That's my father! That's him on the trumpet!" But in order to hear the entire solo without missing a beat I kept silent. Afterward, I really felt speechless. I had felt you near to me, and I just wanted to relax and enjoy the feeling.

Then class began. I don't know how to explain the immense pride and musical wonder I hold for you except to simply say thank you for the radio.

~

It seemed that whenever I had a final exam week, my mother would have an emotional requirement of me to be there for her. She would call late in the evening, early in the morning, anywhere between midnight and 4:00 a.m. to talk. No matter what I said, she ignored my school schedule, as it had nothing to do with her agenda. Can you say Narcissist?

Once I had a final exam at 8:00 a.m. on a Friday, and my mother had called me that Thursday after 11:00 p.m. sharing with me that she would kill herself on Friday if I did not come home. I did not truly think that she would kill herself, but I felt responsible for her. I stayed up all night worrying instead of completing my study for the final exam and when I went into the exam, I was the first one finished. That was a first for me in class, being the first to finish. I got up in a hurry so I could drive home and save my mother. My professor rushed into the hallway and asked me why I was leaving so fast. My defenses were low because I was tired, so I told him the truth. He felt for me deeply and said if I had only told him he would have let me take the test upon my return and not risk my grade. I told him I felt I had no choice. My mother had only called the night before, so I needed to leave to get back to Cleveland as fast as I could. I ended up with a B in his class instead of an A, which I deserved, just because of that final exam, which I did not do as well as I could have due to my familial circumstances.

Another semester I had an educational statistics class in which I informed the professor of my dyslexia and my need for extra time on all tests. I even offered to take the tests early and orally, but he refused to help me. He didn't believe in dyslexia, and he didn't believe in easy outs, which is what he said I was trying to obtain. I ended up with a D in his class. I was so disappointed because my grade point average had then fallen. Without discussing this with the guidance counselor, I added it to my list of things to do that summer; retake Educational Statistics at Kent State University while living with a girlfriend whom I had known from high school and holding down jobs that would support me. With the proper modifications and accommodations, I got a B in the class while working three jobs that summer.

I experienced another situation at Bowling Green State University with my history class professor who also was ignorant of the effects of my diagnosed dyslexia. After getting none of my modifications and accommodations in his class met and ending up with a D as a grade, I took my problem straight to the dean of the college. I was scared, but I knew I was right, and I stood up for myself again. The dean discussed my case with my professor. After all was said and done, I was given a B for the extra work I had accomplished. I was always doing extra work. I stood up for myself even though I was alone.

When I walked across the stage at the Bowling Green State University graduation ceremony, this same educational statistics professor was on stage with his hand outstretched to shake my hand along with others. He was the only one I did not accept congratulations from, for he said snidely to me at that moment, "Oh, so I see you made it after all." I ignored him and that was not my normal good-girl style of behavior. I was exceptionally proud that I graduated with accolades and letters of recommendations and an extreme amount of workforce experience.

I graduated college with a Bachelor of Science in
Education with a minor in Psychology.
One waving happily in the crowd of graduates.

My father never knew of all the jobs I held through my
five years at college. I was a waitress at three different
restaurants, a hostess, a gas station attendant, an overnight
child development center coordinator for troubled
children, and a cable television saleswoman for a start-up
cable company. I also sold appointments to learn of new
software over the phone and was a telemarketer for
re-subscriptions to magazines. I began the telemarketing
job while I was at Kent State University for the summer.
That job taught me telephone skills, which advanced my
communication skills.

I worked full-time while going to college full time, and I chose jobs based on what I thought would support my résumé well and help to teach me. "Learn something new every day." That's a Zauder motto.

Every job I accepted I chose to be a woman of my word. "On time" to me meant ten minutes early, and if I was later than that, I was late. I chose to be the one who others could always count on. I knew the importance of a good first impression, and I wanted a reputation that would make me proud later in life. I was always thinking that way as I moved toward my goals. The actions you take today often don't pay off until tomorrow. But the actions you take today speak to the person you are right now, and I had high morals, high values, and high expectations of myself. I was going to help change the world for the better, and I was on a mission to do so.

My first job that first semester was as a waitress at a Bob's Big Boy restaurant. This was very difficult for me with my learning disabilities. I adjusted my sail because I knew my boat was in the water and it was my responsibility not to sink; I chose to be successful. After three days of barely any training and very few tips, I asked the best waitress there if I could come in the next day and silently shadow her for three hours. She said sure, but she thought I was crazy. I did not care. I needed to know what she did that made her a great waitress. I needed her to demonstrate to me how I could be good at this job. I was willing to spend the extra, unpaid hours to learn. When I arrived, she rolled her eyes, and I said thank you. Then I began to watch what she did.

Prior to my training with her, I would walk up to a table, introduce myself, welcome the patrons, and would just stand there without water, silverware, or even menus. She walked up to the table with all the items and took their drink order immediately. It was a huge wake-up call to my executive dysfunction. Then I watched her make another pot of coffee even though the original pot was more than half filled. I asked her why, and she responded that two of the four people at her table had just ordered coffee and that half a pot would not last through their second fill up. She was constantly thinking two steps ahead. I had never been good at that, but I was getting good at it now. I watched her fill the salad station, replacing items that needed added, and I watched her handle six tables at the same time with ease. The next day when I went into work, I was the second best waitress they ever had. I held that job for two years.

I once had a job interview and it was raining. I didn't have enough money to take a taxi, nor did I have enough money to put gas in the tank of my Ford Pinto, which I purchased for $375.00 in high school with money I had earned. So I rode my bike. In the rain. It never occurred to me that I had a choice to cancel the interview and reschedule, because I am a woman of my word. I hold this value close to my heart. The man who conducted my interview ended up being the owner of the company, and I was the only one of the twenty-eight scheduled applicants who showed up for the interview process, because it was a gloomy, stormy day.

I got the job. That one job. That one relationship I built with that cable company tycoon changed my life.

No, I didn't go into the cable business as a profession. I was studying to be a teacher. However, that job helped me to branch out while working side by side with him as my mentor. I continued to grow new leadership skills that helped to build that cable company. I helped them think out of the box.

As a saleswoman for a new start-up firm selling software to construction companies over the phone, I further grew my skills and my understanding of working for others. I had that position created for me because the owner of the company wanted to date me, and he needed help selling his software. I missed his nonverbal cues. He was telling me about his company and about his new software, and I knew I could sell it over the phone. I sold him on my skills, and then I made many appointments for him and his partners to share what their software product could do for potential clients' companies. Each sale amounted to more than twenty-five hundred dollars and they paid me ten dollars an hour. I held that job for a year and a half, even though a part of my duties was to show up early enough to start the coffee for the men who worked there. I was very aware that I had chutzpah, and yet I needed to keep my place to remain in that job, so I made the coffee.

Chapter 4

My Father's Survival

In any free society where terrible wrongs exist, some are guilty-all are responsible. ~Abraham Joshua Heschel

My father's story of survival is an incredible one. I cannot provide all the horrific details of what my father had to do to survive the atrocities perpetrated against him and his family and the friends he lost during his Holocaust experience, because he refuses to share them all with the public. He still lives with me, and this is his request. There are many resources to obtain the evidence and the facts that prove the Holocaust happened. There are many books written by Holocaust survivors who share and recount many of the inhumane details. He always shared that Elli Wiesel's book *Night* was most like his story.

My father participated in Steven Spielberg's USC Shoah Foundation Institute, videotaping firsthand accounts of testimony. My father's account is eight hours long and is in the Holocaust Memorial Museum Library and Archives in Washington, DC, as well as other museums and universities around the world. Although I don't disclose my personal discoveries in this chapter, it can be noted that I spent days researching both my father and my uncle Solomon's Holocaust experience, documented by both the Nazis and the American army. Some of those documents appear in this chapter. My father only recently discovered that his real birthdate is September 14, 1928 which alters the actual ages that are depicted in chapters 4 and 5.

Here, my intention is to give you one eyewitness account, my father's, and how it, through him affected me as a second-generation survivor. You need to know what he lived through to be able to forgive him as I have and to comprehend the enormity of loss he endured. This type of life experience does alter people. Yet, they still have the responsibility for their actions as well.

> *To the living, we owe respect but to the dead we owe the truth.* ~Voltaire

With my father's permission, this is the *Cliffs Notes* version of what he survived:

My father, David Zauder, was born in Kraków, Poland, on September 14, 1928 to Rose Lucks and Karl Zauder. This is Karl and Rose's engagement photo.

Engagement photo of David Zauder's parents,
Rose Lucks Zauder and Karl Zauder

He had an older brother, Solomon, who was born in 1922, which made him nine years older than my father. My father had an older sister who was most likely born in 1925, but she died of an illness as a toddler. They lived on the corner of 13 Gazowa Street and 7 Bochenska Street in Kraków, Poland, in a one-room apartment in a mostly Jewish apartment complex with a Jewish theater attached. His father was a tailor, a drummer, and a leader among the community.

My Grandmother Rose with Solomon on the left
and blonde haired blue eyed David on her hip.

His mother, Rose, was a seamstress and a mother of three to Solomon, David, and a middle sister whose name was not known to my father. Rose had three sisters, Anna, Bronka, and one more, Leah possibly, who my father doesn't remember her name for certain, but we think it was Leah. His mother was a volunteer at the Jewish theater.

Bronka, Anna, and Leah—Rose's sisters.

They lived a rich Jewish life eating kosher and celebrating high holidays together and within their community. Although my father never knew his father's side of the family, he knew he had been a descendent of the Cohen tribe, one of the twelve Hebrew tribal descendents from Moses' time. His father had told him so. His brother, Solomon, was very successful in his violin studies and had made the family very proud. He studied with Henry Rosner.

HENRY ROSNER
Appearing with his Continental
String Ensemble nightly at the
Baronet, Madison Ave, and
84th St.

Henry Rosner

The Catholics stoned my father every time he crossed the street because he was a Jew. It was not an easy life to live then, and he lived in constant fear. His father would often send him across the street to the corner store to buy kerosene and bread. Often, my father would return without the money or the items, and the Catholics would have beaten him. His father would beat him for allowing himself to be caught. This was not a good life or a fair life, and as a child, no one protected him from all these terrible things.

On September 9, 1939, when the Nazis invaded Kraków, Poland, my father remembers he was a week away from his tenth birthday. He went with his brother, Solomon, and a few of his friends to watch the Nazis march in across the Vistula River from under the Slashi Bridge, which was three hundred yards from his home. That day, my father's life was forever changed.

He witnessed the Nazi commandant accept flowers and wine from the mayor of Kraków. We know from history that the mayor also sent away the Kraków army to fight elsewhere so that they would not be forced to fight the Nazis. This surely saved many Polish lives. We also know that the mayor pulled all the Jewish children out from public school the year before the invasion due to public ordinances against Jews, which he supported. My father, therefore, only had achieved the completion of the first grade. Watching this mayor on the Slashi Bridge welcoming the Nazis in this way clearly indicated that their world was changing quickly and with a negative impact.

After that day, his family was sent to the Kraków Ghetto, along with his father's mother, Sophia Zauder, who was wheelchair bound. My father only referred to her as Bubbe, and he never quite made the connection that she was his father's mother. They lived there together for a short while before the Nazi's murdered Sophia Zauder, as she was crippled, in a wheelchair, and unable to provide labor. They remained there for more than a year, 1940-1941.

During this time, the SS came for Solomon, to put him to work in the next work camp to labor as an electrician. He fought back, and they beat him severely. It took weeks for him to recover while my father and grandmother tended to his broken hands and other wounds. They returned for him, and again he fought back. This time they beat him within an inch of his life. It took two months for him to return to a capable work state, and when he did, they took him, and he did not fight back. My father watched this transformation and learned from it. They sent Solomon to Płaszów work camp to be an electrician and help open it for slave laborers.

My grandfather, Karl, had arranged for the supply of food with his friend the non-Jewish butcher, and paid him ahead of time, for fear of what might happen next. When my father was in the Kraków Ghetto, his father gave directions to him on how to get to the butcher shop at which he had made prior arrangements.

His father told him, "Get out through the barbed wire at dusk. Don't get caught. Remember where you found an opening so you can get back in. Go ten blocks to the left, stay in the dark shadows, go five blocks to the right, and two blocks straight ahead. Go in the back door."

My now ten-and-a-half-year-old father snuck out through the barbed wire at night, scared to death, and went to this butcher shop. This was very dangerous; if my father were to be caught, the Nazis surely would have killed him. My father collected food from this generous butcher for a year and not once did a word pass between the two. My father, feeling eternally grateful, returned each time with food for his family. He could have gone free and run away, as he had in fact escaped, but familial loyalty was strong for him then; it meant everything.

From the Kraków Ghetto, they were forcefully moved to Płaszów work camp where they remained from the fall of 1941 to February of 1943. My father played the bugle in the morning. A long time went by with him having this responsibility until his father finally said to him, "Stay out of the line of fire." He found someone else to take his place. This was depicted in the movie, *Schindler's List*, except my father's hair was blond, and in the movie, the bugle boy's hair was black.

My father had played drums in the Jewish theater with his parents, and he sometimes played the trumpet, so he had musical skills. But his father's advice served him well.

One evening, a Nazi shot his father. He received a gunshot wound to the head. Karl Zauder was doing his job as a fire marshal making sure all the people were in their barracks at night. An SS lieutenant shot him for sport.

Karl Zauder wearing his fire marshal hat
in Płaszów Work Camp.

My father remembers the way this Nazi walked, with a swagger and confidence, which he utilized to demonstrate his power while he abused, beat, and in this case, shot those he saw as beneath him.

Solomon, an electrician hanging lights at the time, had built some relationships at the work camp. He had allies who helped carry my grandfather to the infirmary to get some comfort, but no medication. It took just shy of three weeks for my grandfather to die from the bullet wound in his head while he suffered in intense pain. My grandmother, Rose, stayed by my grandfather Karl's side while he slowly died.

David Zauder bore witness to his father's pain and suffering, but he also heard his father's last words and had his father's legacy passed on to him. My grandfather told my father that he would survive this atrocity, that he would bear witness to all that had happened, and that he would go to America to live and would contribute something to the world.

After my grandfather died, my father located a Jewish shawl from another prisoner and wrapped his body in it, and then he and my uncle Solomon carried him out into a field in the dark to bury him. Bullets flew overhead going both directions as the insurgents inside the Płaszów work camp fought for their freedom through the night. It took them three full days to do this. On the final night, after they completed their responsibility, they snuck home to their barracks and slept for the first time in three days. They awoke to sounds coming from bulldozers that dug up the field in which they buried their father the evening before. My grandfather had no true burial ground.

Rose Lucks-Zauder in the Płaszōw work camp
thinking and praying someone will come . . .

My father was forced to work. He made horsehair brushes by his mother's side for more than a year, and because he made himself useful, he stayed alive in that horrible Płaszōw work camp. He had to work twice as hard to remain with his mother because he was younger than those who were doing this work, and he wanted to remain close to her as he had already knew the Nazi murdered his father. His fingers were long and agile enough to do the job. More times than my father cares to remember, the workers on either side of him were shot for either working too slowly or for reasons unknown.

When the Nazi's took my grandmother, Rose Lucks Zauder, into a line with mothers and children, she chose to save her son's life, my father's life, David Zauder's life and put him in another line. She gave him her handkerchief, which he has to this day, and told him to remain there without her and instructed him to act older than his age. She was murdered that day, along with many other mothers and children. Placed on a boat, they were sent out on the Vistula River and blown up. My father survived another day.

Rose's handkerchief

Fear was a constant in this environment. His brother, Solomon, had been held back to remain and help while the Nazi's dismantled Płaszów. Solomon tried to sneak into the line for Auschwitz with David who was already being moved into a cattle car bound for the death camp. They were seen and in front of everyone, both were severely beaten. David was sent ahead to reach Auschwitz alone. They were going to close down the Płaszów work camp soon. It would be then that Solomon would be moved to Auschwitz. David's brother arrived there in the death camp in the fall of 1944, after the final destruction of Płaszōw was completed.

In November 1943, David went to Auschwitz, alone, by cattle car. He did forced labor cutting wood for the Auschwitz crematorium for a year and half. It was there, at 3:00 a.m. on November 5, 1944, that he received the painful blue-inked identification tattoo—B-14598. The Nazis, who had held him by force with machine guns, had given him a tattoo in such a barbaric way, branding him—no longer a name, no longer a person, but a number. My father squeezed out part of the last number, through the pain, turning the eight into a three. This one act saved his life.

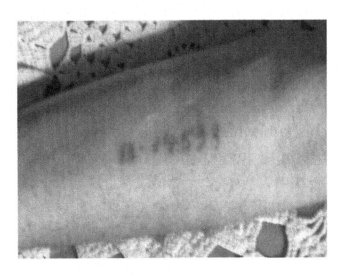

My father's tattooed arm from Auschwitz.
B-14598, he changed the 8 to a 3

In the night, the Nazis often dragged the prisoners out for roll call. Their numbers would be called and sometimes it was decided that all the numbers called were to be marched to the gas chambers. The night they called B-14598, my father did not go forward, because he had changed his 8 to a 3. Everyone who was called that night was taken to the gas chambers and gassed to death.

David was horrified to see in his first barracks, Jews praying with their shawls and tefillin wrapped tightly around their arms and begging God to repair the injustice they were suffering. Nazi guards would come in and machine-gun them down. It was a horrific sight. My father said the Nazis looked down upon any display of religion. He had to change barracks to remain alive, so without being noticed, he changed three times until he reached a barracks filled with captured Russian soldiers, other Polish people, and some Jewish-Polish people he knew from Płaszów. He had blond hair, until they shaved his head, and blue eyes, and he wanted to blend in and not bring attention to himself. "Stay out of the line of fire," his father had told him. He kept his religion to himself, because any outward displays of Jewish rituals got others murdered.

Where there is life, there is hope. ~ Talmud

In the month of December, deep into the fall of 1944, he was put on the Auschwitz Death March that continued until April 1945. He and the other prisoners walked by night and scavenged for food, and they slept by day in the forest. They had to travel this way to avoid being spotted by day walking in a line in fields and being shot at by Americans in planes thinking they all were Nazis. The Americans did not yet have the technology to see that the people were mostly slave laborers. My father lost one of his truest friends walking during the day. An insurgent's bullet struck his friend. My father kept the bullet to remember his friend.

He was only walking with men, about three thousand of them, including about three hundred teenagers who were able enough to walk. My father ate leaves, grass, grubs, and bark off trees to survive. He ate snow to keep hydrated. Having lived through such an ordeal was a miracle.

This was taken by the US Army in 1945. My father in a striped uniform, not his own, but very similar to the one he wore during his Holocaust experience.

The death march was a terrible experience for everyone involved. My father was wearing his black and white striped uniform and wooden shoes without a strap. The Nazis would start out marching to move their slave laborers to the next location where they needed a workforce. After his friend was killed, my father was alone and still on the death march.

In the middle of December and in the freezing cold dead of night, five weeks into the death march, my father fell. He fell into the snow on his knees, and he could not get back up. He was freezing, he was starving, and he was exhausted. He knew he could not give up, but it was the first time he worried that he would not make it. He looked up, turned around, and saw masses of people on this death march walk past him. The well-known rule was if you stopped to help a weak person, the Nazis would kill you both if they witnessed it. My father spoke five languages—Polish, Yiddish, Czechoslovakian, Russian, and German—and at this moment, he looked back and saw a man approach him with a blanket across his body. My father chose to speak in perfect Polish, saying, "Please help me. I cannot die here." As the man with the blanket bent down and picked up my father from the snow, their eyes met. My uncle Solomon looked at my father and smiled just before my father passed out. My father knew he was now safe. Solomon carried him for the majority of the death march, surely saving his life.

Many times during forced work duties, my father would stand on his own, without Solomon's help, but he was, as he has shared, one of the walking dead at this point. Together, the brothers boarded into cattle cars and were transported first to the Sachsenhausen and later to the Flossenbürg concentration camp to work as slave laborers.

Cattle car list from Nazi documents with both David and Solomon Zauder listed below each other. My father's birth date noted here is 14.9.23 which is different from September 14, 1931.

During one of the cattle car transports, it was so crowded, so cold, and everyone was starving. At one point, my father said to his brother that his leg was burning and he did not know why. My uncle, Solomon, squeezed down between the shoulders of the people they were surrounded by to look at my father's leg. He found a man eating my father's leg at the calf. My uncle stopped that man and, again, saved my father's life.

It was an excruciating death march, which seemed to my father would never end. One day, they finally heard American tanks coming up in the distance, and my father felt everyone was in a state of pandemonium. It was General Patton's Third Army, Tank Division.

The Nazis gathered all eight hundred Holocaust survivors remaining of the original three thousand who had started the march. Less than thirty were teenagers like my father. They were told to lay face down in the snow. My uncle Solomon laid his body on top of my father and waited for the bullets to begin to fly, willing to save his brother's life again. But nothing happened. It took quite a while, but some brave prisoner looked up and saw that all the Nazis had fled into the surrounding woods.

At that moment, General Patton's Third Army, Tank Division came up over a hill and liberated the prisoners. It was a crazy time. Everyone was screaming, running this way and that. My father and my uncle climbed onto one of General Patton's tanks and helped shoot into the woods after the SS who fled. They spent a few days with the American soldiers and were given food rations, but not enough to get them healthy, their bodies having been starved for five years.

When they were close to a farm southeast of Frankfurt, Germany, they walked on to this property where they and others ate until they became sick from the rich cheese and milk that their bodies were unaccustomed to digesting at that time. They were very ill and taken care of by the farmers for two weeks, but David was still very ill when they left the farm.

At this time, amazingly, my father still had the belt a friend had given him in the Kraków Ghetto to hold up his striped pants, which kept falling due to his losing so much weight until he made new holes. He was so incredibly thin! He also had his mother's handkerchief wrapped safely inside.

They traveled by way of horse and cart which my uncle Solomon obtained to carry my father. He was too weak to walk, but they needed to get the displaced persons camp organized by the United States Army. Both Solomon and David were hopeful to find any other members of their family who survived as they had survived.

Solomon left the DP camp in order to search for others they knew and he went back to Kraków to learn the fate of their mother and other relatives. Since David was alone again, my father chose to escape the barbed-wire encampment and went to an area in Frankfurt, Germany, where the army barracks of the American soldiers who saved his life were living.

My father begged his way into the army barracks and convinced a guard to let him in to stay. The guard placed my father in the barber's care. In exchange for his keep, my father learned quickly how to cut hair and keep up the barracks and shine shoes.

David Zauder in front of the US Army Service CD.
Supply Room in Frankfurt, Germany

Months later, Solomon returned to the Displaced Persons Camp. He had already met and had fallen in love with Bella, his wife to be, a Holocaust survivor herself. He did not find my father there, so he inquired to the US Army and found my father. Solomon told him of his plans to go to Brazil to live with Bella's family, as they planned to raise their family there.

When they got married in Paris, my uncle Solomon did not even attempt to be certain my father attended the wedding. My father did feel abandoned by his brother, but he understood that they had different fates, and he did not begrudge his brother's choices. When they met again, Bella was already with child.

My father wanted to remain with the American soldiers. Only one light was in the barbershop where he was lucky enough to work, and he used this one light for reading comic books until dark. He read for so long this way that he finally lost his clear vision. The soldiers took him to an army doctor, and he received his first pair of glasses. Then he met Corporal Alex Stroll, his American GI friend who was in the Seventh Army stationed outside of Frankfurt, Germany, in a suburb called Hurst.

My Uncle Solomon Zauder seated and dressed as a civilian and my father, David Zauder, on the arm of the left of him here on a chair dressed in a US Army uniform.

The photo of my father used for the Detroit, Michigan newspapers, with Corporal Stroll's getting it to the Red Cross.

Corporal Alex Stroll in Frankfurt, Germany.

Corporal Alex Stroll assisted my father in finding his aunt in Detroit, Michigan, by sending his picture to the Red Cross and having them put it in the Detroit, Michigan, newspapers. Her name was Anna Lucks-Holtz, and she had been married and then honeymooned in America. Her husband gave her the choice of cities, and she selected Detroit because she had an uncle there. Her husband had no intention of returning to Poland, so after their honeymoon, they stayed to live in Detroit, and that was earlier than 1920. She was the oldest of the four sisters, and she arranged with some help from her family for my David's passage to the United States of America.

Aunt Anna Lucks-Holtz

Instead of returning to the displaced persons camp, my father stayed with Corporal Stroll and Sergeant Larry Forward, the barracks chief who graciously took him in, as well as Lieutenant Frank Bond who was also friendly toward my father.

David lived with the American soldiers for one year. He learned to speak English, how to run errands, shine shoes, cut hair, and he even learned to drive a Jeep.

One of the stories my father shared with me that he experienced while living with the American soldiers was how he learned to swim. Apparently, the soldiers had an assigned pool that was fairly deep but with curved sides. It was very difficult to get out of if you did not know how to swim. One day, while watching the soldiers enjoy time in the pool, one of the soldiers said to my father, "Today is the day you will learn to swim," and he threw him in—clothes and all. My father began gasping for air, kicking his legs, and flailing his arms. However, in his mind, after all he had lived through and survived, he knew he would not die in this swimming pool. He took a deep breath, relaxed his body, and slowly edged his way to the side. Other army soldiers who witnessed this wrongdoing helped to pull him out. My father and I have discussed the experience he had on that day and the irresponsibility of the soldier for thinking that teaching a fifteen-year-old Holocaust survivor how to swim in this way was a good idea.

My father was in Frankfurt, Germany, from May 1945, when he was fifteen years old, until the following year, May 1946, working with the United States Army.

This photo is of the Holocaust Death March survivors
who had been with my father, who was also a survivor
of the same with a motorcycle. My father is seen
to the right of the motorcycle, in shorts. Some of
these survivors are outfitted wearing American army
clothing.

My father liked the safety net of being with American soldiers. Here he is with other death march survivors, he wearing shorts on the right of the motorcycle. The other Holocaust survivors, the other children, hung out in a hotel in Frankfurt for eight to ten days. My father joined them for that short time. They shared their stories about how they survived, and many tried to find their families. Some shared their hopes for the future. Most went to Israel, some to Paris, France. David wanted security and to get to America, so he went back with the American soldiers to stay.

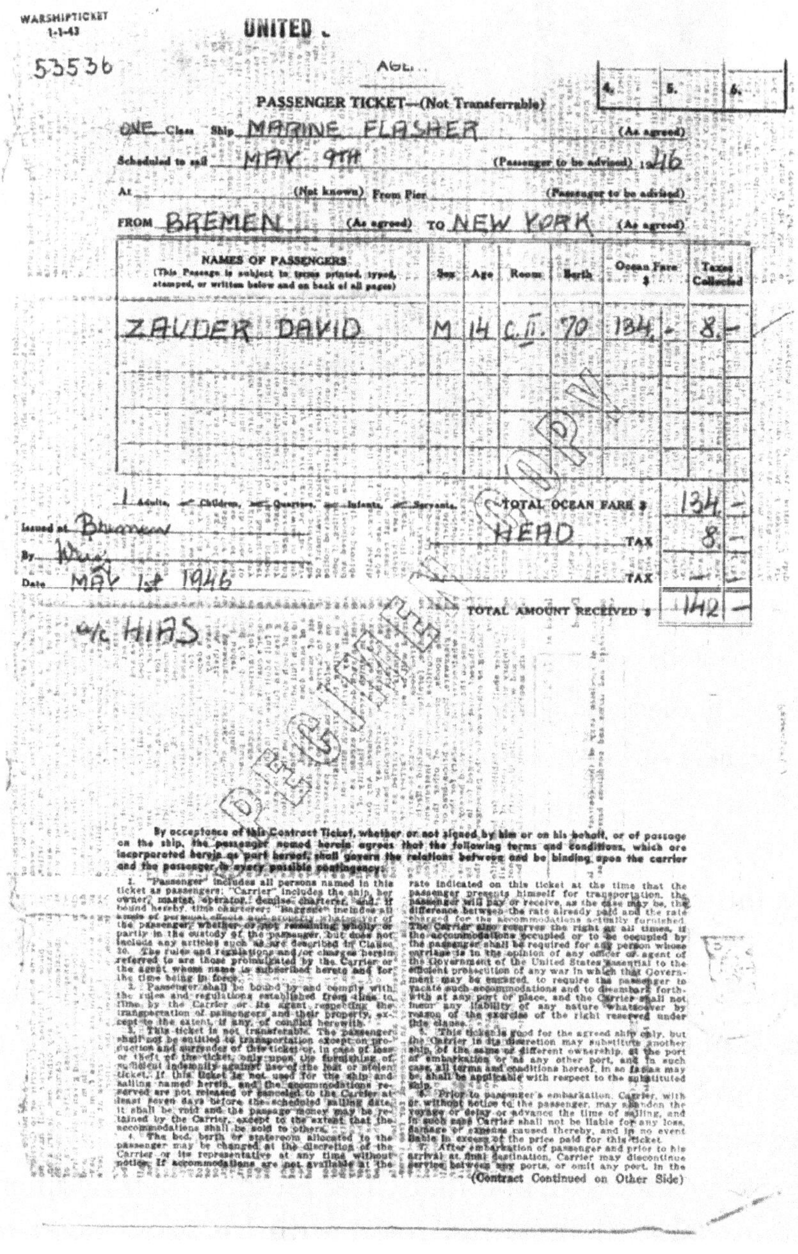

WARSHIPTICKET
1-1-43

53536

UNITED

AGE...

PASSENGER TICKET—(Not Transferrable)

4.	5.	6.

ONE Class Ship MARINE FLASHER (As agreed)

Scheduled to sail MAY 9TH (Passenger to be advised) 1946

At (Not known) From Pier (Passenger to be advised)

FROM BREMEN (As agreed) TO NEW YORK (As agreed)

NAMES OF PASSENGERS (This Passage is subject to terms printed, typed, stamped, or written below and on back of all pages)	Sex	Age	Room	Berth	Ocean Fare $	Taxes Collected
ZAUDER DAVID	M	14	C.II.	70	134.-	8.-

1 Adults, — Children, — Quarters, — Infants, — Servants. TOTAL OCEAN FARE $ 134.-

Issued at Bremen

HEAD TAX 8.-

By [signature]

Date MAY 1st 1946 TAX —

TOTAL AMOUNT RECEIVED $ 142.-

a/c HIAS

SPECIMEN COPY

By acceptance of this Contract Ticket, whether or not signed by him or on his behalf, or of passage on the ship, the passenger named herein agrees that the following terms and conditions, which are incorporated herein as part hereof, shall govern the relations between and be binding upon the carrier and the passenger in every possible contingency:

1. "Passenger" includes all persons named in this ticket as passengers; "Carrier" includes the ship, her owner, master, operator, demise charterer, and, if bound hereby, time charterer; "Baggage" includes all kinds of personal effects and property whatsoever of the passenger, whether or not remaining wholly or partly in the custody of the passenger, but does not include any articles such as are described in Clause 10. The rules and regulations and/or charges herein referred to are those promulgated by the Carrier or the agent whose name is subscribed hereto and for the time being in force.

2. Passenger shall be bound by and comply with the rules and regulations established from time to time by the Carrier or its agent respecting the transportation of passengers and their property, except to the extent, if any, of conflict herewith.

3. This ticket is not transferable. The passenger shall not be entitled to transportation except on production and surrender of this ticket or, in case of loss or theft of the ticket, only upon the furnishing of sufficient indemnity against use of the lost or stolen ticket. If this ticket is not used for the ship and sailing named herein, and the accommodations reserved are not released or cancelled to the Carrier at least seven days before the scheduled sailing date, it shall be void and the passage money may be retained by the Carrier, except to the extent that the accommodations shall be sold to others.

4. The bed, berth or stateroom allocated to the passenger may be changed at the discretion of the Carrier or its representative at any time without notice. If accommodations are not available at the rate indicated on this ticket at the time that the passenger presents himself for transportation, the passenger will pay or receive, as the case may be, the difference between the rate already paid and the rate charged for the accommodations actually furnished. The Carrier also reserves the right at all times, if the accommodations occupied or to be occupied by the passenger shall be required for any person whose carriage is in the opinion of any officer or agent of the Government of the United States essential to the efficient prosecution of any war in which that Government may be engaged, to require the passenger to vacate such accommodations and to disembark forthwith at any port or place, and the Carrier shall not incur any liability of any nature whatsoever by reason of the exercise of the right reserved under this clause.

5. This ticket is good for the agreed ship only, but the Carrier in its discretion may substitute another ship, of the same or different ownership, at the port of embarkation or at any other port, and in such case, all terms and conditions hereof, in so far as may be, shall be applicable with respect to the substituted ship.

6. Prior to passenger's embarkation, Carrier, with or without notice to the passenger, may abandon the voyage or delay or advance the time of sailing, and in such case Carrier shall not be liable for any loss, damage or expense caused thereby, and in no event liable in excess of the price paid for this ticket.

7. After embarkation of passenger and prior to his arrival at final destination, Carrier may discontinue service between any ports, or omit any port. In the

(Contract Continued on Other Side)

The SS Marine Flasher passenger ticket David Zauder was given by his Aunt in Detroit.

David Zauder, second from left, with the boys who survived and shared their life experiences while in a hotel, for three weeks, deciding who they were going to become, now that survived. Only one went to Paris, the rest to Israel and died in the war there. David Zauder was the only one to go to America.

These documents are evidence my father was there, proof that his birth date was incorrect, proof that he survived, proof that his tattoo number was changed in their documents during the time he was a slave for the Nazis. I did not discover these documents until I had spent three days of research at the Washington, DC, Holocaust Memorial Museum in 2009.

Date	29.7.49		Flossenburg	No.47111 PJ	
Name	ZAUDER	David		File	GCC 5/1/d
BD	14.9.28	BP		Nat	Pol/Jew
Next of Kin					
Source of Information	Flossenburg		Reg. made by Doc. Center Third US Army		
Last kn. Location				Date	
CC/Prison Flossenburg		Arr.	6.2.45	lib.	
Transf. on		to			
Died on		in			
Cause of death					
Buried on		in			
Grave				D. C. No.	
Remarks	volume IV, pg 1232				

Third US Army documents from Nazi records.

** Notice the conflicting birth dates and tattoo number on these three documents.

	ITS Combination card based on orig. transfer				
Date	25.4.51 Ts.		slips to/Flossenbuerg	GCC 5/8,	
Name	Z A U D E R, David			File	II A/3
BD	14.9.28	BP	Krakau	Nat	Pol.Jew
Next of Kin					
Source of Information	Flossenbuerg orig.documentation				
Last kn. Location				Date	
CC/Prison Flossenbuerg		Arr.	6.2.45	Flo.No.47111	
Transf. on			from Sachsenhausen		
Died on		in			
Cause of death					
Buried on		in			
Grave				D. C. No.	
Remarks	Previous CC Auschwitz No.B 14598			P/J	

40. This document includes Sachsenhausen as well.

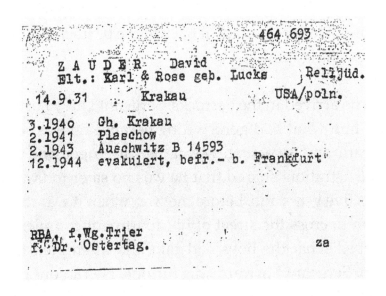

ZAUDER David
Elt.: Karl & Rose geb. Lucks   ;Relijüd.
14.9.31   Krakau   USA/poln.

3.1940   Gh. Krakau
2.1941   Plaschow
2.1943   Auschwitz B 14593
12.1944 evakuiert, befr.- b. Frankfurt'

RBA, f.Wg.Trier
f. Dr. Oetertag.   za

464 693

The Nazi document showing his wrong birth date, his places
of enslavement and his tattoo after he altered it.

My father snuck out at night from the American barracks
to go see movies. Stars like Frank Sinatra, Bob Hope, Bing
Crosby, Esther Williams, and Van Johnson. Seeing these
movies helped him to learn more English. He snuck out
alone through a chain-link fence. He was afraid to go, but
he did it at night when no one could see him and how
he was dressed. He was dressed in a US Army uniform;
however, it was obvious that he was a Holocaust survivor.
On the way back to the army barracks from the movie
one night, there was a gang of three German teenagers
who began harassing him and chasing him while yelling
obscenities. They were taunting him, teasing him, calling
him names, and telling him to go back to where he came
from. They had such hate in their voices, he feared for

his life. My father began to run and they began to run after him. He barely made it back to the barracks without them catching him.

When he arrived in the barracks, Sergeant Larry Forward asked him what had gone wrong because he was so out of breath and sweating. My father, in anger and with great frustration, shared that he was no safer today than he was five years ago, before the war, when it was unsafe for him to cross the street of his apartment complex. He described what the boys had said and attempted to do to him. Sergeant Forward was furious. He ran out of the barracks looking for the German boys who had harassed my father. Since it was late and dark, he came back empty-handed. But the very next morning, he brought two young German boys into the barracks and told my father to take his revenge.

He said to my father, "You've suffered enough; you've been tortured enough, now take your vengeance out on these two and get your revenge."

David was furious, but these boys had not taunted him the night before. He knew that even though they were German boys, they were not responsible for his father's murder, his mother's murder, his aunts' murders, the loss of his childhood, and the way the world was at that time. David Zauder would not use them as scapegoats. The boys were scared, but my he controlled himself and did not touch them. He used his philosophical thought process and determined that hurting these boys would not even the score. He said to them in perfect German, "Go home, and consider yourselves lucky. Think about who you are going to become in your lives. Educate yourselves, and consider; will you be proud of yourself with the actions that you take."

The barrack's chief took the boys by their collars and threw them out of the quarters. The American soldiers looked up to my father for having not taken revenge on these innocent German boys, because they would have understood had he done so. David Zauder had shown them a higher level of morality than they expected to find in a fifteen-year-old Holocaust survivor.

> *What is hateful to yourself, do not do to your neighbor.*
> *That is the whole of the Torah. The rest is commentary.*
> *Now go and study.* ~Rabbi Hillel

David was on the first commercial boat, the SS *Marine Flasher*, with refugees from the war traveling to Ellis Island in New York. He stood in line to get on the boat with his small suitcase made of thin wood; he had all his important belongings in hand. He had saved enough money to purchase a gun because traveling to America alone he believed he needed to be prepared for anything.

One of the American soldiers he knew came up to him to wish him a good voyage and asked him what his plans were. My father told him that Sergeant Alex Stroll, was meeting him when he arrived in America. My father shared with him that he would be okay since he had a gun. The man told my father that he would give him ten dollars for the gun and protect him from not being able to enter America, because holding a gun in his possession would cause him difficulty. My father trusted the man, took the money, and gave up his weapon of protection.

The boat ride lasted two-and-a-half weeks and my father was nauseated and seasick the majority of the trip. He recognized a few people on the boat from seeing them previously in Germany, but he was not friends with any of them. He was alone and afraid, as many people did die on this voyage. He stayed by himself and thoughts ran through his mind about what his past had produced, and he envisioned what his future would become. He was willing to do anything and everything to be free, to grow, to learn the American way, to fit in, and to contribute something to the world because he was a survivor. This was his legacy, passed down to him by his father on his death bed.

He arrived at Ellis Island on May 20, 1946. What my father did in coming to America all alone was incredible.

Proof of David Zauder's arrival to Ellis Island.

Chapter 5

David Zauder's Arrival in America and his Climb to Fame

Corporal Alex Stroll picked my father up from the ferry station in New York after my father left Ellis Island by yet another boat and was brought to the New York Harbor. He took David to his home in Brooklyn, New York, to meet his wife, Ruth, and their two daughters prior to putting him on a train to go to his family in Detroit, Michigan, six days later.

The first thing Ruth did was invite him in and offer him food—a banana. Having never seen a banana, my father took a bite right through the skin and began chewing. Both Ruth and Alex Stroll were quick to correct him, and their two daughters were quick to laugh at his ignorance. They felt the sting of shock in learning that he didn't have background knowledge and lacked life experiences.

David Zauder with Alex Stroll and his wife, Ruth,
later in life. They kept in touch often.

Corporal Stroll had taken great lengths to ensure my father's photograph was placed correctly in the Detroit newspaper, as well as in the *Detroit Jewish News*. It was because of my father's photograph in the newspapers with his name David Lucks Zauder that his family found and claimed him. His mother had a sister, Anna Lucks-Holtz, and she had three daughters and one son—Lillian, Francis, Kay, and Lou. Anna Lucks-Holtz claimed my father and arranged to raise funds and pay for his passage by boat to America. She was very happy that she could help her sister Rose Lucks-Zauder's son come to America and make a life for himself.

The whole family joined Anna Lucks-Holz to try to arrange for both my father and his brother, Solomon, to get the money for their boat passage to join them in America.

I mentioned earlier that my uncle Solomon had other plans. He had married Bella, and she was now caring for their first child, Henry. They had planned to leave Germany and go to Brazil together where she had family. My uncle Solomon had no intention of going to America. Anna Lucks-Holtz was now a widow and very old. She counted on her three daughters and son to take in my father, each of whom was married with children of their own. After all, David was her sister's son who survived the Holocaust. It was Lillian, the oldest daughter and her husband Harry, who decided to take in my father.

Lillian Lucks-Markle and Harry Markle

When David arrived in Detroit on May 28, 1946, the Markle's had a four-year-old daughter, Sheila, and their son Alan was almost three years old. Diane wasn't due to be born until the fall. They did what they could to make my father feel at home when he arrived, and he deeply appreciated their generosity. Lil was known for saying, "You can always add one more cup of water into the soup."

When David was taken to the train station to meet up with Anna Lucks-Holt's youngest daughter's husband, he became very frightened. He shared with me later that he had never met these people, and just because they were family, it did not mean they were safe, trustworthy, or good for him.

He remembers a time when meeting his mother's brother, his uncle, who had lived in America since the early 1920's. This uncle had given him a five-dollar bill. Through the grapevine, this Uncle told everyone how he was paying to help my father financially. This upset Lillian and Harry Markle very much, as they were housing my father, paying his upkeep, and assisting in his well-being. My father gave me that example to show me that just because people are family, blood relatives, it doesn't mean that their motives are clear and selfless and they mean no harm.

I do find the decision the Lucks family made at the time, to send the man who picked my father up from the train station, very humorous. They sent Marcus Sonny, Francis' husband, the least talkative and most stoic-looking man in the family. My father said they traveled in silence. David was good with the silence, but as a fifteen-and-a half-year-old boy, having survived five years of concentration camps, a loving, compassionate experience would probably have been preferred. However, on this man's behalf, he probably had no idea what to talk to my father about, knowing that his parents had both been murdered, and he was now an immigrant orphan. Back then, in 1946, it was the expectation that no one talked about the war. Whether you were a veteran returning from war or a Holocaust survivor immigrating to America, there was no discussion. David Zauder turned sixteen before he began as a sixth-grader in an American school Elementary school. The process of integration, of fitting in, was so difficult; I still cannot believe my father did not have a mental breakdown.

> *Nobody is stronger, nobody is weaker than someone who came back. There is nothing you can do to such a person because whatever you could do is less than what has already been done to him. We have already paid the price.*
> ~Elie Wiesel

The societal pressure and trying to gain peer acceptance was very difficult for my father in the public school.

David Zauder beginning in the 9th grade as a sixteen-and-a-half-year-old at Durphee Elementary School

David began Durphee Elementary School in the fifth grade as a sixteen-year-old, and he was tall for his age. He passed into the seventh grade before the school year was complete. He took summer school classes as well, and in 1947, he passed both the eighth and ninth grade. He was on a mission of success.

He had not formally learned to read or write when the Holocaust began. It is a miracle that he was able to get educated in English as quickly as he did considering his past. He wanted his accent gone, his naïveté gone, and his American expectations met. He attended school through the summer as well, and jumped two grades per year without a tutor. My father decided the way he was going to give back, to contribute something to this world as a survivor, would be through music. His instrument of choice was the trumpet. He loved the sound and the loudness of the instrument. His way of contributing to America was playing beautiful music, and he practiced all the time.

David playing a solo at a school function.

Lil and Harry, understanding my father's musical arts choice, sent him to the Jewish Community Center, and told him to introduce himself to the musical director of the orchestra there. He began playing with the orchestra after that first audition.

Julius Chajas, the music director of the Detroit JCC Orchestra, met my father very early in 1947, a year after his arrival. Mr. Chajas, after hearing my father play, recommended that he study with Leonard B. Smith, and Mr. Chajas arranged for them to meet. Mr. Smith was a world-famous cornet soloist, and the principal solo trumpet of the Detroit Symphony Orchestra. Mr. Smith agreed to take my father on without charge as a scholarship student, which was the only way my father could have afforded lessons. English was still a challenge to my father at this time, so Mr. Smith utilized an English-to-German dictionary to communicate with my father. Mr. Smith could not read Polish.

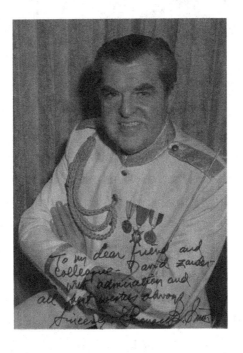

The Leonard B. Smith, David Zauder's
first official teacher and mentor.

121

*David Zauder, seventeen years old, with his first cornet
given to him by Leonard B. Smith*

Both Lil and Harry often discussed whether or not they should formally adopt my father. However, after much time had passed, they noticed that my father's trumpet playing was at such a high level that he deserved to honor his name, his family name, and therefore they did not formally adopt him, allowing him to keep his name and remain David Zauder. Both Lil and Harry were grateful for my father's willingness to contribute to their household. He woke up at 4:00 a.m. daily, never being woken up or told to do so, and helped Harry with his milk delivery business, pulled by horse and wagon, before school. David was always amazed that the horse knew which houses to stop in front of while he was told how many glass bottles of milk to carry up to the front step for Harry.

By 1948, he was seventeen years old and in the tenth grade. He had made a place for himself by playing in both the school orchestra and the school band. He was recognized for his strength in playing his trumpet and was given many solos. His hard work ethic, taught to him at a very early age under much duress, came into play for him in America.

As my father's daughter, I have heard multiple versions of when he first played the trumpet. His first cousin, Steve Zauder, now of Australia, said he saw and heard my father play the trumpet during the insanity of the Plaszów work camp when he too was there with his own mother. My father has not disagreed with this scenario, but he does not discuss it. If you have seen the movie, *Schindler's List*, directed and produced by Steven Spielberg, then you have seen the little boy who plays the morning bugle at the Plaszów work camp. That was my father. Because his father had attempted to keep my father safe and out of the line of fire, he told my father to "get a replacement and stay out of the line of fire." So, my father did what he was told.

When my father saw *Schindler's List* in the movie theater, he disappeared for two days afterward. He told me later that he hadn't trusted his memories of what he had lived through. The movie was very accurate, and they even recreated the Płaszów work camp so that my father believed his memories again. He did know that the white horse ridden by the commandant at this work camp was always with two man-eating dogs released at will, not one. This he saw with his own eyes too many times to question the fact; however, the movie showed only one dog.

Many people in America, when he told them he was at the Płaszów work camp after the Kraków Ghetto, told him the camp did not exist, because they had not heard of it. He also has on occasion said he did not play the trumpet until he came to America to avoid having to discuss that occurrence as well. After a few attempts to discuss his Holocaust experiences, he met with such negative reaction and requests for silence that he stopped sharing his experiences.

Steve Zauder's father, Ignatz Zauder, was my grandfather Karl's brother, making David and Steve first cousins. My father has no memory of his uncle Ignatz or of ever meeting Steve Zauder. However, Steve has been calling my father from Australia since the late 1970s, wishing him a happy and healthy New Year during the high holy days. His daughter, Debbie Zauder, and I have become close since the 1980s. She is my only Zauder cousin I know from the extended family besides Solomon's daughter, Rosa, originally from Brazil, now in Quebec, Canada.

The other story told to me was of the tower of St. Mary's Cathedral in Kraków, Poland's town center. To this day, at the top of this tower, every hour on the hour, a trumpeter will play the song, "Hey Now," which is a warning song.

In the early 1500s, the Tartar's invaded Kraków, Poland, and the trumpeter's job was to warn everyone in all four directions. During this particular invasion, the trumpeter was playing the warning song and an arrow hit him in his throat, disabling him to complete the last note. Today, a trumpeter still plays the "Hey Now" warning song every hour on the hour in all four directions with the final note cut off in memory. When my father was growing up, this was the tradition. He used to run from his apartment to the center of town to hear the trumpeter play.

There also was a story I heard about a Kraków police officer who was his father's friend and played the trumpet. My father, surrounded by music while growing up, saw this man who smoked nonstop and was ill affected by his smoking, but still able to play the trumpet. He used to announce himself present by playing his instrument, not knocking on the door. My father said to himself, "Surely, if this man, so short of breath, could play this instrument, so can I."

My father's decision to play the trumpet was most likely a combination of all three stories I have recounted here.

My father had a difficult time in public school with the student community. Bullies took advantage of the younger, the weaker, and the outsiders within the student body. Every chance my father had to attack bullies and right the wronged, he took it. My father had no tolerance for discrimination, bullying, or taking advantage of someone smaller, younger, or weaker. So when he saw the playground bully pushing a student against the chain-link fence and taking his lunch money, my father beat him up. The student who bullied the younger student went to the hospital, and as the story is told, he took a significant beating from David Zauder.

My father developed quite a reputation very early on in his public school career. I call him the original Standupster!

The original Standupster!

His trumpet teacher, Leonard B. Smith, heard about these difficulties, and agreed with the Markle family that a move into the New York Military Academy would be smart for my father. He knew my father would receive discipline for such behavior, as well as live in a very strict structure, which he knew he was used to from his Holocaust experience. At this time, after my father's actions, he too, did not trust himself and his rage against those who were abusers.

Leonard B. Smith arranged, with the Markle's blessing, to get my father enrolled at the academy on a full-ride scholarship based on his trumpet playing and excellent grades.

My father continued working during school and the summer prior to attending NYMA, as he needed to purchase his own uniforms and supplies for the academy. He worked in a fur factory, rode a bicycle with an ice cream cooler and sold ice cream to the neighborhood, and he continued to help Harry deliver milk in the early morning.

David did well in NYMA's structured environment

Unfortunately, he also experienced hazing while in NYMA. After he had taken all that he could from a hazer, my father beat him up too. He would not allow himself to be a victim ever again. He took action. However, there was a penalty for taking such action at the academy. He was taken to the commandant who said we do not accept this behavior here, but my father explained what had been done to him. He pulled up his sleeve, showed his tattoo, and said, "I've been tortured by professionals, and I will not be tortured and bullied here in America." With full understanding, the commandant gave my father a promotion, and there was never another incident.

*NYMA Band. Third in line behind the two saxaphone
players, with the most medals of honor!*

*David Zauder, Aunt Anna Lucks—Holtz, and Cousin
Lillian Markle at David's New York Military Academy
graduation in 1951.*

I am my father's voice through which I share his strength, his perseverance, and his ultimate decisions to continue to conduct personal, forced marches on to himself while he focused on his commitment to contribute something to this world. Much of what he has achieved as an immigrant he accomplished with sheer internal motivation and a desire to succeed and to prove his life was worth saving. It's with this context I am continuing to share the life he has led, and mine as well, having been under his influence as his proud daughter.

After my father graduated from the New York Military Academy, and while in New York on his way home to Detroit, Michigan, he stopped by and auditioned with Les Brown and the Band of Renown. Les Brown was the musical director for Bob Hope. The audition went well, and Mr. Brown hired my father to join the band in August 1951 and to work with them as they headed to the West Coast. However, as destiny would have it, when my father arrived home, it occurred to him that there was a war going on. He felt he needed to enlist on behalf of his country though he was not yet a fully naturalized citizen. So at the end of one weekend of rest and relaxation, he headed back to New York to enlist in the regular army. He was very aware that he did not understand all the rules regarding enlistment, so he went back to the New York Military Academy and spoke to the commandant in charge. My father trusted him and asked what he should do. With one phone call, my father was enlisted, stationed, and appointed to the West Point Band, which was located at the 1802nd Special Regiment. The following year my father studied and took the exam to become an American naturalized citizen. He was already a sergeant 1st class with five stripes.

Naturalized citizen at last!

Later in August, my father had a weekend leave. Dressed in full army uniform, he took a train to Detroit and showed up to see Les Brown. Mr. Brown was conducting, but out of the corner of his eye, he spotted David Zauder and put everyone in a holding pattern and said, "Oh no! What am I going to do without my next trumpet?" They parted ways and my father dutifully and with high respect and great moral integrity gave his time to the army. He even played in the West Point Military Band during President Dwight D. Eisenhower's inauguration in Washington, DC, in 1953, and he saw

Walter Winchell there who was a New York staff writer and wrote honestly about the Holocaust that happened in Europe while America waited.

*With Cousin Kay {Markle} Kahn
at West Point visitation day.*

When he enlisted and joined West Point, USMA, he added to his extracurricular activities swimming, of all things. He was exceptionally talented at holding his breath, and they utilized him as a safety trainer for practice, letting others pull him to safety as he pretended to drown. He also learned to be a very strong swimmer and placed first for the breaststroke and the butterfly for two consecutive years. He was also a sharpshooter and managed the shooting range.

Butterfly—first place two years running!

*David was an expert rifleman and
was put in charge of the shooting range.*

In 1955, David Zauder was honorably discharged from the army with many honors.

163620

Honorable Discharge

from the Armed Forces of the United States of America

This is to certify that

DAVID ZAUDER RA 12 211 334 SERGEANT FIRST CLASS REGULAR ARMY

was Honorably Discharged from the

Army of the United States

on the 27th *day of* June 1955. *This certificate is awarded as a testimonial of Honest and Faithful Service*

William T. Gleason

WILLIAM T. GLEASON
Lt Colonel, Infantry

David Zauder's Honorable discharge paper

After his military service, my father went to New York to look for a trumpet-playing job. He was a freelancer, but he joined the union immediately in New York. He played at Radio City Music Hall, in churches, the Metropolitan Opera, and he continued to audition for full-time paying jobs. Working for a symphony orchestra often required a twenty-two week per year commitment, so during each summer of 1955 and through the summer of 1960, my father played principal cornet for the Leonard B. Smith Band in Detroit.

He also played Broadway shows, proudly showing me each program, which he kept including, but not in order: *The Pajama Game, Harry Belafonte's "Sing Man Sing"!, Lady in the Dark, Sadler Wells Ballet,* every car commercial and TV show he could get in on, *Ringling Brothers Circus, the Ice Capades, South Pacific, Damn Yankees, the Ice Follies, My Fair Lady, Liza Minnelli, Isaac Jones in the Black Moses, Shaft, the Aqua Follies, Guys and Dolls, Student Prince, Billy Graham at Grand Central Station, the Great Sebastian show at Shubert, Lynn and Fontaine,* Easter Sunday at St. Bartholomew's Church, *The Tonight Show with Steve Allen,* with singers; *Eydie Gormé, Steve Lawrence, Andy Williams, Pat Kirby.*

While all this was going on my father was taking lessons with Harry Glantz and studied with Eric W. Leidzen to learn harmony and composition. He had joined the union in Detroit, Michigan, and enrolled in college taking classes at Wayne State University from 1956 to 1960 during the summers. He studied business administration and humanities. In 1956, he auditioned for the Boston Pops in Chicago under the direction of Conductor Arthur Fiedler and earned the first trumpet position for the 1956-1957 and 1957-1958 seasons. He traveled the United States as a Boston Pops member.

Trumpet first chair with the Boston Pops!

Teacher, mentor, and friend, Leonard B. Smith, 1956
celebrating Boston Pops job.

In 1958, David Zauder auditioned for the Cleveland Orchestra. He was hired to play the 1958-1959 season by the great and well-known Conductor, George Szell. He was placed in the trumpet section, generally playing third trumpet and first cornet. Since orchestras generally have a fall to spring-length season, they are referred to as such.

David Zauder with maestro George Szell on tour in 1959.

When Mr. Szell found out my father had transferred to Case Western Reserve University to continue his college education, he made my father's return for the 1959-1960 season contingent upon his additionally becoming the assistant personnel manager to Mr. Olin Trogdon. In

1966, Mr. Szell gave my father a contract for a job he had already held and been doing successfully for six years prior.

From 1959 to 1969, my father was the assistant personnel manager. From 1970 to 1997, he was appointed the personnel manager of the Cleveland Orchestra, in addition to playing second trumpet and first cornet. My father played these positions from 1968 to 1998. He is the longest-tenured trumpet player in the history of the Cleveland Orchestra. He was heavily involved in organizing the recordings that the Cleveland Orchestra made during his tenure as personnel manager. He had, at one time, six stopwatches that tracked performance time and properly paid employees their fair wages, while he himself played in the recordings as well. On tour, he traveled extensively and many times throughout the United States, Canada, Mexico, Europe, South America, and Asia.

*Conductor George Szell led the Cleveland Orchestra to a top
rate AAA rated orchestra, making recordings
for the world to enjoy.*

Conductor George Szell was an incredible musical leader. He knew everyone's part, and he was high above the rest in his expectations for orchestra excellence. One of the memories my father shared with me was of an orchestra tour in South Carolina. The manager of the hotel would not allow a cellist, Mr. Donald White, to walk in through the front door with the other musicians because he was a black man. He was The Cleveland Orchestra's first African American musician. Mr. Szell said sternly to the hotel manager that if Mr. White were not welcome to be included with the entire orchestra, then they all would leave and not play the concert there that night. The hotel manager allowed Mr. White to enter, and my father saw human rights respected by Mr. Szell and his respect for the man grew to new heights. My father had the distinct honor of working under Conductor George Szell from 1958 until 1970 when Mr. Szell passed away.

My father met my mother in 1957 while they were attending Wayne State University together. Friends had actually introduced them. He bought his home in Cleveland in 1959. Although he felt very insecure in his musical career, as he had not received a contract until 1966, my mother was now a college-graduated school teacher and willing to work. So, together they decided to marry; he an un-contracted musician and she a school teacher. They were married on May 30, 1960.

My parents marriage, and my grandmother Jean Ribiat
to the left of the bride.

David was asked to do commercials selling mutes. A mute is put into the end of a trumpet to "mute" it's sound to be softer, quieter. He is second from the back.

My father was feeling insecure working without a contract, so in 1960 he auditioned for the Pittsburgh Orchestra and in 1961 for the Philadelphia Orchestra. But he chose to remain with the Cleveland Orchestra and work both jobs.

In 1980, my father joined the Cleveland Institute of Music as a master teacher and remained there until 1997. He carried no more than three students per semester and he taught master classes to all interested students, many of whom have gone on to become successful in their musical positions.

Hundreds of students from CIM are thankful for my father's honesty with them, as he shared that they may want to look into another primary career while allowing their music to become their secondary career. There are too many students to recount here; however, one has become a family member: Ryan Anthony, first trumpeter in the Dallas Symphony Orchestra today.

Ryan Anthony, now principal trumpet in the Dallas Symphony Orchestra

Ryan, put in front of my tree by my father in front of the
Compton house, making him "family".

David Zauder's professional photo
from the Cleveland Orchestra

As the personnel manager, my father had the responsibility to make certain that the Cleveland Orchestra maintained its high AAA rating by bringing in the highest-quality visiting conductors until the next conductor could be hired after Szell passed. He collected professional photos from all these great musicians and kept them on display in his practice room.

The next conductor was Lorin Maazel who led the orchestra from 1972 until 1982. My father was honored to be a cornet soloist on the highly acclaimed "Romeo and Juliet" recording which is available as part of the orchestra's wide collection of recordings.

Lorin Maazel recorded Prokofiev's "Romeo and Juliet"
with the Cleveland Orchestra

Lorin Maazel with David Zauder
listed on the record as coronet soloist

Lorin Maazel with David Zauder on tour in Mexico 1978

Brothers Solomon Zauder and David Zauder reunite in 1972

While on tour with the Cleveland Orchestra in São Paulo, Brazil, and without having seen each other in thirty years, my father arranged to meet his brother, Solomon Zauder.

It was a sweet reunion and my brother, my mother, and I attended. My father had studied Spanish and ranked number one in his class while at the New York Military Academy; however, no one took the time to find out why he was so dedicated to learning the language. My father erroneously thought his brother now spoke Spanish. He was very disappointed to learn that Solomon spoke Portuguese, Yiddish, and Polish. Somehow they communicated using a little of everything. We went to their house and spent a glorious time together.

The Pierre Boulez conductor and composer with David Zauder during a recording in Japan in 1997, which earned the Cleveland Orchestra their first gold record!

Having fun in Japan! David Zauder and conductor
Christoph von Dohnanyi!

Soloing at Blossom Music center on July 4th*. Every year we
attended, with stars in our eyes.*

*David Zauder's solo during the Fourth of July concert with
Leonard B. Smith Band at Blossom Music Center. The 4th of
July Concert was held nineteen years consecutively, each with
David Zauder soloing!*

My father was involved in many and various programs within the orchestra to promote early classical musical arts education for public schools, playing thirty-two children's concerts in addition to belonging to three quintets. This was in addition to his regularly required orchestra playing and administration duties. He also was known for promoting the management's ideas for building a family feeling within the organization; he was a pro at building unity. For example, he was in charge of holding softball game days, picnics on the lawn at Severance Hall, and jazz gatherings for the orchestra members. He did a great job building a sense of community and family among the orchestra members.

From left: David Zauder, Al Couch, Bernie Adelstein, Jim Darling. Cleveland Orchestra trumpet section.

From right: Bernie Adelstein, David Zauder, Ron Bishop, James DeSano, Rick Solis. The Cleveland Orchestra Brass Quintet.

While on tour, my father was often out of the country when I celebrated my birthday, which is in September, just like his. Every year my father would call me from wherever he was, and he would play "Happy Birthday" over the phone on his cornet. It was a tradition. Although I missed his presence every year, I knew he loved me, was thinking about me, and valued me enough to remember me and play "Happy Birthday" as my birthday present. Upon his return home, he always had gifts for us.

He was a unique personnel manager because he managed, as well as played in the orchestra, traversing both worlds—musician and administrator. This was difficult and took exceptional skills in personal relationships, understanding personalities, offering respect for all involved, and maintaining constant balance and compromise. I'm certain there are more stories that I am not aware of; however, what I do know is that gathering his colleagues on his behalf for a surprise birthday, or for his retirement party needed no coercing.

As part of his ability to bring people together, my father began to pull together personnel managers from all over the country for an annual conference. These trips were both invigorating and filled with support, knowledge, shared ideas, and shared triumphs within the classical music business. Specialists were often called in to give day seminars on how to work with others. My father was innovative. He was also the union contractor for twenty-seven years as well as all his other responsibilities.

Me with David Zauder at the Blossom Music Festival, which he helped to launch. The Cleveland Orchestra's summer home. I surprised him.

David Zauder's appreciation for the friendship and artistic excellence of Michael Sachs, current first trumpet, whom he played with for a decade. The 1990 Far East tour

David Zauder with Conductor Christoph von Dohnanyi

On Sunday, April 5, 1992, my father participated in the "Heroes of Conscience," which was a tribute to Dietrich Bonhoeffer, Conductor Christoph von Dohnanyi's uncle. Dietrich Bonhoeffer taught religious studies and philosophy at the Union Theological Seminary in New York City. He decided to return to Germany in 1931 and join the fight against the Hitler regime. He was involved in Operation 7, a plan to smuggle Jews into freedom. He was murdered for his efforts. Christoph von Dohnanyi's grandfather who also fought against Hitler was murdered as well. "Heroes of Conscience" was a memorial benefit concert, and musicians from all over the world participated in this program. The program had one hundred and sixty-two musicians from eighteen orchestras, four countries and included two Holocaust survivors, who were participating musicians, my father being one of them. He participated along with six other Cleveland Orchestra members whom he organized. Within some of the focus of the program, it was shared that those who fought back were murdered. The music of German composers who were featured: Beethoven, Schubert, Brahms, and featured singer, Herman Pry, sang the composition "Survivor of Warsaw" which is a Schoemberg piece. Bill Moyers of CBS covered the event, and it was taped and televised.

My father recorded the entire classical repertoire during his tenure with the Cleveland Orchestra. He and Dohnanyi had much in common, including their deep love and high expectations for classical music interpretations.

They developed a very deep friendship as well as mutual respect for each other. My father's first cornet and second trumpet chair was endowed by Mr. and Mrs. Robert Klein, which was a great honor for my father.

The Cleveland Orchestra in 1996, David Zauder is in the right back stage, third left from the gong.

My father retired from his personnel manager position and played with the orchestra through 1998. As this chapter ends, I needed to share how truly engrossed and committed to his art, his music, and his musical family my father was. I know he was working at a fevered pitch, and he even squeezed in a massive heart attack and open-heart surgery in 1987, but he recovered and continued to play. Here, at the end of his career, he received the coveted Distinguished Service Award. His was the second one awarded in the Cleveland Orchestra's history.

Distinguished Service Award

The Musical Arts Association established the Distinguished Service Award in 1996 to annually recognize one organization or living person who has demonstrated extraordinary service to The Cleveland Orchestra in the areas of musicianship, artistic leadership, philanthropy, fundraising, innovation, management, education, governance, and/or dedicated service. Nominations were solicited by the Award Committee from Orchestra musicians, staff, trustees, and volunteers. The inaugural award was given to Dorothy Humel Hovorka in September 1996. The 1997 Distinguished Service Award will be presented to David Zauder at the beginning of this evening's concert.

DAVID ZAUDER

Formal portrait by Herbert Ascherman Jr.

Caricature drawing by retired Cleveland Orchestra member Jorge Sicre, created in May 1997 for David Zauder's retirement.

At the close of the 1996-97 concert season, David Zauder retired after thirty-nine years as a cornet and trumpet player in The Cleveland Orchestra. He holds the distinction of having the longest tenure of any trumpeter in the Orchestra's history. In December 1996, Mr. Zauder stepped down as the Orchestra's Personnel Manager, a post he held for twenty-five seasons after serving as Assistant Personnel Manager from 1960-71. "Overstating the impact David Zauder has had on The Cleveland Orchestra would be impossible," wrote Executive Director Thomas W. Morris in May 1997. "His attention to detail, always within an unwavering artistic perspective, is legendary."

David Zauder joined The Cleveland Orchestra in 1958. Ten years later, he was appointed by George Szell as principal cornet , a post he held concurrently with his duties as trumpeter and in personnel management. In 1989, the principal cornet position was permanently endowed by a generous gift from Mary Elizabeth and G. Robert Klein.

Born in Krakow, Poland, David Zauder was incarcerated by the Nazi regime in 1940 and spent five years in German prison camps. After five months of a forced march from Auschwitz, he was liberated by Patton's Third U.S. Army. He worked with the U.S. Armed Forces until receiving passage to America from his aunt. Arriving in Detroit, he took up the trumpet and subsequently played solo cornet with the famed Detroit Concert Band under the direction of Leonard B. Smith, who tutored David on trumpet playing and English. Mr. Zauder also studied with Harry Glantz in New York, served as first trumpet for the United States Military Academy at West Point, and performed two seasons as first trumpet with the Boston Pops under Arthur Fiedler. In addition, he played for Broadway shows, television studios, and commercial recordings.

During his tenure with The Cleveland Orchestra, David Zauder earned degrees in business administration and humanities from Case Western Reserve University, and served on the faculty of the Cleveland Institute of Music from 1978-95. He appeared as concerto soloist with the Orchestra on several occasions, most recently for the Opening Night Celebration concert one year ago. He was also a featured soloist in twenty concerts with the Blossom Festival Concert Band, an organization of which he served as spiritual leader from its inception in 1968.

In retirement, David plans to spend more time with his daughter Karen, a business executive in Toledo, and son Karl, a medical doctor in Hawaii. In addition, he plans to become a regular audience member at Severance Hall and will continue savoring rounds of his beloved golf game. He will also continue sharing his experience and expertise with others; during the past two weeks, he presented a seminar on artistic and administrative issues for the New World Symphony.

DISTINGUISHED SERVICE AWARD COMMITTEE

Marguerite B. Humphrey
Chairman

Richard J. Bogomolny
President,
Musical Arts Association

Dorothy Humel Hovorka
Vice President,
Musical Arts Association

Thomas W. Morris
Executive Director,
The Cleveland Orchestra

Ralph Curry
Personnel Manager,
The Cleveland Orchestra

3

In retirement, David plans to spend more time with his daughter Karen, a business executive in Toledo, and son Karl, a medical chiropractic doctor in Hawaii. In addition, he plans to become a regular audience member at Severance Hall and will continue savoring rounds of his beloved golf game. He will also continue sharing his experience and expertise with others; during the past two weeks, he presented a seminar on artistic and administrative issues for the New World Symphony.

The honor and the award

Chapter 6

Discord Continues

My mother had said for years that if he took on the personnel manager's job full time, taking more time away from our family and her needs, it would break their marriage. My father felt that his job as a man, as a husband, and as a father, was being responsible for bringing in more money and resources so that our family could have the American dream. They were completely opposed to each other on this issue along with many other issues.

There is a dining room table incident which depicts more of my literal communication deficits due to my learning disorders. My mother and father were fighting and there was a lot of tension and anger, even though we were sitting down to have dinner as a family of four. My mother was good at bringing up things she and my father were fighting about in front of my brother and me as a means to prove to us that she was correct, and she had to do this in front of my father. It was a very uncomfortable situation for my brother and me even though we were used to it. I saw this situation coming, so I began to act out. I must have been eight years old, and my brother was just six. I was goofing off, being silly, and I apparently got on my father's nerves so much so that he was so angry, he stood up and banged the table with both fists and said, "Karen, if you don't stop this right now, I'm going to give you my belt!"

"But Daddy, what would I do with your belt?" I said in a lighthearted tone.

My father turned bright red, and my mother began to giggle. He stormed out of the room releasing the tension, and my brother and I began to laugh. I knew I had hurt my father, but it was unintentional. In a normal situation, this may have been very funny to every family member. But I remember this situation like it happened yesterday, and I had disappointed him even though I was trying to help him.

My father never hit me, never beat me, or even grabbed me harshly. Never. Although, a look from him or a deep breath perfectly delivered spoke volumes. His body language could also scream his true feelings and really let you know where you stood. I trained myself to read the room when my father was present, and I behaved.

Everyone who knew my parents well can speak to the intense love-hate relationship they shared. They were married with love and had a lot of laughs as well as positive experiences while supporting each other through their very different and unique life-choices. Their marriage of 17 years proved their love, however it wasn't enough to overcome their differences.

My father had a belt given him by a friend during the Holocaust to help hold up his prison uniform, due to the starving conditions. The belt is brown and has two prongs that go through holes in the worn leather. He kept both the belt and his mother's handkerchief rolled inside it and still has both today. The belt was important and has always held multiple meanings for me. Hold on tight to your dreams, never forget who you are, even if *they* gave you a number, and stripped away your name. Keep your head down, stay out of the line of fire, and do your best work no matter who is watching. And remember you are loved. I love my grandmother's handkerchief, and today it is framed in my father's bedroom!

My mother talked my father into putting in an aboveground pool in the early 1970s because she saw it for sale in the country. It was during one of the Cleveland Orchestra strikes, so he had time on his hands. So, as it was my mother's idea, we bought that used, aboveground pool, and my father had committed to digging a trench to lay gas piping from our gas heater to the pool to make it a heated pool. While working hard trenching, which took days, my father never slowed down nor took a break. It was scary to watch, as he was the hardest worker I had ever seen.

He began crawling along the trench, after turning on the gas, to see if there were any leaks. He used a lighter, placing it near the piping, going ever so slowly looking for a leak. He imagined that had there been a leak, the lighter would light the gas leak like a mini lighter.

Our neighbor and friend, Neil Serr, stopped by to see how the job was coming along and said in a stern but calm voice, "David. Give me that lighter now." Confused, my father stopped what he was doing and handed the lighter to Neil. Neil then proceeded to tell him that had there been a leak, he would have blown up our house with his wife and children inside! The way to test the pipe was to fill the trench with water and watch for any bubbles. I do believe Neil saved our lives that day. But my father had no personal experience with these things. My father is a Holocaust survivor, and the thought that he could have killed his own family from his lack of knowledge is daunting. The success of the pipe installation, and we all enjoyed the heated pool for years, was also proof he was tenacious. He also changed the house plumbing from galvanized to copper piping, which added to his workload, but he is very proud of his accomplishment today. He had to rent tools and ask friends for help to complete the job.

After I had failed at playing the piano, it wasn't long before I was asked to pick up another instrument. It was decided that it would be the violin. I instantly felt uncomfortable in my stomach thinking about how this decision had affected my brother, Karl. After all, this was his specialty, and it was something he was very proud of and something that he got a lot of credit for. Although I argued quietly, the debate was over before it began and my first lesson was with Mr. Nate Snader of the Cleveland Orchestra.

I did not do well with the violin lessons, and I still could not read music. Nate was kind, and he was very aware of the tense family atmosphere every time he came over. I spoke to Nate about my disappointment that I was made to take up the violin when it was actually Karl's instrument. Nate assured me that when I got going, it would be fun for everyone when Karl and I would play a duet.

My brother Karl with his violin

On one of the days that Nate came to give me my lesson, my mother picked a fight with my father. During these years, my mother was good at picking fights in public and in front of those who visited our home. She felt she needed support, and if anyone heard her side of the issue, she believed that he or she would also try to encourage my father to agree with her. The problem was she was very disrespectful with her speech, tone, and vocabulary. Most people shied away from getting involved.

On this particular day, she was very angry, and Nate and I closed the door to the study where we were practicing. But the screaming got louder and louder, we could not ignore it, and my lesson stopped. Nate sat down with me and told me that this had nothing to do with Karl or me. He reassured me that our parents loved us very much and that this was an adult issue, not a child issue. I know I felt responsible for a lot of their fighting as many children of divorced families feel. I especially took it personally because I knew my father had been through so much pain, so much loss, especially in the family area. A divorce, I felt, would kill him. Nate Snader was one of my angels.

Other times they would fight and Karl and I would sit at the top of the stairs next to each other and listen carefully. My father very rarely used swearwords, and never used physical violence. I remember Karl and me talking about how lucky our mother was that our father never lost it on her during one of their fights. To our knowledge, our father never laid a hand on her, despite what her words were doing to his ego.

I felt like Karl and I were in a bunker together, surviving emotional blackmail as well as emotional warfare. Our mother often put us in the position to give her feedback on her beliefs about what our father should have done or how he should have changed. There was talk for a long time that she had helped another Holocaust survivor overcome emotional issues through her work as an unlicensed therapist. She stated that the other Holocaust survivor wanted to be cured, and that's why she could help him. But our father did not want to be helped. This line of thought infuriated me. Mainly because my father attended so many therapy sessions and workshops, it was amazing to me she thought he was not trying, but he had PTSD. As I believed, and by this time I knew, I had been affected by being a second-generation Holocaust survivor, and for her to say that I should not be affected, and he should just be "over it already" was just crazy. How could my father not be affected by what he lived through, who he had lost? How could my father overcome his post-traumatic stress disorder, quirky behaviors and need for order, control, and cleanliness?

My father's Holocaust experience was a wound that he woke up with every morning, as it appeared to be a dark cloud hovering over him. Every day my father fought that dark cloud off using his four strategies. He was a part of world history because of what he survived and some of the worst human treatment ever perpetrated. Some of which has been a repeat from other inhumane tragedies in world history, and some which even continues today! Based upon his experiences of loss and inhumanity, I believe he has compensated incredibly well. I never allow his Holocaust experiences to be an excuse for his poor behavior toward me, but I do allow his experiences to be explanations for why he has poor behavior. My mother and I were diabolically opposed in this one area of conversation. Despite the multitudes of documentation on Holocaust survivors and their future experiences and abilities to overcome and live, my mother held on to the belief that she could fix my father of all his problems and difficulties if only he would let her. If only he was willing.

He had great needs for cleanliness and order in our home. I was not witness to this, but my mother did tell me that one day he came home after a full day of work and put on a white glove and started touching things to see if she had properly cleaned the house. When he could not find anything dirty, he finally ran his white-gloved hand across the top of the front door archway. She was so angry that he found dirt there and blamed her for not keeping a clean house after all her hard work and effort to make him happy. According to my father, this never occurred. Yes, they fought over the cleanliness of the home, but he used an example that IF he wanted to use the training he received in the US Army, where they used white gloves, he could. But he never did.

Again, this was a story she told me, not one I witnessed. However, shortly after that, my mother hired a full-time house cleaner and nanny named Mrs. Fletcher who cleaned, cooked, and looked out for Karl and me. Mrs. Fletcher was kind to me. She knew I had difficulties with understanding language, and she was patient. She taught me my colors and that took weeks of repetition. I remember the first time I got it right. She was one of my angels. We were in the playroom, she was cleaning the windows, and I was watching cars go by. She would say the color of the car, and I would repeat the color after her. I saw a yellow car go by and I said yellow before she did, and we jumped up and down together cheering that I had finally been able to process my primary colors. It was a big celebration, one that I don't believe my father or mother participated in. I loved Mrs. Fletcher, and I actually saw her again before I got married. She wished me well and we hugged tightly. I felt like she was a surrogate mother for me during those years, and she wanted and enjoyed the job.

Our father, babysitting!

My father was working in so many areas, even today it's amazing what he accomplished. He wrote and published three books for trumpet and cornet. The first is *Trumpet Tunes* by David Zauder, and his second practice book is *Trumpet Embouchure Studies*. The third book was published later and called *Trumpet and Cornet Embouchure and Technique Studies*. He was also active in teaching and as a clinician for the King Musical Instrument Company and did a commercial for them. I was so proud.

School photo of me in the fourth grade wearing a knitted red sweater from my grandma Jean.

I remember as a ten-year-old coming home from Hebrew Sunday school at Park Synagogue, and finding my father outside cooking on the grill. I had learned a new word that day—Holocaust. Somehow, I knew this word involved my father; perhaps it was the teacher asking me to wait in the hallway while they discussed the details of the Holocaust in class.

When I saw my father, he appeared happily focused on the grill, the food, and the intention of a shared meal with the family. Food was important to him, and we always had enough. So you can imagine how devastated I felt when I asked him in my ten-year-old little girl voice, "Daddy, what does Holocaust mean?" My father's face fell, fear permeated the air, and he walked away from the food cooking on the grill. I followed him into the kitchen undaunted, because I did not understand. The mood had changed and the rules were that I was to be good and quiet. But I was insistent, and I was afraid, but I asked again. His answer was harsh and final. He said, "You are too young to know," and he walked away.

Mrs. Stern, my fifth grade teacher at Euclid Heights Boulevard Elementary School, supported and believed in me, so I began to keep a serious journal. She knew I struggled educationally, but she liked me and helped me find my voice. My writing and even some poetry came naturally after that. I wrote this story when I was ten years old to share how my father's past affected me.

~

A Legacy a Choice

It was early evening and I was watching my father skillfully peel, in a continuous circular motion, the skin off an especially large tan potato. He did this so carefully and with so much concentration, I had to wonder why. I was not yet old enough to understand the answers to many of my questions, but I was curious enough to ask them anyway. I had seen him peel apples too, but only when he peeled potatoes did he disappear.

"Why do you peel it like that?" I asked him.

My father just looked at me, smiled a slow, self-containing smile, and gently said, "Someday, when you are old enough to understand I will tell you my story."

I, being slightly annoyed at being thought of as young, yet respecting my father's silence and reasoning, kept quiet and did not ask him again.

Later, I often wondered why he was mysteriously secretive towards me. Why didn't he ever talk with me? What was so terrible that I shouldn't know? But I did know, from some powerful source within me, I had to wait and give him the time to see that I was old enough to comprehend the feelings he so much kept me sheltered from.

So, I patiently waited, steadily growing older and working in vain to act in an adult manner whenever I was with my father. I so much wished to learn of his life, his past, to get to know him. Yet, he continued to deprive me of his horror-filled history.

Finally, the day had come. I was ten-and-a-half years old, and I had learned a new word. I saw my father grilling outside and thought it was a good time to carefully ask my father what it meant. The word was "Holocaust." A look of terror shot through my father's eyes as I could see him search for a sign, a sign that would show him that this was indeed the time I had so much longed for. He finally said, after a testy explanation of what the word meant, that he would now tell me his story.

I was full of excitement and wonder to what was to come. Yet, I felt a severe feeling that this was not a joyous affair. With wild, incomprehensible concentration, I listened intently to my father. The time had come. His story was to mark me for the rest of my life. For now I shared his sadness, his loss, his grief, his guilt and pride, all mixed together as one.

I grew up a little that day, and I felt terribly closer to my father. Although, I have yet to totally comprehend his personal tragedy. Since then, I still childishly and angrily longed for the devastating day to occur again just so that I could take the vicious revenge my father had courageously surpassed.

~

Because my father did not answer my question, as the above poem suggests, this began my Holocaust education, focus, interest, concerns, and passion. Behind my father's back, I continued to learn about the Holocaust. We never spoke of it again, not until years later, in high school. However, it was a known fact that his screams in the night in Polish were a secret in our family that no one shared.

As the years went by, I read everything I could get my hands on starting with Chaim Potok's book, *The Chosen*, and then *Anne Frank*. I list many more books on my website as references. I continued to choose to be Jewish, read Jewish books, and learn about the Holocaust. I felt intense pride that both of my family heritages were seeped in the Jewish heritage and culture going back generations.

This I wrote in fifth grade while contemplating why life was so difficult for me and why I felt such an intense desire to achieve.

~

The More I Wonder

The more I wonder,

The more I see.

The more I see,

The more I know.

The more I know,

The more I search.

The more I search,

The more I feel.

The more I feel,

The more I miss.

The more I miss,

The more I remember.

The more I remember,

The more I hurt.

The more I hurt,

The stronger I become.

The stronger I become,

The less I believe.

The less I believe,

The more I reach.

The more I reach,

The more I need.

The more I need,

The less I find.

The less I find,

The more I wonder.

Karl and I were with our father once during a rehearsal while Lorin Maazel was conducting. We knew our father, sitting in the back, could not see us. We were in third and fourth grade at the time and had not yet developed our ability to think about consequences for our actions. We used our one-foot long, sugar-filled Pixy Stix and conducted from the middle of row four, exactly as we saw Maazel doing. We kept great rhythm, but we also attracted many onlookers from the violin and bass sections. So much so, that when we stopped to giggle, they found themselves off beat from Maazel, and he was beginning to get furious! We were in big trouble with our father that day, but the orchestra members who saw us thought we were very cute and fairly good conductors to boot!

Because of my father's position with the Cleveland Orchestra, I often attended Saturday night concerts with my mother and brother. In fact, I believe that from the age of ten through 14 years old in middle school, prior to our parent's divorce, we spent most Saturday nights at a concert. It was a thrill to have such great seats in the balcony watching my father on the back right side of the stage while he played his instrument.

~

The Day the Bass Fell

One moment, I was absorbed in the program while I carefully filtered out what conversations I wished to listen to, and then the next moment I was holding my breath as I watched the beautiful bass being picked up off the floor along with its musician. My heart skipped a beat as I began to formulate what had actually just taken place in an instant. It seemed almost irrelevant how the trite tragedy occurred. What had been left was what was most interesting. Not only was the performance about to begin, but the by standing musician that had his bass affected also by the fall was obviously examining his instrument ever so painfully and was scorned by his fellow bass player for his incompetence, without words.

I felt for the man who let his bass fall accidentally. He had not even gotten up off the floor before his comrades were on him like vultures. I watched him the rest of the concert and saw him change from what I was used to seeing on the professional stage. His embarrassment and his now felt incompetence humiliated him so. It showed in his newly formed stature, as his frame was no longer proudly squared. His playing stance was severely hindered as I could sense that the memory of the event was not leaving him room to concentrate on his performance. His musical enthusiasm seemed to have been ripped from his very soul as he pushed himself forward to finish up the evenings events. I felt for him and his newly acquired position and the tear I felt rising up deep from within my throat.

~

There was a time when we were at the Cleveland Orchestra's summer home, Blossom Music Center, and the famous Captain Kirk, William Shatner, was going to be there narrating the program. I was thrilled! A real, live movie star! I wanted his autograph, so I begged my father to let me accompany him to work early before the concert. Knowing my father ran the guest services and would be talking with Mr. Shatner, I told my father I needed an autograph, but he was busy and did not commit to getting one for me.

The moment had come, and there in the backstage hallway, near my father's office, was my father and Mr. Shatner talking. I walked up slowly, unseen as always, holding my paper and pen to get his autograph. My father ignored my presence completely, as did Mr. Shatner. I waited patiently and thought surely that Mr. Shatner would know I was a huge Star Trek fan and see my pen and paper, and when they finished going over the details of the program, he would smile at me and present me with his autograph. It didn't happen.

Neither my father, knowing my intentions, nor Mr. Shatner, ever looked my way. When they finished talking, they parted ways, both apparently blind to my presence. I was horribly disappointed and hurt, but I remained silent, as I always was in my father's presence.

I often wondered how I could be so fortunate to be able to attend weekly concerts. It was a time of much thought for me, and I truly enjoyed reading about each musical performance and what I was about to feel as well as hear. The next short poem I wrote after one of those nights at Severance Hall.

Me with my father before a concert

~

It's Your Love I See

The brilliant light seems to be aimed through you

as your orchestra hails its sound

and majesty around you and in front of you.

You delight in its magnificence and watch over it

like a mare watches its struggling newborn colt.

You don't help, but you admire its efforts and you offer

your support and maternal-like love.

It is your love of life that I am witnessing.

It is your love through their performance that I see.

It is your life.

~

Chapter 7

My Brother's Keeper

All I can say is that every single person is the combination of his or her experiences subliminally submerged and accumulated, and combined with one's DNA when one comes into a problem. ~ Richard Holbrooke

There were other things that happened while I was growing up that I was pretty sure did not happen in my friends' houses. My brother was born twenty-two months after me. I felt very close to him while we were growing up on Compton Road.

Karl and I arm in arm

Karl and I sharing soup

We were good playmates together, and we were both afraid of making mistakes. We both came immediately home from our distant travels in the neighborhood when our mother rang the big navy ship bell out by our backdoor. We felt we shared more than the average sibling did.

My father named my brother Karl after my father's father, who was murdered during the Holocaust. I remember feeling as if my brother and my father were constantly working out their relationship. I knew my father adored my brother, but I also knew he did not know how to show his affection. My father never mentioned his parents, but

I knew they were watching him, like angels. I felt always emotionally connected in a deeper way to my father's personal life. I bore witness to my father's pain as well as his personal success in overcoming post-traumatic stress disorder through horrific memories he brought into the present, which then became a distorted present.

My brother and I were very close when we were younger, and I remember we did a number of things together that were slightly different from the norm. When walking to public school approximately six blocks from home, we would pretend to be speaking a different language. We used voice inflections and took turns. It was fun. Somehow, I believe we both thought that we should have known a different language, like Polish, unlike our friends and neighbors. So we pretended and it felt right.

We also played a game that I believe is amazing, based on our age and knowledge at the time. For me, it's proof information was passed down by osmosis as second-generation Holocaust survivors.

We used to walk in the snow, always in snow, and whoever was first, up ahead, would fall down and pretend they were dying and couldn't get up. The one who was in the back was supposed to run up to the one who had fallen in the snow, help him back up, and carry him to safety. I don't recall ever discussing this role-playing game; however, my brother and I played this game with each other for years.

The first time we played it, I remember being in third grade, my brother in second grade, and the last time I have a clear memory of playing it, we were both in high school. As I mentioned before, it's important to know that my father had his life saved by his brother during the death march out of Auschwitz, in the snow, and being carried to safety was part of my father's survival. My brother and I did not know this as we enacted it.

I only remember having this happen a few times, though I know it happened with some frequency; my father would scream in Polish during a nightmare. My mother would comfort him, but they would never discuss it in the morning. I began having nightmares when I was in first grade. I was highly anxious due to my inabilities, and I was very aware of how much better everyone else was than I was at most everything educationally. I worked really hard, and I still didn't get the best grades. Nightmares are normal and age-appropriate in the first grade, but I was worried my father would think I was too stupid to be his daughter, and I worried I wasn't good enough. I felt scared all the time.

My brother had a different experience being the son of David Zauder than I did being David Zauder's daughter. For all the reasons that I could come up with for the differences between the ways my brother was treated by my father and the ways I was treated, all it serves to do is to allow for my misinterpretation. With that said, I am only able to give my opinion here; you'll have to wait for my brother's memoirs for his personal opinion.

Fear. There was always a lot of fear growing up with my father and his concerns for us. He had to hold in all his emotions and his fear when he was surviving the camps, but he never could recover completely. Because of me, we were now out of the closet; we were Jews living in Cleveland Heights, Ohio. Cleveland Heights *was* a Jewish section of town to live in; my father made certain of that when he bought the house one block down from the Park Synagogue, a Conservative synagogue. Fear of our way of life becoming known to non-Jewish neighbors and friends, fear for our safety, fear for our ability to get an education, and fear for his ability to provide for us was always in the forefront. I felt it, I saw it; the fear was palpable for me. Fear of losing his job. My younger brother, Karl, dealt with a lot regarding my father's fear as well.

My brother was given the opportunity to begin playing the violin through the Suzuki method at a very early age. He learned to read music by the age of five. My brother was exceptionally talented and he showed promise, which gave my father great pride. Karl continued to master his instrument. He played with the infamous Mr. Leonard Samuels of the Cleveland Orchestra, and then later, he played with the fabulous Mr. Nate Snader of the Cleveland Orchestra. My brother played the violin until he turned twelve, and then he chose to quit. He had mastered Vivaldi and learned it by heart. I was amazed at Karl's abilities, and was so happy for him because I knew it drew him closer to our father. Culture was very important to our father, and we were responsible for continuing to grow. Karl had a hard time practicing because it came so easy to him; he didn't have to practice very much to get it perfect. This was not my experience.

My brother's personality showed weakness regarding work ethic, chores specifically—raking leaves, shoveling snow, etc. He seemed very entitled, due to our mother's influences on him, and he had a poor attitude regarding his responsibilities in the family. I often heard him speaking aloud to himself while doing a chore, saying things like, "He's trying to kill me" . . . "I can never get all this done today" . . . "This is going to take forever" . . . "I'll die before this job is over."

When my father would hear Karl speak like this, he felt infuriated. My father had slaved for five years in horrendous conditions to save his own life, eating one stale piece of bread per week and one bowl of mostly watered-down potato soup per day! And it did not help that my brother looked a lot like my father did when my father was young. They shared a strong resemblance. As my brother reached the age when my father's life turned upside down, the expectation that my father had of my brother to rise to the occasion became extreme. My brother was to prove that he too would have survived the Holocaust to reduce my father's anxiety. But my brother was not aware of this connection or this expectation, not as I was. When Karl failed, my father became incensed. We were to be survivors. No excuses.

Karl looking like his father when he was younger, like on page 102

David Zauder at twenty-four years old

Karl Zauder at twenty-one years old

I remember when my brother was young, my parents were fighting a lot, and my mother would call my father on his unrealistic expectations for Karl's behavior. I had the same expectations given me, but I always surpassed them without complaint, and I worked extremely hard to do so. My mother never had to protect me regarding my father. Karl was more vocal and self-deprecating.

One day in particular, my father went ballistic after finding out that Karl had done something wrong. Remembering that he was young here, it was still a bad situation. Remembering that my father had spent days hiding inside a latrine at Auschwitz, with defecation up to his shoulders to save his own life, keeps the focus on what was expected now that he was in America. His own son was disrespecting the value of freedom and living in a home my father provided by failing to be proud and failing in participating by caring for what our father worked so hard to provide for us.

There was screaming and running, and I remember hearing my mother yelling to my brother, "Don't let him catch you! Run! Run!"

I believe my father managed to get in a few hard swats, but he was not going to be able to stop himself and my mother knew it. My father's rage had been set free, and my brother was getting all of it at once. My brother got away, ran downstairs to the basement, and hid near the laundry room. By the time my father got down the stairs, Karl had squeezed between the machines and made it back to the stairs and ran up and out. It was chaos. My mother felt helpless and could not stop my father's uncontrolled rage.

My father felt disgusted with his own loss of control and abusive rage. I believe my father lost it that day because of who he was, what he had lived through, and what he perceived my brother's life to be, which was safe, secure, and comfortable and filled with love and anticipation for his future. How dare my brother take that for granted?

My father almost lost it two other times on Karl. My brother had made some bad decisions, but my father went after him with such anger and rage, not equal to the offense. Unfortunately, my mother used these examples repeatedly to share with both Karl and me how my father was too emotionally and mentally deficient to be our father. Just hearing her talk like this about my father put me on his side, as his protector, because I knew he did not want to feel that way at such a high level, but often felt uncontrolled. I believe his fear started when he began his family. Would he be good enough to be a father the way he wanted to be? I think he did the best he could with the knowledge he had at the time, just as my mother had, and of course, I was in the habit of forgiving him for everything because of his past Holocaust experience. I have learned how to forgive my mother as well, and have done so.

I remember often comparing and wondering why my brother and I were so different. After all, we were raised in the same house with the same parents. We were told the same rules, given the same amount of responsibilities while our parents were married, and yet my brother had difficulties.

In third grade, some bullies were picking on me because I was different. On one particular day, Karl rescued me from four of them. They had caught me, tied me to a tree with rope, and they were taunting me. I was crying. I was getting rope burns around my middle waistline, and Karl was terribly scared and alone when he saw me like that. He had taken a few years of karate and he overcame his fear. He started kicking and hitting every single one of the bullies yelling the whole time to get away from his sister. He beat them all up and they ran away. He was in first grade at this time; he was my hero. We walked home together, and I thanked him for weeks for what he had done for me.

Unfortunately for him, he had embarrassed the leader of the third grade gang, and they were out to get him for the rest of the school year. He ran home from school every day the remaining school year to avoid another confrontation. They threatened him simply due to his protecting me from their bullying. They never bothered me again, and I was eternally grateful to him for his bravery and his courageous willingness to get involved and help me, to be a Standupster.

My father's four standards for living remain the same today as they have been for his adult life.

Use your mind. Wake up and read a newspaper. Listen to the news. Think!

1. Exercise your mind and wake up and use your mind, read a newspaper, watch the news, read.

2. Exercise your body and keep it strong

3. Exercise your spiritual life through music and faith observance. In his case, hold a memory of murdered family, friends, and community close

to the heart at all times. Be honest, respectful, and observant to your culture.

4. Do something nice for someone else daily. Be a mensch; Yiddish for a human being conscience of others in the world.

He dedicated hours to community service his entire life in Cleveland. The JCC and the YMCA organizations held running marathons. He participated annually for the community fundraisers. In total, the logged miles he ran registered more than thirty thousand, but he ran more than that. He ran probably closer to fifty thousand miles.

After our parents' first divorce, he was living in an apartment two miles away from us. I often ran with him, in silence, of course. I became quite a good runner. He would phone me, and without any introduction or hello say, "I'm going to be leaving my apartment to go for a run; if you'd like to join me, be outside in seven minutes." I would hurry to change clothes; begin to stretch as fast as I could, and when I would see him nearing the house, I would run out to join him. Before he ran around the circle driveway the second time, I would have to be out the door or I would have missed my opportunity. It was crazy, because I needed to stretch out first, and I was never dressed for running when he called. I only missed him once, and I had to run really hard to catch up with him that day. We would run for three or four miles, not talking, just running.

I had a condition where my ears would hurt when the air was too cold, and I learned to wear a bandanna, a sweatband, or even earmuffs during those cooler seasons. He never validated the fact that my ears actually hurt me, so I took care of it myself.

I was never to complain to him because he couldn't believe that I felt pain. If I could acknowledge my physical pain or discomfort, it proved I was weak. Again, proving I would not have been able to survive the Holocaust. He had no empathy for any of my complaints, because he could not allow himself to believe that they existed.

During track, in physical education during my eleventh grade year, I was pushed to run more than I could. The coach yelled at us and told us to go two more laps, and my shins were screaming and burning. I told him that my shins hurt, and he told me to quit complaining and hurry up. I said to myself that this is nothing compared to the death march my father had been on during the Holocaust, and therefore I needed to shut up and run my last two laps. I do give myself credit for complaining to the coach and telling him that my shins hurt because that took a lot of courage for me; however, I should have just walked off the field. I ended up going to the hospital, having x-rays, and being told I had severe shin splints and needed to be on crutches for three weeks.

Me on crutches after my "forced march".

I am certain that my father's sharing with me his torturous death march was never meant to encourage me to allow personal physical harm, and yet looking back, I had made choices many times that were harmful for me because of my constant comparison of his death march experience and whatever current difficulty I was challenged by. These comparisons affected my decisions in undermining my own ability to self-advocate. His experience of pain and suffering always won.

When Harry Markle, Lil's husband died, my father fell ill and he failed to attend the funeral. I don't know who contacted me to share the bad news, I don't remember, but I do remember feeling torn between both responsibilities; going to Cleveland to care for my father who fell ill for the first time in my life, or going to Harry Markle's funeral.

When I spoke to my father on the phone, he sounded horrible, and he told me he couldn't get out of bed. I asked him what he wanted me to do and he said, "Don't worry about me, it's nothing."

I chose to represent his Zauder family at Harry Markle's funeral. I could not reach my brother, and so I was there alone, again. My memory is very clear of how wonderful that family looked together, and how far removed from them I knew I was. Years later, I attended Lil's funeral with my husband, David, by my side. I still felt quite distant from them.

Once, Lil's grandchildren, now in their thirties, commented and shared their personal memories of their Grandmother, as is custom. How terrific they felt receiving homemade zucchini bread while at college from their grandmother Lil. She would wrap the bread in a box filled with real popped popcorn. It was obvious to me that Lil never considered me one of them. I never received a care package in the mail, with or without real popped popcorn from her and certainly never her famous zucchini bread. It hurt to know that was what my cousins enjoyed, and I had not had the opportunity to be treated by my grandparents in that way. The Nazis murdered my father's parents, my paternal grandparents, so they were not alive to treat me well and spoil me while I was in college. My mother's parents died earlier, right before I left for college. I was alone.

When I was in high school, I was forbidden to join or take part in the Holocaust studies conducted by Dr. Leatrice B. Rabinsky, a true pioneer and our Holocaust and history professor at the time. I had been forbidden to travel in the summer for a class trip to see Poland, Germany, and any of the concentration camps.

I remember how frightened I was to ask my father to come in and speak to my high school Holocaust class. Dr. Rabinsky knew my father was a Holocaust survivor and she asked me, in front of everyone, to bring him in to share his story. I tried to tell her he doesn't talk about it, but she insisted.

My parents had been divorced for five years at this time, and having time with my father was very limited. So I had to call him and ask him if he would come in and talk about something he had yet to talk with me about. It took great courage, but I phoned him and asked. He agreed to do it! It was like a miracle to me. He agreed to come into my high school, Cleveland Heights High School, and speak to a class of thirty students and tell those things he had yet to tell me. I was both happy and furious. I couldn't believe he thought that it would be okay for me to hear of some of his trauma in front of my peers.

My father chose to share a small amount of detail with my class, but he also shared a list of R's. Words to live by, like responsibility, reliability, realistic, respect. The list of P's were; Perfect Practice =Perfect Performance. I could not write them down, as I was crying too hard. He wanted to be motivating and inspiring. After the forty minutes went by and all my peers filed out of the class, I found myself hugging my father and burying my face into his shoulder while I cried. It was one of the hardest days of my life, and I felt alone again. I wrote this poem afterward.

~

My Father Spoke to my Class Today

My father spoke to my class today. He spoke of his childhood laced with anti-Semitism.

He spoke of the human race as a whole and why we shouldn't condemn them.

He spoke of his held in feelings, though he didn't explain it that way.

He spoke of his childhood dreams and oh, how limited were they.

He spoke with intense concentration and prepared thought, though he knew he hadn't time.

But I knew his presentation would pay off to the very dime.

He would stick in a joke here and there as he tried to reach the youths.

But there were only a few there that actually sought to learn of his specific truths.

The truth came out in many ways, including one very horror filled happening.

He was in a boxcar when some hunger starved, half-crazed man, my father's leg he started chewing!

I held in my tears of his tragic years and tried to hold my composure. But when all was said and done, I gave him a hug, my tears, like a wild river had no closure.

I can't begin to explain the very sharp pain I feel deep inside me.

I only know that my children will be shown the way, somehow, to a beautiful, fruitful life.

Free from this kind of tragic life changing strife.

The pride and sadness I felt when my father heroically let go and let his feelings show was oh, so great.

No one can mistake his ideas for simple man's fate. I love him oh so dearly, and I can see ever so clearly, that the love I feel now will always be with me through eternity.

~

Rabbi Cohen was a very wise and gifted rabbi, and I was lucky he was my rabbi while I was at Park Synagogue. I spoke with him often of my family life, especially my father's tortured existence. He always showed the highest level of compassion for my father and taught me the correct way, a respectful way to understand what my father had endured and had emotionally been through, a Genocide, how to deal with a father who was a Holocaust survivor. He knew my mother, he knew my situation, he knew I was slow but smart, and he treated me as such. I felt honored to have him counsel me, and I also felt understood and protected being a Jew in his shul, his synagogue.

The day my father spoke to my high school class was a life-altering day for me. I had shared with Karl that our father was going to do this, and told him he should come and he said no. He said he ". . . wasn't living in the past . . ." As much as I was trying to support and protect my brother and trying to share with him our mutual family history, he wanted nothing of it at the time. I had friends who were not in this class with me, who were going to be there for me during this emotional time, but they failed to appear. I was alone. I was alone in a room filled with my peers who did not understand my fear or my father's bravery for choosing to speak because I asked him to speak. Because I asked him to speak, he spoke. Not for any other reason would he "out" himself as a Jew. I was amazed and confused by the amount of information he shared, that somehow I already knew. I couldn't stop crying. In front of my peers, in high school, I couldn't breathe. My father spoke in spite of my emoting. As everyone left the classroom, stopping by to thank my father first, I hugged him and sobbed for the pain he had endured. He was not willing to hear me or understand my pain. He continued to keep us separated.

That was the beginning for me of his sharing directly with me. Dr. Rabinsky was wise and asked me to follow up with my father. She directed me and gave me examples of questions to ask him and to clarify what his experiences actually were during the Holocaust. I audio taped a personal interview with my father. The following Sunday, I had arranged to come over to his apartment with a tape recorder and my list of questions. He was frustrated and short-tempered with me, but he answered every single question.

Fear could have held me back from asking for my father's entire Holocaust story. Fear could have held me back from my future speaking engagements, but I didn't let it. Fear is false evidence appearing real. My father taught me to be quiet about my Jewishness because it would keep me safe. My father taught me more through his actions than through his words that he is Jewish. He is proud to be Jewish, but he is fearful of Jew haters because they still exist today. "It is a private thing," he would say, "like politics, money, and sex."

I knew I was Jewish and I was proud of my heritage and I became more involved at the Park Synagogue Temple. I studied under Rabbi Cohen, and we had a class together. Once he left to go to the bathroom and returned unprepared. What I mean is he left his zipper down accidentally. All the other students began to giggle, and I knew right away that I could not allow my great rabbi to be giggled at while he was teaching us Torah lessons. So even though I was painfully shy within this social peer group, and not truly accepted by them, I got out of my seat and walked up to him and said quietly in his ear, "Rabbi Cohen, I'm sorry to point this out, but your zipper is still down." He was so grateful that I had stood up and spoke out for him in front of my laughing peers that he made an example of me as being a mensch. I was very proud of my choice. I knew the difference between right and wrong, and I knew that my decision would not make me more popular, but I did the right thing anyway.

Later that year, I specifically asked Rabbi Cohen, who was a very famous and well-beloved rabbi, if he would support me in being the first female to lead in the children's services on Sunday mornings at Park Synagogue. I was lucky Rabbi Cohen knew me well and liked me as much as he did, so he approved. I studied alongside the rabbi's son and two other young male students, both within a year or two of me. I was a fanatic at practicing the prayers, each having different musical melodies for each of the different holidays. I loved singing!

One of my proudest moments was when I was leading the singing in the children's service one Sunday morning. I looked up and saw my father sitting in the back row praying alongside the students. My father never attended regular services; he only attended the high holidays, Yom Kippur, and Rosh Hashanah. We never spoke of it. Another example of how close we were through our silence.

I was in high school now. I left the house early in the morning and stayed at school late to avoid my mother. After a brief remarriage to each other, my parent's tried to reconnect, that had lasted less than a year, my parents were divorced again, and shortly after, we moved. I held down two jobs and multiple extracurricular activities at the high school. I had been the first girl to apply to and be hired as a delivery person for the *Cleveland Plain Dealer* newspaper back in the 4th grade, which I continued for years.

My mother was a staunch feminist and activist. She was very proud of me for marching in, respectfully, and asking for that job. I had started with just three city blocks, eighty-five houses, and grew my route to more than 245 homes and later, after we moved, delivered to apartment buildings. It was hard work, but I didn't mind. It was good money, and I was growing my skill set when I had to collect payments. I also worked phones at a construction company trying to sell their services, and I worked at a lawyers' office answering phones. My goals were to move out and get into college.

I had anti-Semitic experiences. The first one was after my parents divorced. My brother and I were sent to the Hebrew Academy, and I was excited to learn Hebrew and get more Jewish in my daily practices, davening and saying all the blessings. But while on the Hebrew Academy school bus, I was sitting by a window when a snowball came in and hit me in the eye. A bunch of private school children were throwing snowballs at our Jewish bus and yelling nasty anti-Semitic statements. All of us on the bus tried to ignore them and the shame for having been victimized we felt, but no one talked about it. It was very painful for me to explain to my father how I got the black eye that day. In fact, I'm not sure I ever did explain it to him.

When I moved out and left for college as a sixteen-year-old with dyslexia, auditory processing disorder, executive dysfunction, nonverbal learning disorder, and a lot to prove, I never thought that I wouldn't regularly be coming home on weekends and for holidays. My idea of family differed much from my familial reality;

however, that is what happened. My mother and I had a difficult relationship, which did not improve while I was away at college. I spent years away from an actual home and felt okay with that, because I saw myself as a survivor. I believe my father thought he was doing his job—concentrating on his career, paying for my college education—though he too did not stay in touch or worry where I was during holiday weeks off from school. I knew he loved me and counted on me to step up. I am truly grateful he succeeded in supporting me financially to obtain my college education, because he never received a free ride. Neither have I. I had three jobs at all times to pay for my food, expenses, rent, utilities, and gasoline.

When I went to Bowling Green State University, I worried about others knowing that I was not so smart. I felt worried often, due to what I know now was my nonverbal learning disorder and executive dysfunction. I worried I wouldn't make it in college. After all, I was admitted to BGSU on probation due to low scores on my SAT tests. The tests were timed, and I was not given modifications in support of my disabilities. I had a wonderful high school student counselor who helped me complete the college requirements for admittance, and she wrote a beautiful reference letter on my behalf. In addition, I had seven other reference letters from managers of positions I had held.

It felt overwhelming to me being in a dorm situation and having to learn all the locations of my classes in such a large, spread-out campus. I remembered being in middle school and not being able to find my way around after transferring from the Hebrew Academy. I finally came up with a plan. I put colored tape matching each book cover and matching folder, per subject, on the outside of the doorjamb where my classes were. For whatever reason, I could not figure out how the classrooms were numbered, even knowing they were even on one side, odd on the other. Looking back, I was dumbfounded that my brain did not allow me to learn that automatically, like everyone else, but all my friends did. It was embarrassing not to know where I was, or how to get to where I needed to go next, by myself.

I remember I worked every summer while in high school as a camp counselor at Camp Wise, as well as jobs at the Jewish Community Center, and the mall in retail sales. I was saving money to buy a car. The time I spent as a camp counselor at Camp Wise was what solidified my decision to become a schoolteacher. I wanted to go to college to learn how to help other students with similar difficulties as mine were, even though my special needs were mostly undiagnosed at the time. I knew other children were suffering. I knew they were teased and bullied as I was and had been. I was committed to learning what I needed to learn so I could help those young, special-needs students who today represent a large percentage of all student bodies. I still am today, and that's a large reason I have chosen to speak and share today.

According to the Learning Disabilities Association of America, more than 50 percent of all students in public school K-12 special education programs have been diagnosed as having learning disabilities. According to the National Dyslexia Association, it is estimated that 30 percent of those with dyslexia have coexisting ADHD. I believed that with the proper education I could be of service to children like myself.

At Camp Wise, I felt special and gifted, and I was beloved by my campers. I held respect for my campers and took my responsibilities seriously. I was honored to be voted best camp counselor two years in a row. I didn't do what most people did at Camp Wise; get a boyfriend for the summer. I was committed to my campers every Camp Wise trip I attended.

Saying good-bye to Karl as I left for the summer
to work at Camp Wise.

Hugging from behind him. We had a good relationship
mostly while in high school together.

One summer I was gifted with a special secret friend, a
male counselor who liked me but didn't want to scare me
away. He wrote me notes and did special things for me
without me knowing who he was. Looking back now, I
had no idea that his being my special secret friend was
his way of wanting to date me. I was socially clueless
in that department. If only I had learned some of those
social skills, I would not have felt so alone.

One time during college, in the middle of the night, my
brother called me while I was working at a night job taking
care of emotionally disturbed children in a lockdown
facility. I am exceptionally proud of my work at the Child
Development Center in Bowling Green, Ohio. I worked

two evening shifts per week with teenagers who lived in the residential facility and considered difficult. I treated them with respect and felt no problems with any of them during my year working there. I was the night-shift person who got them to bed, did their laundry, fixed them all breakfast, and got them showered and dressed in the morning before the school bus came. I'm very proud of the work that I did there especially helping a young woman named Leslie who had an exceptionally traumatic experience.

During the evenings, my job was very busy with all I had to accomplish. I know I was extremely helpful to Leslie, for it was during the evenings that she would wake from her nightmares and share with me what really happened to her. I took detailed notes and provided them to her therapists. When she visited me at my home years later, she thanked me profusely for holding her through those evenings so she did not feel so alone. She looked fabulous, strong, and independent; she appeared healed.

The fact that my brother knew the phone number of where I worked at the CDC shows you how close we tried to remain. On this evening, he called me sounding very upset. He said that he felt he had taken on the worst characteristics of both of our parents while I seemed to have taken on the best characteristics of them. He wanted to know why this was. I shared with him that I felt now that we were both over eighteen years old, that it was up to us to select which characteristics to maintain as part of our personalities, part of our values, and part of who we chose to be as people—second-generation people. We spoke for a long time that evening, and I only can hope that sharing his feelings with me had helped him cope with what he was going through at the time; he was still living with our mother. She often tore us apart, and he let her drive a wedge between us. She required sides be picked, both before and after the divorces. One of my biggest regrets today; I lost my brother for years.

Karl and I while in college

~

I wrote this poem afterward.

Hang on Little Brother

Hang on Little Brother, it'll be all right. Hang on Little Brother, just hold on tight. The trip may be confusing and cut like a knife, but hang on Little Brother, you'll soon see the light.

I've been there too, I know how you feel. It hurts and it's aggravating but your feelings are real. Don't push aside the pain or the ideas you've been pondering. You'll be surprised how close to the answers you've been wandering.

Hang on Little Brother, remember it's all in the name of love. Hang on Little Brother, don't let go of the dreams you're dreaming of. Life gets easier at times, and then more difficult than others. But hang on Little Brother, believe me it's worth all this bother.

Don't worry about proving yourself or anything you wish to do. Don't put extra pressure on yourself behind the disguise of being cool. Just be yourself and let your bright ideas flow right through you. I'll be here always to listen and to share my ideas too.

Hang on Little Brother, for you're the only one I've got. Hang on Little Brother and let's continue to strengthen our love knot. We'll be all right and probably come out the wiser pair. So hang on Little Brother and remember that life can give its fair share.

Hang on Little Brother, for the load alone is not for you to carry. Hang on Little Brother, your soul is too special to lay down and bury. Remember I love you and we'll get through this phase together. So please, oh please, hang on my Little Brother.

~

One Monday in 1986, I spoke to my father in the midmorning. Throughout my day, I sensed that he needed me, so at the end of my first of three work shifts, I called him. He answered the phone out of breath and hurried. Not unusual, but my sense that something was wrong with him was very strong. He shared with me that he had gone to the lawyer's office that morning to change and update his will. This was an unusual circumstance, after all, my parents had been divorced now for more than a decade, and my father had not changed his will until this day. My intuitive sense was that he knew something was wrong, and I was right.

Come to find out, the next day late Tuesday afternoon my father had his first of three massive heart attacks. The first one dropped him to his knees clutching his chest, trying to catch his breath. It lasted less than ten minutes and he chose to ignore it. He made no phone calls, and he did not lessen his work schedule. It was on the same day I called him.

The second heart attack occurred two days later on Thursday after the concert that evening at Severance Hall. He told no one and went off stage like nothing had happened.

The third heart attack was on that Friday while onstage during a morning concert. He could not lift his trumpet to his mouth due to the pain. No one noticed. He went straight to his office and called my brother, Karl, who was to be leaving, himself, to go to the doctor's office for an upper respiratory cough.

My father told Karl that he was going to need to take his appointment time because something serious was happening to him.

When my father arrived at the doctor's office, he stayed with Karl in the waiting room until Karl's name was called, and then he went in instead. The doctor hooked my father up to a heart monitor and found that my father had suffered three massive coronary heart attacks and that his main artery was 98 percent blocked. He told my father that he needed to go to the hospital immediately and would require open-heart surgery, making my father miss the concert that night. My father told the doctor he would drive himself to the hospital, and the doctor quickly corrected him and told him he would be getting an ambulance ride to the hospital.

I have no idea what my brother did next. I don't know whether the doctor saw him for his infection or whether he got the care he needed, but I do know that all the while he worried about our father. Karl had to drive home and somehow obtain a ride back to the doctor's office to drive my father's car back as well.

All I know is that I had arranged to take time off work from all four of my jobs to come home that weekend. When I arrived at my father's house and saw my brother standing there waiting for me, I knew something terrible had happened. Karl grabbed my arms and told me something happened to Dad and that he was in the hospital. I dropped to my knees, began to cry, and said, "I knew it, I knew it, I knew something was wrong!"

Karl and I drove to the hospital and waited in the hallway while the medical staff proceeded to do multiple, painful tests on our father. From the hallway, I could see his feet shaking with pain and discomfort. It felt awful to watch, as I knew in his Holocaust experience he had been tortured, and I was both scared and protective of him. The only person I remember calling was our mother, who now lived in Hawaii. Her only comment to me was, "It serves him right. He's been asking for a heart attack for a long time."

Karl and I were alone again. The entire orchestra was aware of his heart attack, but not aware that he had suffered three. They had to do open-heart surgery on him, and he had a single bypass that was successful. Karl and I waited in the hospital deep into the night by ourselves.

We got a phone call from Mr. Nate Snader, the violin teacher that both Karl and I had studied with, offering for us to come to his home for dinner. We received only one offer and we accepted graciously. Karl and I went to Nate's house and had dinner with his wife and his young daughter, and it was a lovely evening. I thank him today for his willingness to reach out to us, the pseudo-orphans, while I was left to parent my brother, Karl.

Nate and his daughter, with Elsa Z. Posell on back left

Because my father had separated us from his personal life, and because of my father's beliefs and values, I had no one to call on his behalf. We heard on both the television and radio news broadcasts that *the* David Zauder of the Cleveland Orchestra had suffered a massive heart attack and was in recovery in the Cleveland Clinic. It appeared everyone knew, but Nate Snader was the only one who reached out to us. Remember, this was before cell phones and e-mail.

I visited my father in recovery and without being informed of his condition ahead of time, I saw him on a ventilator. I had not been afraid until I saw that. I had no idea they had put him on a breathing machine after his surgery. My trumpet and cornet-playing father was hooked up to a breathing machine. I had no idea if he would fully recover, and I worried if he would ever play again. I knew this was going to be a make-it or break-it deal for him. Without asking permission, I walked around the circle of recovering surgical patients, as if I had the right, and I went straight up to my father and using my freshly washed finger, applied moisturizer to his lips. His lips were so dry, the worst side effect for a trumpeter to withstand. He had memory of me doing this for him, even in his unconscious state. When my father was moved into his own room, they gave him a plastic spirometer to practice breathing into to regain his lung capacity. He was very upset by having to use this device, and he sent me home to get his mouthpiece from his trumpet.

When I returned to the hospital with his mouthpiece, he sat straight up, the staples visible down his chest, and he played the national anthem on his mouthpiece. Then he said, "I do not need this piece of crap plastic that they charged my insurance hundreds of dollars for . . . I'm fine!"

I took him home and began nursing him, but he only allowed me to stay for two weeks. At the end of the second week, he asked me to leave because he said he had someone else who wanted to come in and care for him. He did not disclose who this other person was. I was hurt, but I also knew that I had spent more time with him during those two weeks than we had in the last fifteen years, so I felt grateful for the time together.

For two months, my father continued his recovery without me, with some strange person caring for him whom I did not know. During this time, I was not on the receiving end of any details regarding his recovery. Although I called every few days, the report was the same. He was continuing to improve, and he expected to be back to work in short order. Later, I discovered he had a girlfriend who took care of him in my place. She was a woman whom he had been with for a number of years.

My father used to wake up every day under a gray cloud. One that he could not dispel without doing specific things that he had determined to be his top four morning rituals. The same four rituals I've mentioned before: mental, physical, spiritual, and doing something nice for someone else. After he accomplishes these four things every day, then he allows himself to feel joy in his life, and he has successfully dispelled his enforced gray cloud. After I learned of her existence, I was grateful that he had allowed himself some personal happiness, not just more punishment for having survived the Holocaust, feeling survivor's guilt, and the loss of his family through repeated divorce.

While he was in recovery, his focus was to get back to his jobs: playing the trumpet and cornet, being personnel manager for the Cleveland Orchestra, and trumpet teacher to student, Ryan Anthony, at the Cleveland Institute of Music. My father recovered very quickly and in record time. No one could believe how fast he was back on stage blowing his trumpet—hard! I believed it.

One night he revealed to me with pride that during a performance, he blew so hard he heard popping. It was six of his staples popping out of his chest incision and into his shirt. He found the staples later that evening while undressing to go home. That's the kind of man my father is.

Chapter 8

Thanksgiving for the Divorced Family

My parents divorced in 1976, when I was in the sixth grade, and then they remarried each other in 1978, and promptly divorced again in 1979. I was very shaken by all the turmoil. In 1980, my father moved back in for six months. I began to feel even more splintered when he moved right back out. I was a person living in America without a true family. This was not what my father had had in mind. I had to keep Karl close to me so he would be safe from all the chaos.

The first time my mother divorced my father. Then they got back together and were remarried, and I was present at that wedding with the Serr family and a few other friends. Karl and I didn't think it was going to work because of the nature of the fighting that they had been doing. We both hoped they could make a go of it, because we didn't want to be a broken family. Within that first year, they separated, and then my father divorced my mother. It was never discussed where the children were to live. It was obvious to both Karl and me that we were to live with our mother. But there is a story involved.

I remember hearing that my father had shown my mother many houses when they were considering moving into a bigger house in a neighborhood closer to Severance Hall where he worked. I remember hearing that the house my mother first saw and fell in love with, when she came from Detroit to Cleveland to be with my father, was finally up for sale. It was a Tudor mansion on the corner of Overlook and Edge Hill Road.

The Tudor house Mansion

View of me when we moved into the Tudor house, 11
years old and in the Hebrew Academy.

She adored this house, seemingly built for a queen. There
was a carriage house in the back, but that was being
sold separately. This house had twenty-seven rooms
and seven-and-a-half baths. My father's first response
regarding this house was money pit, because there
were so many things wrong with it. It wasn't up to code
and the city was going to demolish it if it didn't sell. If
it did sell, the buyer would have two years to fix it up.
My father's second response was not feeling worthy or
financially capable of living in such a mansion. He wanted
to live an assimilated life, not draw attention to himself
and his family. I recognized both problems, and as an
eleven-year-old girl, I agreed with my father. The calm

one, the one who never criticized me openly, the one who I could spend time with, and even without talking, felt good. I don't remember the details now, but I do know that not siding with my mother was always a bad choice for me. She took her sides seriously. It was war.

So while my father was touring in Europe in 1977 with the Cleveland Orchestra, as he did every year from August through September, my mother sold the house we lived in and bought the Tudor mansion. I still don't know how she did this without my father's signature at the bank, as it was his house, even though they were still married. We moved into the new giant house during my twelfth birthday weekend. My birthday went unnoticed. Every year, from wherever in the world my father was, he always called me on the telephone and played, "Happy Birthday" to me on the trumpet. This year, the phone had been disconnected.

When my brother and I, along with my mother, went to the airport to pick up my father and bring him to the new home, Karl and I knew all hell was going to break loose. And it did. Our mother drove our father to the new house he did not want and said, "Welcome home!" My father stormed out yelling that she had no right to do this without considering his feelings, knowing how he felt about this house, and he shouted that he was done. This was the beginning of the first divorce.

Afterward, my mother enrolled both my brother and me in the Hebrew Academy. I was there during my 6th and 7th grade years. She felt we both needed the intense structure as well as the Jewish education, and I believe she knew it would hurt my father to have us in such a location due to his fears of the intensity of the Orthodox Jewish religion, as well as being located in one building filled with Jews. Due to his past, he felt we were not safe in such a building filled with Jews waiting to be blown up.

The first year, Karl thrived and mastered the educational portion as well as the Hebrew instruction he received. He was getting straight A's and began to believe he would grow up to be a doctor, which his maternal grandparents and our mother told him he needed to become. He is currently a doctor of chiropractics working in a successful practice.

Because I was now in the sixth grade at the Hebrew Academy, the girls swarmed around me supportively. I was the new girl, and they tried to teach me everything I needed to know to fit in. It was the perfect modification and accommodation for someone with as many disabilities as I had. I never needed to know what was next, because they always told me, so I was always aware. My anxiety began to wane and I developed friendships. As a severe dyslexic, nonverbal learning disordered, executive dysfunctional preteen, I felt like I finally understood what I felt my brain never picked up earlier. With their constant supervision and attention to the details I was missing, I was given what I needed academically on a daily basis. It was like being in a three-tiered school. It was both an educational experience and a spiritual one as well. The test was would I become an Orthodox Jew?

I was invited to many different family's homes after school on Friday through Sunday morning. They were all Orthodox Jews, so there was no travel by car from Friday sundown until Saturday night after sundown. The problem was, I couldn't return the favor and have them come to my home because my mother did not keep kosher, and she always drove on Saturday.

By the following year, my peers ostracized me, and it was painful. I had become fairly good at reading and writing Hebrew, which was difficult with my disability; however, we spent every day for five hours a day in Hebrew study. The repetition is what did it for me. We chanted the Bar'chu after lunch every day, which is a beautiful prayer thanking God for the ability to eat, to share a meal with others, and for those who prepared the meal. Because it was in song, I memorized it, and it became part of me.

As I shared earlier, my mother had a very strong personality, and although it was often overwhelming for others, living with her prepared me never to feel overwhelmed by anyone else. Compared to her, no one compared. I had the confidence to question everything I did not understand while studying the Torah at the Hebrew Academy. So much so, that on a regular basis

I was sent to the principal's office to think about what I had just said. However, that put me in close proximity with the rabbi, the principal of the Hebrew Academy. He listened to me, he answered my questions, and he was happy I was so outspoken. Another lesson learned.

Having my peers at the Hebrew Academy turn their backs on me in the seventh grade because I wasn't like them in my Jewish upbringing made me very aware of what it must have felt like to not be accepted by the non-Jews when my father was in Kraków, Poland. Far from it, but I felt isolated, and I felt extremely disturbed that I would be judged based upon my mother's choices of not having two sets of dishes upon which to eat from and becoming an Orthodox Jew. Not that it was a little thing; being kosher is a spiritual ritual and a commitment. But knowing my mother's beliefs, we were not going to be kosher. We ate mostly kosher food, but we did not separate our meat from our milk. The experience made me look deeper at what religion, spirituality, values, rituals, and morals meant to me, personally.

My mother was still not happy with me, and in fact, she complained often. It actually seemed to me that now that my parents were divorced, all of my mother's attention was on what was wrong in her life, and that included my educational difficulties. In the seventh grade, the Townsend Reading Center therapists finally diagnosed me with severe dyslexia, but they offered no real therapy or follow-up. I attended the center, but my mother told the therapist that due to money issues, she would only allow me to come back for three sessions. So the therapist spoke fast and intensely with me about my diagnosis. I was in the seventh grade, but reading only at the fourth grade level. My fluency was also low, but my comprehension caused her the most concern. The therapist shared with me a few tricks that would help me maintain a level of organization and be able to be educated, but this required extra work, above and beyond the norm. That worked for me, because my work ethic was very high and hard work did not scare me. I felt horrible that I had so much compensating to do and my hands began to peel again. The anxiety was so great in my life, especially then, because I was again proving to my father that I wasn't good enough. It was one thing to prove that to my mother daily, but it was on another level to provide that evidence to him. My hands peeled from high anxiety.

At the end of my parent's second marriage, I wrote this poem, which shows my deep Jewish roots, belief in God, and my willingness to reach out for help, which has since become a strategy enabling me to live my life more successfully than had I not asked.

~

The Wall

Even when I had the chance to wish for anything in the world, I wished for the restoration of your marriage. The wish would be on a little slip of paper and would be delivered by an Israeli scout to the great Wailing Wall in Jerusalem—not to be denied. Had I been a little further ahead in my emotional development, I would have realized that it was not possible and I would have asked for something less damaging and more realistic for all involved. I felt, when alone, that the second marriage had been my fault, as it had ended in the second divorce and it was I who had, after all, wished it of the wall. My wish had been granted, even though I thought at the time it was not a blessing, it was, for I learned so much more the second time around. My belief in love was tested and strengthened, and I learned more of what to yearn for and that which to let go of.

~

I remember having a meeting with my high school counselor regarding how to get into college with my abysmal SAT scores. I was not given extra time for the tests which, had I had an individual educational plan (IEP), that would have been an accommodation that would have helped me reach better scores and share the true level of my intelligence. She shared with me that I had done so many extracurricular activities and had so many letters of recommendation, including one from her, that four universities had accepted me. I did get into the school of my choice, but I was on probation.

The first semester at Bowling Green State University, I was only allowed to take four courses, or twelve credit hours.

So I sought out two paying jobs and got straight A's in all four classes. I was quickly removed from probation.

One semester I retook an English writing course; the professor was so kind to me. He understood that my dyslexia had made me a horrible writer, and he helped me rewrite all my papers from the earlier semester without having to attend class. That semester I carried twenty-one credit hours and worked two jobs. This is another reason why writing this book was so difficult for me. As a child of divorce, many emotions emerge and sometimes, as in my situation, the children are severely affected.

I continued to try to emotionally help and save my parents when I was in college. I remember scheduling off work so that I could come home my sophomore year for Thanksgiving. I planned the whole thing out. I first called my father to make certain he hadn't accepted anyone else's invitation, as he had done so for years. Then I called my mother to tell her that my father wanted us all at his apartment for Thanksgiving, which was not true. However, he did agree to have Thanksgiving at his apartment upon my request. Then I called my brother to make sure he would be there so I would not be alone between the fighting ones, and he committed to being there. Next, I went to the library and checked out books and copied passages, and literally assigned readings to outline our Thanksgiving meal. Not only am I a second-generation Holocaust survivor, I'm also an adult child who has not been truly parented. I orchestrated the evening. The following describes what happened.

~

Thanksgiving for the Divorced Family

After nine years of the sometimes vicious sparring of love, we paused.

We paused in our paths of the separate lives we've acquired to retrieve the family feeling once again. For one short evening of thanks, we dropped our arms. With the table set and the champagne poured, we welcomed each other. Arms outstretched and embraced in anxious hellos and holiday greetings. Dinner is cooking and so the evening's endeavors begin. Smiles grow and tensions relax as all continues to go well. Even though there was an isolated incident, even though I felt like fading into the blackness of the old, worn, omniscient chair, even though I held in my wounded soul from any onlookers, I was partially rescued. My natural instincts of yesterday returned, and I got that sick feeling in my stomach all over again. It was all too familiar in the turning and aching felt like I was falling,

falling,

falling,

into a land of mistakes, and old ways proven wrong, only to prove themselves wrong all over again. The same pain. The same loss, the same tears formed in the corner ducts of my childhood eyes.

~

Karl and me that Thanksgiving Day

During one of the rare weekend visits to my father's second apartment on Monticello Boulevard, my father had both Karl and I over for the weekend, and we were listening to music and playing bumper pool on my father's special table. It had bumper pool on one side and a card game with poker chip spaces on the other. At one point, I noticed that my father had gone into the small kitchen, and I went to check on him. I witnessed him hunched over the sink crying when the mid-1970s song, "Never Going to Fall in Love Again" played on the radio. I had left my brother in the living room zoned out emotionally, as he often was during these times in our lives. I saw my father crying for the second time in my life. The first was when Anna Lucks-Holtz died, and we attended her funeral. Seeing my father crying, no, sobbing, with his chest heaving, trying to catch his breath, I became the adult and I held him. I felt that was the beginning of my mothering him. I always felt like it was my job to take care of him anyway, after all he'd been through, but now it was obvious he needed help, and how dare I withhold such help. I became emotionally married to my father, a surrogate spouse, and many times, I gave to him without receiving.

I wrote this prose poem after my parents remarried each other, then re-divorced five months later. We had spent a weekend together, Karl, my father and me.

~

Being There for Each Other

I remember a day, long ago, when the pain had been so deep that just a song from the radio moved, even you, to tears. In your second apartment one Sunday afternoon, when you shared a few scant hours with us, we all were quieted by a song called, "Never Going to Fall in Love Again." It all hit me like the final curtain falling at the end of the first act. Even you had a hard time and removed yourself in your twisted emotions into the small closed in kitchen. I felt the extremity of the moment and I felt too alone to remain in the small living room with one who didn't want to be close, so I took a chance and went into the kitchen to see if I could reach you. When I came around the corner and saw you hunched over the sink as if you were going to be sick, or in horrible pain, it stabbed me in the heart. All your dreams seemed to fly around the room and I caught a glimpse of them as one almost hit me in its flight. You somehow heard me and turned and invited me into your world and we embraced, hard. I didn't let go right away as I was afraid of your usually silent emotions, but as you let go and began to cry on my shoulder, I lost it. I cried too and we stood in the lost embrace of love, a lost hold of dreams, lost hopes for the future, yet hanging onto the reality of being Father and Daughter and being there for each other.

~

My mother knew that her marriage was insufficient for her needs before the first divorce. You'll probably have to read her book to get her whole side of the story. My father accepting the personnel manager's assistant job was the beginning of her unsatisfactory lack of time spent with him, so she shared with me regularly. When he took the job full time, no longer just the assistant, she began complaining regularly.

She really loved this Tudor house. For years, she had been collecting furniture in our basement to fill up the mansion. Seeing the writing on the wall, I asked my father if I could move in with him. He said children should never be separated from their mother. Silently, in my head, I said, "But she's not my mother."

She and I would continue to have large-scale arguments, many of which she began by coming into my bedroom while I was sleeping at 2:00 a.m. and yelling at me. I never knew when she would do it, and I never knew what set her off, but I always knew that I was a disappointment to her and that no matter what I said or did in her eyes, I was not going to do it right. I was managing my own type of survival.

I wrote this poem in hopes of having her hear me.

~

Enough — No More

Such complicated communications

so many high expectations

Enough — No More

feelings of guilt and alienation

accompany feelings of anger and frustration

Enough — No More

confused have I choose to follow

seeing you in the same rut while you choose to wallow

Enough—No More

wondering why I feel such deception

it's all leading to my personal dissatisfaction

Enough—No More

passing the carving knife between us at will

making you proud of me and my cutting skill

Enough—No More

no more role switching, or skilled carving

no more hook catching, or soul bargaining

Enough—No More

no more pain, no more fears

no more lies, no more tears

Enough—No More

no more evening the score;

it's been enough

No More.

~

One day, after I'd had enough of her attacking and yelling at me, I said I was leaving. I went to the front door closet to grab the purple winter coat that my father had bought me for my birthday that September. She said I could not have that coat because she had bought it for me, and if I was going to leave, I was to leave with nothing. In addition, if I left, she said she would never let me come back home. I went through the front door, slammed it as hard as I could, and wished to God that her words had been heard.

She called my father, as she seemingly always did to complain about me, and told him that I had left the house in the snow with no coat on and he was to go get me. When he drove up alongside me and told me to get in because he was taking me back home, I said, "I don't want to live with her anymore. You got to divorce her, why can't I?"

He was frustrated with me because he knew I had been so angry, which is an emotion never to be shown, because it indicates a weakness of self-control. But he did not know the whole story. He only knew what she had told him, because our relationship was based in silence.

My plan had been to go to a girlfriend's house, which was just two miles away. I knew I could walk that far in the snow and cold without a coat. After all, my father survived the death march. I had gone to seek refuge in her home in the past, and my friend had eight brothers and sisters. They would never know I was there. I had slept on her bedroom floor before and always helped and cleaned the kitchen, so her mother loved me.

Many days, avoiding my own home situation, I would go to a different girlfriend's house, two cities away. Even at this moment in time, I cannot count how many Shabbat meals I ate with them on Friday nights, how many times I slept over, or how many times my girlfriend's mother was more like a mother to me than my own. She brazenly rescued me on one special occasion when I quietly shared with her about a man of authority who had recently begun molesting me. Without question, she supported me, faced him, and told him that she knew what he was doing, and if he continued, she would take action. The next week he quit his job and moved away, and I credit her 100 percent for her courage and her belief in me. Thank you, Estelle; you are one of my angels. I felt as if I was a member of her family, and I knew they loved and cared for me. We stayed close for a very long time until a tragedy occurred in their life. And I became orphaned again.

On this snowy day, my father made me get into the car, and I knew it hurt his heart to think that he would participate in separating a mother from a child. This was from his past, not my present.

The following week I tried to make amends with my mother because it was always up to me to do the hard work of mending the relationship. I went to an antique shop and spoke to the owner about getting her a beautiful China bowl that I knew she would love, as she collected them. I spent every penny I had saved and bought it for her. When I gave it to her I said, "I am sorry for all the fighting. I love you and please forgive me."

My mother smashed the China bowl on the ground and said, "Nothing can make up for the things you've done."

My father knew she did this and later, quietly, and without her knowledge, apologized to me for her insensitive and unforgiving behavior. But to my knowledge, he never spoke up for me to her. Her love for me was always conditional with terms hidden from me at all times. I knew I was done trying to appease her at that very moment, but apparently, my father was not done trying, and they reconciled and got back together. My brother and I were present at their second wedding, along with some friends of theirs, all of us holding our breath for the first fight. I was really alone now.

Me in 8th grade at Roxborough Junior High School

Me in 9th grade Cleveland Heights High School

Me sitting on the front porch of the mansion,
my senior year in high school.

My grandfather, Ben Ribiat, during his last summer,
my senior year summer after graduation.

During my senior high school year and directly after graduation, I cared for my grandfather, Ben Ribiat, while he suffered with bone cancer and was in a wheelchair.

The day I had to go to college, he would not look at me, he would not talk to me, and he did not say good-bye. He knew I held many jobs while I cared for him, including being a custodian of some apartment buildings, a camp counselor at Camp Wise for one three week trip, and I kept my *Plain Dealer* newspaper route. We were together approximately two months before I departed for college, and he was in a lot of pain due to his lung cancer metastasized to bone cancer.

Even though it was summertime, he preferred to have a fire burning all day and all night while he stared into it, remembering. He was the type of man, who before his illness and when he was young, had run a race against Jessie Owens once, unofficially, in the early 1950s, and won!

The year before his cancer, at the age of seventy-four, my grandfather was still doing handstands and walking across our floors on his hands. That's the kind of man he was.

Chapter 9

Great Man—Distant Dad

I have always felt close to my father, but this is an accurate account of my life with him so I'm not going to lie. My father is a great man and a distant dad.

I remember wanting to interview him for more details about his Holocaust years, as well as learn more about his family prior to the war. I wanted to go with my high school Holocaust class to Europe with Mrs. Rabinsky, but he forbade it. Later in my adult life, I studied under her to become a docent and a speaker for the Anne Frank traveling museum exhibition when it stopped in Toledo, Ohio. I was thrilled to be trained by her and under her tutelage.

Years would go by and my father and I would not have a conversation. I once wrote him a thank you letter when I was a freshman in college. I thanked him for working so hard that he could afford to pay for my college education; something no one did for him. I thanked him for believing in me despite my disabilities and allowing me to reach my best self and work toward getting an education degree so I could teach and help others similar to me. The letter came back with red pencil marks everywhere that I had improperly used the English language in my punctuation, spelling, or content. I never wrote to him again.

During my middle school years, when I was 12 years old, after the first divorce was over, my mother began dating a great deal. There was a man, Bill, who she brought into our home who was unsafe for me. He was inappropriate, took advantage of me behind my mother's back, and he was seventy-three years old. He began slowly, trying to develop a manipulated relationship with me despite my obvious disgust. The problem was I could not see the red flags. I was very trusting, innocent, naive, and with my nonverbal learning disorder, I missed many of his signals.

I was incapable of telling my mother more than the first offense. His first offense, when he stuck his tongue into my mouth pulling me backward, while holding my neck. My mother was getting dessert from the kitchen after the dinner we had just shared. He was abusive, but I knew that my mother held on dearly to this relationship because she needed to be involved with a man. When I told her later that same night that he abusively kissed me while she was in the kitchen getting dessert, she began to yell and scream at the top of her lungs that I was trying to steal her boyfriend away because I did not want her to be happy. I couldn't tell her later, after that, what else he was doing to me. I was, again, alone.

However, like so many abused girls, one out of every four today is molested, according to a report on Wikipedia, under "Child sexual abuse in girls." I did not know why he selected me, and I did not know how to stop it. He had all the power and all the authority. After all, I was the only girl there, and my mother didn't believe me.

I was one of the lucky ones because I was saved. To afford to live in the Tudor mansion without my father's full financial support, my mother rented out the apartments on the third floor to cover our expenses.

One of the many people who rented for a short time was an old family friend, Herb Grossman, who was going through the process of divorce. He noticed a big change in me that summer while Bill molested me. I was now twelve and-a-half years old. In his kind and gentle way, Herb began to investigate through conversations with me, why I was having all these changes. I used to be so happy and outgoing. I used to hug Herb every morning when I saw him. One change was that I stopped hugging him. He also knew that I refused to take phone calls from my father, and I refused to spend time with my father on our regular one Sunday a month father/daughter times. Herb also noticed I wasn't smiling and happy-go-lucky anymore. I was withdrawn, mistrusting, and even jumpy. I felt a large amount of self-loathing and I couldn't make it stop.

Looking back now, what Herb did was perfect, and he was one of my angels. He asked me if I had a friend who was in trouble — the perfect question. I answered in full detail all about "my friend" who was in trouble. I told him of the forced car rides to the mall, forced to buy something she needed like tennis shoes, and forced to remain in the car on the return trip when he pulled over on the side of the highway to molest her. Saying "no!" and "don't!" and "stop touching me!" was met with, "If you tell anyone, I'll kill *you*!"

I had believed Bill, and I knew that my mother would not believe me. After all, she didn't even believe me regarding the kiss. But Herb Grossman believed me, and he went straight to my mother that same day and told her. He forced her to listen, but unfortunately, she was not able to treat me with kindness or respect, because I had ruined her relationship after all. She told Bill to come over to our house where she forced me to apologize to him for not telling him to stop. As he left my house, he winked at me over his shoulder. Both Bill and my mother, in this sorrow-filled transaction, abused me. She did not protect me, believe me, or even see the changes I had gone through. I thanked Herb then and in my adult years for being so strong and protective of me.

When I was older, there came a time where I researched why my family was not able to be, nor chose to be a source of support to me and my molestation, especially from Bill. The book is titled; "Family Fallout: a Handbook for Families of Adult Sexual Abuse Survivors" by Dorothy Beaulieu Landry. It explained why my mother had to turn against me and why others I had shared with going forward in my life would rather blame me for such abuse rather than be honest and compassionate. This behavior ruins family relationships for generations going forward and is very much a loss on both parties. I was and am still very grateful for this knowledge and it helped heal me even more deeply.

I didn't dare tell my father any of this for fear of hurting him so badly with the recognition that due to his absence, harm had come to me. I protected him and never shared why I didn't take his calls or spent time with him that summer. However, when I was dealing with my memories and my feelings of this painful time later in my life with a therapist, and I tried to share with my father what I had gone through, he was unwilling to listen. He literally put his hand up and walked away. Even in trying to share a past, which I had survived, he could not be there for me. I lived through it. However, he did not view me as a true survivor, which I longed for from him.

I thought of myself as having had survived, and yet I still knew that even though this was a bad experience for me, it was still nothing compared to what my father had endured in the Holocaust. I compared myself and my problems constantly with those of my father and his terrorized past. My problems never measured up. God was with me through Herb's strength and courage. Herb was one of my angels. Because of him, I knew I was not alone.

I believe my nonverbal learning disorder affected my inability to read the red flags of the experiences I had with Bill and with others whom my mother put in my life that followed later. I have since forgiven myself for having had more than one episode of this nature because I know it was not my fault. I should have been a protected child. I believe every child deserves protection.

I have had many angels in my life, one of whom is Charlie Sullivan Jr. My mother knew his father, and she hired Charlie Jr. as a sort of handyman. I met him when I was twelve years old, and we've been friends ever since. He witnessed many of my mother's attacks on me and felt defensive on my behalf. We've been best friends for decades!

Charlie with me on a recent family trip back to Cleveland in 2010. We visited the house, but were not allowed to enter..

What is interesting about Charlie Jr. is that he has always been a World War II book collector and historian. Charlie Jr. was and is one of my angels.

After that second year in Hebrew Academy had ended, my mother enrolled me in Roxborough Junior High School. I made many friends there and began to strategize through my educational experience. I remember how difficult it was for me to figure out the building and know where I was going. I became good at memorizing who I attended classes with, and then I looked for them in the hallway and followed them there. With my disabilities, I could not figure out where each of the rooms was located. The skin on my hands would peel due to my high anxiety.

I know my father had fear about me and my obvious forgetfulness, or rather, small underdeveloped, short-term memory. He worried that if the Holocaust were to happen again, I would surely not survive. Again, all by osmosis I received these messages.

My father knew that my grades were pretty good, that I succeeded to the best of my abilities socially, and that I was fully integrated as an American. I believe he was proud of me, although my grades were never top-notch due to my disabilities and my lack of parental over-seeing, support, or advocacy. When I went to high school, I had a few good friends who followed with me from junior high school. I knew something was wrong with me, possibly more than just dyslexia, but it didn't change my reality.

I always felt nervous and alone as well as painfully shy. Most of my good friends from that time, share that they didn't think anything was wrong with me. I guess that speaks to how well I hid my inadequacies and how well I strategized around my limitations.

Being a second-generation Holocaust survivor comes with many automatic scars and seems to deliver post-traumatic stress disorder passed down through osmosis and DNA from the Holocaust survivor parent. This is true in my case, though it may not be in all others.

My mother was always searching for answers to our family problems after the divorces, and I give her a lot of credit for the extra work she put in looking for help. We attended therapy sessions with groups of other people, anger workshop weekends, many healing programs, and a lot of healing arts like kinesiology, ego states training, iridology, "I'm okay you're okay," Gestalt psychology, Reiki, and many more.

One particular appointment was scheduled by her with what I think was a psychologist in Beachwood, Ohio. She took me there with the sole purpose of fixing our relationship, mine and hers, which I had been done with a long time ago. But I appeased her and went on my best behavior, as always. This psychologist sat behind his large wood desk and laid out the ground rules for both of us. He said he was going to ask us to say we were sorry for all the things we've done in the past and that we were ready to move forward into the future with new skills, which he would provide. This sounded good, but I knew he was in over his head because he did not know my mother. I knew that she was relating her anger and disappointment from her second failed marriage to my father and substituting it on to me. So this psychologist had me apologize first, which I did, sincerely. Then he turned to my mother and said, "It's your turn now." My mother began screaming at the top of her lungs, "Never! Never!" with a ferocity that seemed to me to have her head rotating 360 degrees! Can you say Sybil?

While she continued to scream, this mental health specialist jumped around the corner of his desk, grabbed my arm, and took me into the hallway, closing the door behind us sharply. Then, while holding my hands in his, he said the most important words to me up to that point in my life. "This is not your fault, you've done nothing wrong, your mother is both bipolar and schizophrenic, and I did not see this coming from our earlier appointments. You could have been any person in the room at this time and she would have still yelled, 'Never!' You are not to blame here, and I am so sorry I didn't see this coming, because if I did, I would have protected you."

He changed my life. He was the first adult to recognize and validate whom I had been living with. I had a reason not to take it personally now.

My father had shared a story with me that when he was attending Case Western Reserve University one day, when it had rained so much in Cleveland that the road was closed on Carnegie Avenue. University Circle was flooded and he had driven in from Detroit to take this final exam in Business Law. He had the final exam scheduled that afternoon. He parked his car several blocks away and began walking toward Case Western Reserve University. When he got to the road that was flooded, he put his books over his head and began to wade out into the road, ultimately swimming across, to reach Baker Hall, where his exam was to be held. He and only one other student arrived for the final exam. The other student lived uphill from campus and did not wade through any water. The professor gave both students an automatic "A" for the final exam and sent them home. I remembered this when I was headed out to my cable interview. Rain never killed anyone, and I knew I could towel off later. I had a strong belief in myself and an unyielding willingness to do what was necessary, I had tenacity.

Only one time did I come home during my college years and ask my father to help me financially. When I was working for the cable company, as I had mentioned earlier, they were having a celebratory party for winning the Bowling Green State University contracts that I had helped to secure. What I did not have was enough money in my budget to buy a beautiful dress to wear to this party. This was back in the day when you used your credit card for emergencies or in a situation where you knew you would have it paid in full at the end of the month. I did not have extra money to pay for the seventy-dollar dress I found and fell in love with. I bought the perfect dress on credit, and brought it home to show my father how wonderful I looked in it and asked him if he would help me purchase it. I had 40 percent of the total available. While watching baseball on television, my father said no. I returned the dress and wore a borrowed dress the night of the reception. He did not say no to hurt me, he thought the money he gave my mother should have been enough to cover the cost. My father provided child support for twenty-five years, but my mother shared none of it with me to support any of my costs after I moved out to attend college. He did not know this fact, and I remained silent so as not to upset him.

When I was at Bowling Green State University from 1982 to 1987, I came up with things to do to make me feel close to my father. Every time I went to an orchestra concert where he was a featured soloist, I bootlegged a tape recording of him on the tape recorder I had purchased to help me with my studies. I kept these tapes of him.

One day, while waiting for a professor to show up for class, I found myself listening to my father play. I wrote a poem about it. I wrote poems a lot. It was a way in which I found my voice and worked on healing myself. Just hearing my father's music helped me feel grounded while in that cold classroom waiting for the professor.

I remember traveling back to Cleveland to watch my father play a solo at Severance Hall. He had let me know about it in time to take off work and come into town. For some reason, I knew this was going to be a difficult solo for him, so I made sure I was present for both the rehearsal and the opening night concert. I tape-recorded that show too. A female Russian composer, Pahkmutova, wrote the trumpet concerto solo. It was extremely emotional to listen to, and I'm certain it was emotional to play as well. Again, we did not speak specifically about my being there for him, but he knew I was bearing witness to his pain on stage.

In 1984, my father traveled with the Cleveland Orchestra to Warsaw, Poland. I don't remember what courses I took that semester, but I do remember how worried I was for his well-being, traveling to his country of origin, loss, and betrayal. This is before I owned a cell phone, but this did not stop me from calling the American Embassy. I had tenacity; that I got from both my parents. I called and spoke with many people until I reached the right person who gave me the phone number to the American Embassy in Warsaw. I called them next. Eventually, I managed to reach a man who was heading into the evening party program with the orchestra management and Christoph Von Dohnanyi, the conductor of the orchestra. I knew my father, being both a musician and the personnel manager, would be present for this event, if he were emotionally well. I spoke to this embassy ambassador and told him of my concerns for my father's well-being because of his past. He understood my worries and promised he would give my father a message on my behalf, should he see him this evening.

As my father tells the story, he was busy posturing and working the room when the ambassador came up to him and said, "Are you David Zauder?"

My father began to worry immediately, deep-seated fear creeping into him in a flash of memories, and he had to decide whether to admit who he was. The ambassador recognized my father's hesitancy and said, "Because if you are, I have a message from your daughter, Karen. She wants to know that you are okay, and she asked me to give you a hug."

My father couldn't believe it! How did I manage to reach this American ambassador all the way in Warsaw, Poland, and convince him to give my father this personal message!

When he came home from that particular tour, he called me and with a bit of threat in his voice said that I was never to do that again. I couldn't believe it! Didn't he get that I understood that what he was doing by returning to Poland was so difficult and so deep-seated with fear and mixed with loss and mixed with love? Didn't he know, that I knew, that he partially loved his home country and feared it at the same time? Didn't he know that I knew this?

Two decades later, he shared that he had lost it twice on that tour, once with a German guard who refused to let the tour bus pass from one country to the other, unless he could check all the orchestra's instruments. My father pulled up his left sleeve, displayed his Auschwitz tattoo, and yelled in perfect German, "I have already been through this once, and I am *not* going through it again, now let us through!" His reaction surprised all his musician colleagues. The other time, he couldn't leave his hotel room for two days due to fear and past memories. I had been correct in my worry for his emotional well-being. During this particular tour, on our birthday month, I wrote the following poem.

~

Too Far Away

You're so far away.

And yet thoughts of you move me so. Your love is a source of great comfort and yet your embrace is far too distant to comfort me.

I miss you.

Thoughts of your location disturb me

I reach for you in my mind and my heart weeps as your past devours me.

How are you working in the exact location of your past?

How do you feel when left alone to think and to feel?

Do you feel my love and soak in my strength?

Are you sleeping soundly through your lonely nights?

Do I feel your sadness, or my own?

Do I anticipate your reaction, or is it a bad premonition?

I want to reach you—even the American Embassy is too far removed from you.

I feel so far away!

Tears burned my eyes and your smile is

Fading . . .

~

Chapter 10

Family—Zauder Style

Family has always been an interesting vocabulary word for my father and me. With all of his travels around the world with the Cleveland Orchestra, he always searched in the White Pages in every town he was in for his family name, Zauder. One time while in New York, he found the Zauder name. He took a moment, gathered his confidence, and called. The story goes that a woman answered the phone and said "Hello?" My father said, "Hello, this is David Zauder," and she fainted. It seems they had a death in the family and that day was the funeral. The family member who died was named David Zauder! The coincidence! Uncanny!

Later in the week, he met with the family. They were concerned because they felt he was interested in their money, not a family reconnection. Because my father was missing so much family information, there was no way for him to know if they were related or not. He was not aware at the time that his father had two brothers and one sister, since he had never met any of his father's siblings; he believed there was none. Remember, his family was torn apart when he was only nine years old.

In high school, I felt things at home had gotten worse to the point where I never wanted to be there. My mother was always criticizing me; from not eating enough food to working too hard on my homework—which I did because of my learning disabilities—to having the wrong friends, the wrong boyfriend, to not spending enough time with her, etc. So I immersed myself in school activities. I joined choir, was the student council secretary, volunteered with special-needs students, worked after school for a good friend of my mother who was a lawyer and who I continued to work for into the summer. I worked in retail at a store at the mall, and was a camp counselor at Camp Wise for multiple summers. I left a boyfriend behind for two of the summers I worked at Camp Wise. I could never quite fully explain to him why I had to leave and not be around my mother. Camp Wise was a haven for me.

In 1983, for the New Year, my father decided to take my brother and me on a short weekend vacation from Cleveland to Florida, by plane. He did not ask us, he told us we were going. Not that we were unhappy about having to travel with him for New Years, it was just that we hadn't spent time as a family since 1976.

Once again, I felt my father's loneliness, as he apparently had no significant other, but at the time, my brother and I didn't have one either. The three of us flew to Miami, had fun, went dancing, and rang in the New Year together. I remember my father being a little overwhelmed with the nature of the youth at the time. Partying teenagers were overrunning Miami Beach. Our time together on this vacation was so good, but it was not hard to remember that it would be over soon. His work schedule with the Cleveland Orchestra, his master teaching at the Cleveland Institute of Music, and his personnel manager position and union work were consuming his time. He hardly ever called just to check in, and we never spent quality time together. This vacation was wonderful.

Karl and I on the beach in Miami

David Zauder golfing, his favorite past time, left-handed.

When I was in high school, our father used to come to the house and drive Karl and me to school so we did not have to take public transportation. We lived too far away from the school bus route. He made certain once a week, every single week, that he would drive us to school. I don't remember a week going by where he did not lay eyes on us and have a vocabulary word to teach us. Time and space separated us, and he was so dedicated to his employers that I remember it being bittersweet when he had his twenty-fifth anniversary with the Cleveland Orchestra. I wrote him a letter and participated in making a party for him in his honor. The letter is below:

~

Congratulations

So often you speak to me through your eyes.

So loving,

> *so sensitive,*

> > *so very insightful.*

I feel you through them, and yet, something else too. I am often aware of this undertone of feeling that seems to consume me so at certain moments. So often in my memories do I hear your music.

So distinctly,

so very crystal clear do I hear you. You speak through your music and I hear you.

Yet, I am moved to tears too often by your song.

Why does your song sound so tragic?

> *Why?*

Why must your song touch me in such a strong, overbearing way?

Why am I moved to quaking sobs while listening to your record?

Why can't I simply be relaxed and enjoy your beautiful sounds like so many others?

Or is it because we are cut from the same cloth?

You are such an intricate person at times, yet I have only the most un-embellished emotions concerning you . . .

I think of you; so strong, so wise, so domineering. So very set in your ways of the world. I feel a sense of pride, joy, love, and accomplishment when I think of you and your life. You've been such a big part of my life; I feel you in everything I do. You've been there for me whenever I've attempted to reach out for you. "The Summer Knows" has always reminded me of you and your silent ways of reaching out to me in teaching what you've painfully learned yourself. Though, if I were to try to converse these things to you I fear you would not understand. Worse than that, I fear you would understand and avoid me. Me, your daughter, who only wishes to love, help, and understand you. This fear I've acquired probably will interfere with my giving this letter to you. But maybe it won't. Maybe, at the risk of being so profound in your eyes, so wise to the ways of the world not to mention the universe, I might take a chance and give this to you. Please understand. I love you so much. Maybe I've just gotten off the track a little. Maybe all I should have simply said was how much I love you, how much I appreciate you, the way you are, and how you seem to learn and grow with and through me. Maybe all I needed to say was congratulations on your 25-year service and loyalty to the Cleveland Orchestra. I don't know, maybe. Despite whatever the appropriate words are and whatever you expected, I hope and pray you understand why this was so hard for me. There are many more things involved here than your 25-year membership to me. I do believe you know. I love you, Dad, and congratulations. Love always, your daughter, Karen

~

Sometime in the 1980s, my father's cousins, the Markle family, held regular family reunions. Apparently, they invited my father, and also my brother and me, through my father. Which means my brother and I never heard about these family reunions since my father was barely talking to my brother and me at the time. This was very disappointing to me, as I had felt very much like an orphan during many of my years while in high school and college, as well as when I was a young adult.

I spent most of my college years not speaking with my mother at all. I was actually in therapy regarding my not speaking with her, and hardly ever hearing from my father. My mother had been an only child and therefore I had no close relatives from her side of the family, save for one, the daughter of her father's sister. I became close with Eileen Rosenberg in my adult life. I was exceptionally close to her son, Andy, while in high school. He and I use to write letters and speak on the phone regularly during my junior and senior years in high school. He had visited once, to give his parents a break, and he and I became best of friends. I feel fortunate that my cousin Eileen and I share such closeness. My mother did not support that relationship then or now.

I did not feel like I was welcome to call on my Markle cousins and to have them be there for me during those years. Since I had never heard about the family reunion invitations, I thought that they wanted nothing to do with me after my parents divorced in 1976.

Prior to the divorce, my memories of seeing Lil and Harry Markle and all three of their children were scarce but consistent, and I enjoyed every visit. We also visited many of my father's friends who were orchestra-related in Detroit, Michigan. I was actually too young to remember Sheila and Diane's visits, although the pictures look lovely. I do have memories of Alan's visits, as he came closer to the time of the divorce and was very aware of my bat mitzvah. I still have the beautiful turquoise Jewish Star of David necklace he gave me in honor of my bat mitzvah. I felt he understood me, and he cared about me. He liked it when Karl and I called him "Uncle Al the kiddies pal." When I was in college dating a non-Jewish man, I felt comfortable enough to write him a long letter asking for his opinion. He wrote back a beautiful letter filled with love and understanding, and a universal ideal of both tolerance and acceptance.

While growing up and going away to college, feeling so alone, I sometimes asked myself that if the Markle's believed that my father was their brother, and felt very close to him, then it stands to reason for me to wonder, where were my uncle and two aunts? Why did I have no family contacting me? I think my mother had a lot to do with their decisions pertaining to staying in touch with my brother and me. Enough said.

Because of my father's failure to inform me about their family reunions, and my obvious failure to communicate with them regarding their invitations, which I never received, we had no relationship. My loss. I do not wish to be misunderstood here; his loss of family murders and experiencing first hand Genocide, loss of home and a way of life being destroyed during the Holocaust vs. my not having a connection or a communicating family life is not the same loss. It is not equal. I was alone. Mimicking the loss that my father experienced by losing all his family members as well; loss is loss. My father had no idea that by not inviting me to be included, he was excluding me—leaving me virtually without a family. In a very strange way, making me even closer to my father emotionally, and through feeling similar experiences, making me feel even more enmeshed with him.

I'm happy to say that today my relationship with the Markle family is a strong one. When my father moved in with my family in 2007, the phone calls began to trickle in, and when he was diagnosed with terminal bone cancer in 2009, metastasized from his prostate, they honed in their care and concern for him and began checking in on my family and me. Each of Lil and Harry's children has visited my home since 2009. Sheila and her husband, Len Gursky, have visited multiple times and have kept us knowledgeable on how their two daughters and families are doing as well. Alan Markle's entire family, wife Joanne, Philip, and Michele have joined us. Diane's entire family has also visited—husband, Bill Sarnat, daughters Lauren Sarnat, married to Branden Paoli, and their son, Jacob. And there's Adina and her husband, Rob Miller, and Diane and Bill's son, Jeffery. We have all turned the page of the past together as well as the loss of being able to be there for one another over the years. I am truly grateful for that and for them and their love for my father, my family, and me.

The Markle's and extended family in the late 1980's, for Jeffery's Bar-Mitzvah. I am on the left, next to Karl's first wife and then Karl and DZ are in the back left.

Markle/Sarnat/Gursky/Miller/Paoli/Brass extended
family's recent visit, 2009, on our porch,
DZ is third from the back left.

The Sarnats; Diane and Bill with son, Jeffery and daughter
Adina and her husband Rob Miller and DZ and David
Brass in the back right and Shannah and Adam Brass, front
and center.

The Sarnat's, Miller's, DZ and me!

My father has a distorted view of family. Just recently, he excitedly shared that he had a cousin whom he had not heard from in thirty years, just connect with him by phone. When he was finished explaining in an enthusiastic way about how he felt to reconnect with whom I now know is Francis's grandson, I asked, "Does this mean I have a new cousin?"

My father looked at me confused. I continued, "I'm so excited! Who is my new cousin, what's his name, how old is he, does he have children? Where does he live?" I did not get the answer to these questions because in my father's mind, these are not my people, and he is still alienating me. I do believe there is a deeper meaning behind his behavior. Specifically, to spare me from hurt, pain, and disappointment, these were his words, "mishugina," craziness.

The actions you take today often don't pay off until tomorrow. But the actions you take today speak to the person you are right now and I had high morals, high values, and high expectations of myself. I was going to help change the world for the better and I was on a mission to do so.

My story here includes my father's relationship with Ryan Anthony, a former student of my father's from the Cleveland Institute of Music, who is currently the first trumpet with the Dallas Symphony Orchestra.

Ryan Anthony and I are close like a brother and a sister. He and I know so much about my father's intricate ways of behaving, feeling, celebrating, and ranting and raving, that we often have to share stories from our past to include each other in our individual memories of David Zauder, just for fun.

*Ryan and me for the first time meeting
at my father's retirement party*

The three of us

Mustaches for all, even Conductor Christoph von
Dohnanyi, in honor of DZ!

My father taught Ryan at the Cleveland Institute of
Music between 1988 through 1992, and continued to
mentor him, be his friend, be a source of information
and offer him professional advice. He was his friend and
many times called Ryan saying, "This is the voice of your
conscience calling." I believe that Ryan is correct when he
shares that he felt he was helping my father understand
how to be a better father to Karl and me through working
with him as a professional trumpet and cornet teacher.
My father did not speak to me for years. Not because we
were in a fight, but because he didn't know what to say.
It was during these years that he was investing a lot of
time, energy, care, and concern into Ryan Anthony. Ryan
Anthony is by far one of the best mensches I know. I'm
grateful to have him in my life now as I care for my father

in his later years. We celebrate together the good times, now and through memories of the past, and we support each other through the difficult times.

"You're my press agent. You tell me why Dave Zauder is in PEOPLE and I'm not!"

David Zauder knew he had made it
when this appeared in the 1996 paper!

The first time I met Ryan was in 1997, the year my father retired from the Cleveland Orchestra, and we were at his retirement party, which I was slightly involved in helping to plan. I was hurting financially, but I managed to find a wholesaler to sell to me two hundred black mustaches that everyone would wear at the retirement party as a spoof on DZ. I was responsible for getting my father to the party that he did not know existed.

I had done this once before for his surprise sixtieth birthday in 1991. I remember he would not go with me, not anywhere, and I finally had to say, "Daddy, please just get in my car." My father does not like surprises and not knowing where I was taking him was almost offensive. It puts him in a defensive mode, as he is use to being in complete control.

I was drawn to Ryan, as I felt he was like another younger brother, and he was there bearing witness to my father's retirement. My brother, Karl Zauder, chose not to attend the party. Retirement from a lifelong commitment that separated my father and I from communicating, from living a life together, and from supporting each other in all ways, was difficult. I knew that Ryan had so much support from my father throughout so many of my lonely years, and I knew that my father had never allowed us to meet prior to this date for a reason. After we met, nothing could keep us apart as friends.

In the years since, Ryan and I have often shared with each other comments that my father makes. You see, he calls Ryan and tells Ryan about me, and talks to me about Ryan. So, though Ryan and I don't hear directly from my father what he thinks about us. We vowed to inform each other at all times because some of the most deeply felt compliments about each of us are told to the other. We would miss so much if we did not share.

Ryan with a written quote to DZ

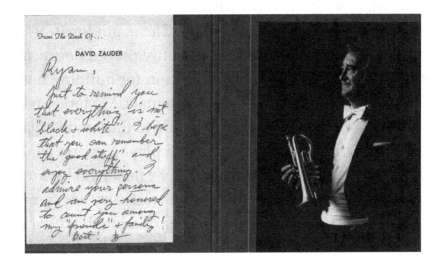

David Zauder—portrait and letter given to Ryan
at his CIM graduation

All of us at Thanksgiving together, two years after my father retired. Ryan and wife, Nikki, David and me, 5 months pregnant, and Karl taking the photo at Thanksgiving 1999

I remember Ryan shared with me a story back in the days when he was going to school at the Cleveland Institute of Music with my father. Ryan apparently played poorly an etude, which is a musical composition for building both musicality and technique—fundamentals. My father had a little fit, ran out, and never returned to the lesson. Ryan told me he didn't realize that he had played poorly at all, and he still had to pay for the lesson he never got because my father never returned. My father was very angry, but it was about something else, orchestra related. So Ryan, in a way, was like a stepson to my father. He put up with his antics, his emotional instabilities, and learned from his amazing talents. I am lucky that my father brought Ryan into my life because going through the last stage of my father's life now is much more bearable with Ryan in my second-generation support group.

Ryan has gotten very close with my family, and I had the chance to visit with him and his family recently in Dallas; Medieval Times!

A quote from Ryan;

How does one express the importance of a mentor? How do you put into words the proper thank you and gratitude towards such an individual? I don't think you can, you can just live your life as an example to the teachings and dedication bestowed upon you. My lessons with DZ were not just about playing the trumpet, but about how to be a man in this industry and world. It was beyond notes but about personal experiences and the choices given. Yes, he made me a better trumpet player but the reason I was successful was the wisdom and life lessons I learned during our time together. Why did David Zauder choose me to invest his time and share his life and knowledge? I'll never know, but I'm thankful for it every day and choose to make this world a better place and share what DZ taught me to others. Perhaps that's how one says "Thank you".

Follow Ryan on his website: www.RyanAnthony.com.

~

Chapter 11

Life Happens and We Learn

Looking back now, it really wasn't worth the time, the money, or the energy to raise my grade point back up by going to summer school at Kent State University for the educational statistics class. No one since then has ever asked for my graduation grade point average. I graduated from Bowling Green State University with a 3.6 GPA and a dual major—an early childhood education degree and a K-12 education degree. I would have had an additional major in psychology as well, had I just taken one more psychology statistics class and not failed it. So I settled for a minor in psychology. I had a friend, whom I considered one of my angels during this time, my college years. He was a graduate student, and we spoke deeply about how our actions validate and consecrate our values. Doug Hahan was very intuitive, but I still kept him in the dark as to how truly bad my personal life was getting. He was and still is one of my rocks!

Speaking with many second-generation survivors, there seems to be two ways to live. One, in constant comparison with the survivor and comparing every life experience to get current validation; and two, letting the past be the past and the present be the present. It seems that I witnessed my father living in the present so much that I felt I needed to bear witness to the past for him. This is another example of the definition of codependency.

There are two ways to live your life. One is as though nothing is a miracle. The other is as though everything is a miracle.

~ Albert Einstein

In college, I had a friend my entire freshman year with whom I was close. We shared stories and felt like family. During Hanukkah, I had a menorah in my college dorm room and this friend stopped by and saw it on the windowsill. In shock and with awe, my friend asked me, "Where are your horns? I never knew you were a Jew because you never showed me your horns!" I was shocked! I couldn't believe the question and found out that it was a grandmother who warned my friend of Jews having horns on their head. I learned since then that the myth began with the stone sculpture of Michelangelo's statue, *Moses*. The two tufts of curly hair on Moses' head could be seen or interpreted as horns, and many wives tales shared it as such; Jews have horns on their heads. Much education is needed to cure generations of ignorance and misinformation.

During my final year as a senior, my fifth year in college, the university had a job fair for teachers. I signed up for as many interviews as I could, so that I could get a job, as well as become well versed in the interview process.

My favorite interviewer was a principal who was an African-American woman, and we got along as though we knew each other for a long time. I interviewed well and her questions were very in-depth. One of the questions she asked me; what did I believe qualified me to work with the needs of special children. I shared that because of my learning disabilities, I was special as well. I told her that I had struggled all my life and was exceptionally patient with my students, because it was easy for me to see things from their perspective. She asked how I felt about differences and perhaps lower-income students. I made the erroneous assumption that she was a principal of an inner-city school, which most likely had a large population of African-American students. Being from Cleveland and having attended school with 50 percent African-American students, many of whom I called my good friends, I had no problem teaching in such a school. So, I answered that I felt I was highly qualified to work with students with differences. First, I was a woman working in a man's world, and I felt I had to work harder to maintain the same status. Second, I was Jewish and therefore a minority and knew I would be successful and capable of working with such a demographic.

She was so excited as well as impressed by my answer that she said I was her favorite interviewee so far. It turned out she offered me the job as a fourth-grade teacher in Washington, DC, for a predominantly Jewish school. That taught me the lesson of making improper assumptions! I would have been excellent as a teacher at that school, but I wasn't quite ready to leave Ohio yet, as I was in a relationship that I felt I needed to commit to. My life would have been so different then had I had adult intervention, involved parents, and mentors to help me make that decision.

Directly following graduation, while seriously attempting to obtain a local teaching job, I was hired to work at a child development center at St. Charles Hospital in Oregon, Ohio. I worked with four-to-eighteen-month-old children of the doctors and nursing staff from the hospital. I loved that job, and Nicholas was one of my favorite children. He toddled over to me each morning with a giant smile on his face! I was successful in assisting a nine-month-old little girl who was just precious, who had not learned how to roll over yet. She was the youngest in her family, and her next oldest sibling was already ten years old. I don't think her feet hit the ground at her house! I taught her to roll over and begin to crawl, which thrilled her parents. I learned about office politics there. I was still too naive. The director was kind and agreed with my ideas, but the women there who had their jobs for twenty or more years did not want a young, enthusiastic, newly-graduated teacher making stimulating charts, graphs, and cotton ball lamb posters for the children. I remained there for only six months.

Next, I taught school as a substitute teacher in three districts, teaching kindergarten, fourth grade, and even physical education for six months while the physical education teacher was on leave to care for her dying mother. Then, finally, I got a full-time teaching position. One of the evaluations I had received from a principal whom I respected, stated after much praise for my work ethic, and what I accomplished during the school year, that she worried about me burning out working in the public school sector. I had no idea what burning out meant, and as it stood, I never did burn out. That would be failure and failure was not an option.

I left teaching not because I didn't love it, but because it wasn't paying the bills. Yes, I was now married, having just turned twenty-one the month following my wedding. My first husband was a full-time college student, and he had a part-time job at a pizza restaurant, but we had expenses to manage.

> *Kavanah; God is that aspect of reality which elicits from us the best that is in us and enables us to bear the worst that can befall us.* ~MMK Mordecai M. Kaplan

We had first met in a psychology class and later that same day I had written in my journal that he was a very troubled young man, and I was not to ever date him under any circumstances. He had shaved his entire head because at work, his boss had told him he needed a haircut. He had classic problems with authority and respect issues. But as many romances start out and despite my inner-voice warnings, I had romantically fallen for him, when on Sweetest Day he bought me a dozen red roses. His IQ was very high. He had been exceptionally kind to me during an exceptionally difficult semester I had while in school due to problems with relationships at home, and we had become friends. The roses made us more than friends; we now were officially dating.

My mother had come into town unexpectedly, unwanted, and unannounced during finals week of my junior year. She knew this was my schedule, as she had called and wanted to speak to me late at night, and I told her I was studying for finals. So, as usual, she ignored my schedule and my needs, and put hers first and showed up. He found out about it, came over, and confronted her. I couldn't believe it. There they stood toe-to-toe exchanging words about me. He fought for me, for my goodness, my honor, and for my respect without showing any respect to my mother. I thought of him as strong, smart, and unafraid of my mother, which instantly made him more attractive to me. His hatred of authority afforded him such bravery. Having never been fought for before, or never been protected from my mother by a male, it was a new experience for me. Now he became not just the guy I was dating at the time, but also my guy I could count on.

During my senior year and his junior year, we both found ourselves needing new roommates, as mine had graduated, and his had gotten married and moved. So we made the decision to move in together. It was economical, and I did not want to be alone.

Since we were dating, we agreed to become roommates out of necessity, but I had also fallen in love with him and felt loved by him. I did not believe we were living in sin. It had been against my principles to live with a man before marriage, but some of my principles, due to my family situation, had gone by the wayside.

Both a minister and a rabbi married us in August following my college June graduation. Not by Rabbi Cohen, as he could not condone my choice. We remained married for five years. We were actually together for eight years, counting our years of friendship.

My first marriage. Karl and my father were there. My mother showed up late, dressed in white.

My dad and I danced

He had blond hair and blue eyes, was of German descent, and his father was a Presbyterian minister. I had great respect for him and his ideals, and the morals and values he shared with me at the time. He was very smart, but also tortured and stunted emotionally. I naively thought we would help each other. He would help me be smarter, and I would help him be less fearful of enjoying his life and being angry. Relationships are complicated and this one was more so than the average.

I paid for my rented wedding dress and the flowers for the wedding, taking on yet another job to cover the expenses. My father paid for the country club, and my mother paid for the disc jockey at the last minute, just to aggravate my dad; no live musicians. His divorced parents paid for the alcohol. All my girlfriends, all six of my bridesmaids, wore dresses they selected. All I asked was that they were of different solid colors. I had a rainbow-themed wedding.

I had one girlfriend, AnneMarie, whom I've known since I was four years old, share with me that she thought he was a jerk. I thanked her for her honesty and told her his behavior at the rehearsal was just because of the wedding itself, and he did not like authority. We had the rehearsal two hours before the wedding; it was an all-day event. Told what to do, where to go, how to stand, and what to wear put him in a horrible mood. She was right, and I was making excuses. I was, after all a codependent adult child. She was the first one I called when I began my divorce proceedings.

My maternal grandmother had gifted me when she was still alive, a ten thousand-dollar CD note that I would receive upon graduation from college. She told me this in my junior year when I visited her in California and saw her for the last time. She advised me never to cash it in, but to borrow against it whenever I needed serious money. She believed a woman should have financial security. That way, she told me, a woman could make better decisions; she would not have to rely so much on a man or love. She also shared with me that upon her death, I was to inherit more, but that never materialized. My mother had power of attorney.

With that CD note and other money I had earned and saved, I bought my first house. It was a duplex, and I thought myself very smart for investing in one. I rented out the top half, and we lived in the bottom half. It was a fixer-upper, but I was certain that together we could do anything. My first husband was not very involved in this endeavor at all, but he did agree that the duplex was a smart idea. The house was in my name, as all of the funds for the down payment and the future improvements came from me.

When we married, I had a hard time with the idea of giving up my maiden name of Zauder. After all, my father had told me we were the last ones living. After much thought, I decided on hyphenation. I thought it was a good compromise and he didn't seem to mind. I was proud of us, proud of the way we were making things work. He shared that he valued my Jewish heritage, and he promised to participate in all Jewish holidays. However, he missed every single one I planned and shared with others.

My duplex in Bowling Green, Ohio, with my first personal
dog, Puma! I trained her, and she me.

We had lived a few years in the duplex on the first floor when the city ran a special for homes located in the center of town. If you owned a home that was a duplex, you could involve yourself in a program that would allow the city to invest half of the cost in updating everything and bringing it up to code. All the utilities and the home itself could be improved under the program. All I had to be willing to do was rent out the top half of the duplex to low-income families for ten years and then the loan would vanish. Brilliant! I registered and began making my list of things I wanted our house to have. Updated plumbing, updated electrical, new siding, fixed leaky roof, updated heating and furnace, updated windows, and a bathroom that worked. This included my kitchen widened from 11' x 6' to 22' x 22' and a laundry room added next to the new bathroom.

I documented everything including the phone calls I made to city hall complaining that they had given more money to the contractor than the work that had actually been completed. I had already given my half of the total cost, accepted by the city for the project, and in increments according to the contractor's requests. The contractor was on the city's list for acceptable contractors; however, they had some bad experiences with him in the past, and he should have been taken off the list. After six months of all the utilities failing to be updated and living with the back end of my house exposed to the elements, I scheduled a meeting with the mayor. I had tried to set up the meeting during those six months; however, it wasn't until I made a call to my city councilwoman that the mayor would agree to see me. With the help of City Councilwoman, Marcy Kaptur, currently representing the ninth district of Ohio, I was successful. I was a Standupster®.

I was at the meeting alone. My husband refused to support me as I presented my side of the story, including documented evidence of phone calls made, dates, times, and photographs of work left uncompleted. He said I would never win. I stayed up all night reviewing my data so I could do a good presentation in the morning. After hearing my side of the story and seeing the evidence I had compiled, the mayor was so angry at what had been done to me that he stood up and hit the city project manager in the back of the head for having made such a fiasco of my home and the project. The city canceled another project to use earmarked money to complete the work on my home, and within four weeks, an entirely new contractor completed my home. I was grateful I stood up for myself even though I did it without my husband's support, attention, or pride in me.

I was an excellent teacher and I loved my kids, but I was always financially underwater. I paid for my first husband's undergraduate degree and most of our expenses on my small teacher's salary. I accepted his limitations, his inability to balance his college responsibilities, his ten-hour per week position at the restaurant, and his unwillingness to pick up a few more paying hours at another part-time job. I was used to accepting limitations in men from my family history, and loving them anyway, while my needs went unmet. He worked hard at both, but I was always working harder. I accepted our differences, but I believe that my ability to work harder made him feel less of a man. It was during this time that his friend accepted a job with a shipping company and told him there were night-shift openings. My husband quit his part-time restaurant job and took this new one with his friend, which was part-time at night and paid better. This was when my father stepped in and suggested that my first husband accept a loan from him to pay for his next two semesters. This offer was with the understanding that he would then use this additional income to pay off the debt I co-signed on, then graduate and get a full-time job of his career choice and then pay DZ back. I was very surprised my father stepped in to help financially. It felt good to be supported by him. My first husband accepted the loan, but it was not a heartfelt agreement, as he never met the terms of the loan.

I had summers off from teaching but needed a job to try to get out from under the bills, and then I saw an ad in the paper that my old boss from my Kent State University days was looking to hire a telecommunications operations manager. I promptly called and told him I could do the job. I had a very good reputation with him, as I had been a model employee and one of his best saleswomen. Prior to the scheduled interview, I spent ten hours preparing by researching potential locations to open the office and determined pricing for the phone systems that would be required. Unfortunately, I held the interview without a clue about what kind of income being an operations manager should have pulled in. So when he asked me how much I made as a schoolteacher, and how much more I needed to make, I told him the truth and that is what he paid me. I was underpaid to start by fifteen thousand dollars compared to my counterparts within the company, and I was the only female in the role of operations manager.

I ran a very tight-knit group, had the highest numbers in the division, and was very successful. I worked two hours per day more than the other operations managers did 'because I had to go over all the financials twice, due to my learning disabilities. I did improve my math skills running that office, but not to the extent one might have expected. I hired and delegated to phenomenal supervisors and assistants whom I trained, including some I'm still in contact with today. I also personally trained every single telecommunications sales person.

When the school teaching year began, I had already informed the administrators that I was resigning because I needed the additional income I was making in the operations manager position. After five years working as an operations manager, my teaching license was out of date, and I had no options beyond the current position I held.

Then my marital life took a very big turn for the worse. He had not treated me very well for quite some time.

One night we were watching a taped movie, and I had a serious allergic reaction to, of all things, celery. All my life while growing up I would eat celery—plain, with cream cheese, with peanut butter—like everyone else. However, every time I ate the equivalent of one stalk, my lips and tongue would go numb. So I stopped eating it. I thought since no one ate a lot of celery that was how everyone felt. It never occurred to me to double check the feeling. A favorite meal during college, as well as after, was chicken wings, which included two pieces of celery and blue cheese dressing.

One weekend, my first husband and I were watching a movie on our separate couches and eating chicken wings. He always got hot sauce, and I always got mild. However, on this day, I ate his celery stalks that he didn't want in addition to mine. During the movie, he began to yell at me for making too much noise, as I had begun rubbing my hands and my forearms. I hadn't realized it until he said something, but I was having an allergic reaction, and my hands and forearms itched like crazy. I also had developed a slight cough, more like an irritation. So while he continued to watch the movie, I went and took a hot shower thinking that perhaps I had touched some of his hot sauce and my skin was reacting from it. After the shower, my cough had gotten worse and more continuous, and my hands and forearms had a visible rash all over them.

My first husband ignored me and continued to watch the movie; a norm that I had settled for within that marriage. But I was worried, so I called my girlfriend who worked the phones at the emergency room and told her what I thought had happened. After every fourth or fifth word, I had a cough, and she was horrified for me. She said that if I wasn't at the hospital within fifteen minutes, she herself would have an ambulance at our house to pick me up; she knew I was having an anaphylactic shock reaction.

So I got dressed and my first husband said, "Where the hell are you going?" I told him I was going to the hospital.

He was looking right at me, saw what I looked like, and said, "Wait, let me get some books, and I'll come with you so I can study while you're in there."

I waited the five minutes until he came out, and then I drove myself to the hospital with him and all his books. When I walked in, my girlfriend who armed the phones did not recognize me, as my face had swollen so badly I looked nothing like myself. She screamed and ran down the hall for the doctor who met me in the hallway and pulled me directly into a room, bent me over a hospital bed and gave me a shot right into my hip. I passed out.

When I came to about four hours later, I was told that I was fifteen minutes away from experiencing cardiac arrest, all due to a celery allergy. Had I taken one minute while at home to look in a mirror, I may have noticed the severity of my situation. With house under construction . . . they weren't strategically placed. But that's still no excuse for my first husband's behavior and lack of empathy, let alone care and concern. I was not in a safe environment, and even though that was very familiar to me, it was not healthy. My ability to wait and persevere through an adverse situation without care and concern for my physical well-being was taught and therefore caught.

Then, my first husband's brother called me a "dirty kike", a very anti-Semitic term, in front of a crowd at a party. He said his brother was using me for my financial stability and that he never loved me. Can you say wake-up call?

The conversations my first husband and I had prior to marriage regarding our religious differences were both respectful and, I thought, honest. There was a part of me that thought this was my way of healing my father's past, not holding them responsible, in reference to those of German descent like my husband was. Then my first husband began threatening me. He would lay books around the house like *The Nazi Doctors*, and I felt his hatred. Hatred abounds, as does ignorance, and both must be fought against.

Looking back it was a very difficult time for me. I loved him, but I knew he was not good for me. I remember when we first discussed moving in together because of our individual circumstances.

One day, I was outside in a parking lot crying. I was cleaning his motorcycle, a deed of service that I was doing out of love. He came out and said, in so many words, why are you crying? I told him because I knew his personality was currently stronger than mine was, and he was so angry all the time. He would yell at the TV commercials as if they were there to harm him in some way. I was worried that I would begin to swear like he did, complain like he did, and begin to act like it was he and I against the big bad world, and I would begin to believe him. I did not believe the world was bad. I had a very positive outlook on life. We were virtual opposites, but it never occurred to me that one day he would change and put me into the category of the big bad world that was against him.

For many reasons, most of which this book is not about, I still married him, despite the warnings he gave me when I think back. The week before our wedding, he was angry with me for sharing about the kindergartners that I was working with, as it seemed I had story after story to share from my teaching experience of the day. Instead of respectfully communicating his desire for me to stop sharing, he took the chair from my desk where I did my classroom and teacher planning, and broke it over the top of my desk destroying everything in the area. It was his first display of intense physical aggression and loss of control, but it was not his last. At the time, I believed it was wedding jitters, and I wrote it off as such.

Within the first year of our marriage, I began marital counseling due to his anger, verbal abuse, and consistent destruction of the property we had together. He did drink alcohol but not daily, and it was not often the cause of his misbehavior. He was a mean drunk, and I felt when he drank, he was the most honest with his demons. He did not join me in counseling.

A few years later, after one particularly horrible abusive incident, I knew I was in physical danger again and would not put myself in the position to be physically hurt a second time. He grabbed me before I had a chance to get out and hurt me badly. I landed in a woman's shelter that evening.

I called my father crying; it was the first time we spoke that year, which was 1994. I told him where I was, and the first thing he said to me was, "What did you do to make him so angry?"

He acted as if it was my fault that my first husband chose physical violence and hurt me rather than to use calming words to discuss the issues. I hung up on my father and we didn't speak again the rest of that year. He could not handle what I was going through. My father lacked empathy for me as a separate person.

I struggled with the thought that he couldn't handle what I was going through compared to what he had gone through in the Holocaust, and no matter how I thought about it, he should have been strong enough for me. After all, he had survived abuse by professionals. I felt unsupported by my father, not because of a lack of love, but because of a lack of willingness to be in a bad situation again. He had limits.

When my father snuck out of the Kraków Ghetto and walked ten blocks in the dark to get the food his father had arranged for him to receive from a non-Jewish butcher, he always came back with the food for his family. Perhaps he had been able to sacrifice and give then, but no longer did he have it in him to sacrifice for me. I forgave him for not being strong enough for me; I forgave him for choosing not to be involved in my life, and not to know whom I was married to during my first marriage.

I began self-esteem classes in the early morning while in the woman's shelter before I headed off to my eighty-hour-a-week operations job. I felt frustrated because I knew all the information that the shelter was providing, but because of my warped thinking, I was not using my knowledge. I was exceptionally codependent, an adult child, and very hopeful that my first husband would grow and change so he would not be so angry. Notice the focus was on him.

After my third month in the woman's shelter, I had arranged to meet him for lunch before work in an attempt to convince him to join me in marital counseling. I said I would not come back home until he did. I was paying the mortgage and utilities, but not living there in our house, and he was frustrated. He agreed, under duress, to attend a session with me.

A week later, we arrived in separate cars at the therapist's office. When we got inside and sat down on the couch, side-by-side, he stated, "For each day she makes me come here and have a session with you, I will retard my personal growth by one full year. Go."

My therapist thought carefully, took a deep breath, and said, "This session is over, as I am not willing to take personal responsibility for his refusal to grow, change, and heal, to save your marriage. Karen, I'll see you next week, and we'll plan your divorce."

I was not ready to give up, as I had thought my parents had done so twice. I reluctantly stopped seeing that therapist because while he focused on a divorce, I focused on survival.

My first husband began drinking more regularly and blaming his poor behavior on his drinking. I stayed married in an unhealthy marriage for an additional three years. I was on a personal forced march, as I knew how to do that.

Chapter 12

My Life Shift—High Gear

While preparing for this book, my father and I were looking through some old photographs together and he found the one with me in high school on crutches. He was very angry when he asked, "What happened that you were on crutches?" I recounted the situation and he said, "I never meant for you to behave that way when I told you my Holocaust death march story." I told him I knew, but it was the cross I was to bear while growing up; always comparing myself and my experiences to his story of survival and pushing myself to be better. To be a survivor.

It was a lucky day for me the day I found my next therapist. His name was Dave Lewandowski, and he worked with me for ten years. I still keep in touch with him today. I was so disconnected from my needs and myself. I remember he once gave me an assignment. The assignment was to write a list of twenty things I could do for myself to make me happy, to make me feel good inside. It took me three weeks of writing lists of twenty items before I finally got it right. It amazed me how others-focused I had become.

Finally, my dog, Puma, a half-collie and half-springer spaniel mix helped me to learn to sit on the edge of my porch next to her and just breathe while watching the traffic. Apparently, I wasn't good at that either.

I felt that if I wasn't doing something productive, I shouldn't be alive. I put a lot of pressure on myself. Dave L. helped me tremendously, and he suggested Al-Anon. I decided I was tough enough; I could try anything to learn how to overcome my craziness. I went to Al-Anon to learn how to become mentally tougher.

I recalled, as an example of mental toughness, how my father, learning to swim at the hands of an American soldier, was forced to use his survival tactics even after the war had ended.

I believe many older children and adults drown, or fail in their endeavors, today because they do not have the skill to prepare themselves mentally for what happens when their mind and body is exhausted. They have not learned the exercise of mind over matter, and they have not learned how to survive a physically difficult situation. A primary thing that happens, particularly in a drowning situation, is that panic sets in, and the skill of controlling panic is a mind-over-matter issue, which is not commonly taught in these times; perhaps it is a survival skill more related to a less urbanized life. They have not learned how to use mental toughness. Again, a primary mind-over-matter survival skill is largely un-taught today.

I thank my friend, Katie Joe McDonough, for sharing with me this knowledge, as she was both a past pool guard, and she taught others how to save lives in and around water. She agrees with me that those inexperienced have no way of pulling from the experience of physical and mental trauma and lived through it to rely upon it for inner strength as my father had. He had determined that he was not going to drown in that pool. After all, he had survived all he had been through; a pool was not going to take him out.

The idea is the concept that "Necessity is the mother of invention." My father, because of his experiences which were harsh taskmasters, learned mental toughness and mind over matter, or whatever you want to call it. These days more of the world's educated population lives a relatively easy life, which encounters fewer traumas, and therefore less life learning in the survival-skill mode. This statement does not include war-torn and genocidal areas still being adversely affected today.

My father has used this mental toughness in all his life endeavors and has passed this mental toughness on to me, a second-generation Holocaust survivor, and through me, to both of my children who are third-generation Holocaust survivors.

One night while working at a Fortune 500 company job, I heard the back door open thirty minutes after my last employee had left. I went back to look and see who was there, only to find three punks had entered my office. They had begun kicking the vending machine to get free food and soda. I took four steps toward them and using a very loud and powerful voice I said, "Stop right now, or I'll take you across the street by your collars to the police myself."

My demeanor and my courage shocked them. I am five foot two, and at this time weighed one hundred twenty-five pounds. I continued to walk toward them but they did not move, so I pushed one aside as I opened the back door and sternly sent them out on their way as I would when I was teaching disobedient students. They did leave; however, they left laughing that a young woman my age and stature would consider taking them on. The next day on the wall across from the backdoor of my office, they spray-painted my initials and some type of symbol, which I took to mean I was cool with them. I never painted it over. Like father like daughter: fearless.

After my first visit in the rooms of Al-Anon, I knew I was home. I joined Al-Anon in 1988, since Dave Lewandowski suggested it, and he was usually right, as he was one of my angels. Al-Anon is a 12-step program for those affected by the disease of alcoholism. I became immersed in my personal growth and healthy responses to my life situations. When I arrived in those rooms, I felt so responsible for both my first husband and my father's emotional well-beings; I had almost given up being there for myself. I was close to feeling homicidal, and that rage stemmed from many things, including having been alone emotionally for so long. I had not been supported during most of my childhood and for most of my young adulthood, and yet I had a very high level of expectation from both others and myself. I still work on that problem today, but I feel I am successful more so because of my 12-step program, than I would have been had I not invested so much in supporting my own well-being.

Live and let live, one day at a time, just for today, the serenity prayer, the daily readings, time to pray and the rest of the slogans were lifesavers for me. Most of what I learned in those rooms I had heard in Torah study years earlier; however, I needed to act on these strategies not just know them in the back of my mind.

I remember during my first marriage, after sharing at my AlAnon meeting for my five minutes during one of my home group meetings—"... and then he said ... and then I said ... and then he said ... and then I said ...,"—to get credit and validation within the group that I was not the crazy one, a beautiful woman named Joy stopped me. She changed my life. She said, "Now honey, just jump off that merry-go-round right now! You have no control over this, you didn't cause it and you can't cure it. Now what do *you* need to do right now to feel good all by yourself?"

I couldn't believe what I just heard! She was suggesting I stay out of other people's business and focus on my business, which apparently I was not good at doing at all. Normally, in my home group, there was never any cross talk, or telling someone specifically what to do. In this case, I think the entire group was grateful to Joy because I never spoke like that again. It was the beginning of my deeper personal growth and accepting my personal responsibility of where I allowed my mind to spend time. I was no longer going to let other people and their problems live rent free in my mind.

I thank my home group, my first of many sponsors, Pat H., who helped me to learn how to detach with love, to understand, and get clarity on my personal needs by sharing how they did it for themselves, and she made certain I made it to weekly meetings for years. Had it not been for her invite to go with her, I would have stayed home and continued to work. My sponsors helped to parent me and teach me things healthy parents teach their children. They helped me to reclaim my part in caring for myself. My maternal grandmother, Jean Ribiat, had always told me, "No one is standing in line to care for you except you. So take good care of you because no one else will."

My maternal grandmother, Jean Ribiat in my mother's
kitchen when I was in high school.

Detaching from negative circumstances is helpful.
Remembering first things first, easy does it, and the
serenity prayer. I chose to stop jumping into quicksand.
I chose to stop enabling others to show up in my life and
live in their weakest states. I chose to step aside, to stop
judging others, and to focus on my gifts and my talents.
I heard, "Doing something is not necessarily my job."
"Everyone is in the middle of writing their own personal
story." I learned to respond instead of react, which I still
practice today. I hit the pause button and ask myself,

"In five years will this really matter?"

Growing up as a second-generation Holocaust survivor and knowing that I was to suffer in silence, equated for me that I was to be alone. Teaching me to be strong enough to survive alone might have been my father's goal, but it was not a healthy one for me. Through Al-Anon, I found my family, my functional family. Wherever I live or wherever I have moved to, I have found a new home group to grow with, and accept and love, be loved, be accepted by, and support, love, and nurture back.

It occurs to me now that five years of my first marriage went by and I have no memory of how my house got cleaned, who did the grocery shopping, and who wrote all the checks to pay the mortgage and expenses, even though I know it was always me, and who did the laundry—even though I know that was me, too.

Once, while married, I had gone into counseling called "The Courage to Change," which was a therapy focused around being molested, being a survivor of it, and the healing that needed to take place. I had begun having nightmares while I was still married and I wasn't sleeping. I was remembering the times of my abuse. Something I had stuffed away for twenty years. The woman who was my therapist worked with me for almost seven months. We had made great headway, until one day she announced that she had to move because her husband had taken a new job in a new state, and that this would be our last session. The first word out of my mouth was, "Congratulations!"

I held in my sadness and personal disappointment that she could not complete therapy with me on such a sensitive and personal subject so deeply embedded in my heart and soul. I focused on her and not myself. When I got out to the car, I sobbed and felt alone, again.

On several occasions during those last three years of my first marriage, I begged my first husband to let me go, get divorced, and go our separate ways, respectfully. He refused, and then he would treat me well for a week or two to prove his intent.

It was while still holding my job as an operations manager that I joined Mary Kay Inc., and I added being an independent sales consultant to my life. I was first introduced to Mary Kay when one of the people who worked for me, in my Fortune 500 company, offered me a Mary Kay makeover, sharing with me that I needed it. Not a cool way to introduce me to self-improvement. I was offended, having worn no makeup at all at this point in my life, and I told her no thank you.

However, Mary Kay Inc. was going to become a major force in my life for positive change. Every week I went to the bank to get a draw on my petty cash for my operations business and one of the bank tellers, Diana, said to me during one of my bank runs, "Karen, you work really hard at what you do. You deserve some pampering. Do you want to come over to my house for lunch before going to work tomorrow?"

I was excited! When I showed up the next day, on her kitchen table was a pink mirror and tray, and I knew she was going to give me a Mary Kay facial. I was not happy, I felt tricked. However, I felt Diana wanted to become my friend and not just the bank teller whom I saw every week, so I invested my time getting a Mary Kay facial. While she read the flip chart giving me the information on the company and the products, all I kept thinking about was how I could read it better. As a schoolteacher by trade, I had developed some skills while reading to others and one of them was entertainment value. This woman did a fine job, and I did want to buy everything I had on my face that day, but I was frugal and investing in my home's renovations at the time. I bought just two eye shadows and a cleanser. Every week I saw her, I bought something else.

Diana had told me definitively that she felt that I would make a great Mary Kay consultant because I was so smart. It shocked me to think that Diana thought of me as smart. She invited me to go with her to a Mary Kay unit event to learn more. So I went and I was confused about what I saw: women dressed in business casual, having fun, cheering one another on, and winning prizes. I had asked to go along with her to another event, thinking that one was just a fluke. But it wasn't and I saw more of the same. Positive uplifted women having fun, learning new things, and growing their businesses. Diana suggested that I let her Sales Director interview me. That sounded like a challenge, so of course I accepted. During the interview with Sales Director, Trudy Miller, who is now my Executive Senior Sales Director with Mary Kay, my strong personality came out as I actually suggested to her that she update her interview folder with colored paper. It was the teacher in me.

Looking back now, I'm horrified to know that I was that abrasive and direct in my communications. However, those qualities come in handy when working with kindergartners and when running a business surrounded by men. So it had worked for me up until then. In addition, I was a bit black and white when it came to nuances.

After nine months of attending Mary Kay meetings, sometimes with Diana, sometimes without her, and meeting Sales Directors like Pat Carr who I felt emulated all that I was not yet at that time; poised, beautiful, caring, calm, saying to me each time she saw me that I deserved to be a Sales Director like her and earning the recognition and accolades I was missing from my corporate job. She believed in me and I got to see Pat Carr and her wonderful husband Dick Carr so often, they felt like family. With Trudy seeing something in me, believing in me and my potential, and calling me every other week to re-invite me to join her Unit, I finally joined Mary Kay Inc. in May of 1991. I was a true business owner now, and I was still working eighty hours a week as an operations manager.

I had earned a trip to Atlantic City with the operations corporation because of my office's top revenues. I took forty dollars with me to gamble with, as I was going to be there three days and two nights. As it turned out, the roulette wheel loved me, and I turned that money into four hundred dollars! It was almost enough to join Mary Kay and place a minimum six hundred dollar wholesale order, which was my goal, not a company requirement. Unbelievably, my mother loaned me the difference that I needed because at this time we had begun to speak again. Within two months, she was paid back and still proud that she was able to help me, and I was very grateful because it was a first. I joined Mary Kay to get the products at cost, to earn some tax deductions, and to learn how to look better on the outside while feeling better on the inside. Then I learned I could help others feel and do the same. I began to build my team!

Executive Senior Sales Director, Trudy Miller and me
at Seminar

Along with Mary Kay Inc.'s values and ideals, all the women who mentored me gave me what I needed to believe in myself and to grow the skills that allowed me to become the leader I am today. Trudy Miller was a true mentor, and I will thank her forever for not giving up on me those first nine months. She was a fine example of a leader while I was learning the ropes of being a business owner. I continue to share what I learned from our company's high standards with those who choose to work with me within my Mary Kay unit, and have done so for the past twenty-one years. Here is what she has to say about me today:

> I met Karen in 1990 when she was in the process of realizing that, to take control of her life, she needed to start her own business and work for herself instead of someone else. She has always been bright, beautiful, and passionate with an incredible work ethic.

> Today I see that her life priorities of God, family and career continue to guide her decisions. She has experienced challenges that she cannot change and has learned to see the opportunities they present. What separates her from so many is her ability to act on those opportunities. She is a mentor to many because not only does she believe that although you cannot control what life may deal you, you can control how you respond . . . and she responds with

passion, focus, and grace. I count myself lucky to call her my friend.

Trudy Miller
Independent Executive Senior Sales Director
Mary Kay

I've loved the company's golden rule philosophy and have been gifted with many mentors along the way during my twenty-one years and counting. I cannot name all the women here, but in addition to my Senior Director, Trudy Miller, Executive Senior Sales Director Pat Carr who told me I belonged in Leadership with Mary Kay the second time she met me, giving me the vision, Senior Sales Director Heather Fitch who said, "Yes you can! What are you letting hold you back?", Senior Sales Director Kay Roth who said, "Never give up until you reach your goal!" National Sales Directors; Arlene Lenarz who said I had high integrity and that was what stood out with her working with me for 20 years, and Debbie Moore, who attended and spoke at my Sales director's Debut, Senior Sales Director Konie Slipy-Jestes for believing in me enough to loan me my first gown when I received my first diamond ring of four, Senior Executive Sales director Kelly Willard-Johnson who has always included me and made me feel I have great things to offer and achieve, and Elite Executive National Sales Director Anita Garrett-Roe who shared my vision for the speaking I do on behalf of Holocaust Awareness and Anti-bullying through my Standupster® Program and endorses my book as well.

All of these precious ladies are all very important to me. They have given me their priceless mentorship.

My first year at seminar, Konie Slipy-Jestes walked across the seminar stage in a gorgeous purple velvet and silk gown. This Seminar is annually held in Dallas, Texas, to train, motivate, mentor, and inspire us to go forward each fiscal year. I thought Konie in that dress was the most gorgeous woman I had ever seen! What an honor to do so well in the business that you could earn a diamond ring, wear a gown like that, walk across a stage after being handed down the stage staircase by one white-gloved gentleman after another! I gathered the courage and asked Konie if I earned a diamond ring the following year, would she loan me that gown? She amazingly said yes, and I was fully motivated and inspired to do what I had to do. I *did* earn that diamond ring, and I did walk down those seminar stage stairs in Konie's gown the following year. I felt like I had arrived!

*Me with Mary Kay Ash and my SSD Konie-borrowed purple
dress and earning the first of four diamond rings!
So truly excited and empowered!*

*SNSD Emeritus Daleen White and NSD Debbie Moore
with me in middle management!*

*My first company earned Mary Kay car out of ten! Two
Grand Ams, six Grand Prix, two Grand Achievers!*

ESSD Pat and Dick Carr at my Sales Director
debut—so supportive and inspiring!

*Me with Mary Kay Ash during my Sales Director-training
week in Dallas, Texas 1994.*

Applause magazine *and I earned another diamond ring,
and to date seventy-nine stars on my Ladder of Success! Fun
photo op!*

At Leadership Runway Banquet with SD Heather Fitch
who taught me, "Yes, I Can!" 2012

*NSD Arlene Lenarz who always said she admired my high
level of integrity.*

My third diamond ring with NSD Lisa Madson
at the royalty reception!

*My ESNSD Anita Garrett-Roe and I; she supports my
Standupsters®! And dreaming about growing
Mary Kay in Poland.*

*Me and ESSD Pat Carr. I love seeing my sister Sales
Directors each year at all our company events!*

I earned my third diamond ring!

Our company's thirty-fifth anniversary and I earned my
fourth diamond ring! And I'm wearing all four!!

Mary Kay Independent Senior Sales Directo

Karen Brass

Congratulations on achieving your new status in Mary Kay!

"You're the ones who have proven that there's nothing that cannot be accomplished, that there are no restrictions on success. It is with the greatest pride, as I'm sure you all know, that I congratulate you on the goals you've already reached...the goals I know you will be reaching tomorrow."

Mary Kay

Gary Jinks
Gary Jinks
Senior Vice President
Sales

Mistye Roché
Mistye Roché
Director, Sales Development
Diamond Division

inspiring **beauty**. enriching **lives**.™

FORTY YEARS OF WOMEN HELPING WOMEN

My favorite certificates earned by Mary Kay, helping another leader of women have what I have in becoming a Sales Director, while keeping my priorities in order; God first, family second and Career Third.!

My good friend and leader in my unit, Brass' Braveheart
Flyer's in Mary Kay, Darcy Yates!

*My tenth Mary Kay car. David Zauder and me and my kids
picked it up together 2012!*

I have often said, take back all my earnings, just so I know how to live a good life being a woman with God first, family second and career third!

The month of May has a lot of significance in my family, as every year I personally celebrate my father's immigration. May is a month of change and growth, and it was Mary Kay Ash's birthday month as well. She began to be a mentor to me, as she was to thousands of others as well. I saw her as a mother figure. I gained back a lot of positive self-worth, which my first husband had broken in me, and soon after joining Mary Kay Inc., I felt strong enough to begin to work on getting myself a divorce.

I called my father in early June, before seminar, and informed him that I was coming in to see him to tell him some details about the direction my life was taking. I was sad but I was strong, too. After I arrived and informed him that I was planning to get a divorce, he began telling me that I would sell everything, quit my job, come live with him, and work at the elementary school down the street from the house he had bought. He had never visited me at work during my five-year stint as an operations manager, a job I thought he would be proud of me for taking, as it was similar to his. I was responsible for 118 employees that I hired, trained, and personally motivated to invest in our corporate family. I had opened the doors of that job site, and I had a great atmosphere in which to work—positive, uplifting, and fun.

I told my father that I had no intention of giving up my Mary Kay business or moving it to Cleveland. I was very successful where I was living and had planned to quit my full-time job soon. He did not listen to me well and continued to repeat how I would just sell my house and move in with him. I told him he had nothing to worry about, and that I would not die a spinster. Actually, I said a "sphincter." My dyslexia plays good, hard vocabulary games with me, similar to Archie Bunker, who had excellent sitcom writers. I use the wrong, similar sounding words often, and it frequently leaves those with me laughing in stitches, as my father did that day. I had to ask my girlfriend, an editor who was one of my closest friends and who knew me well, why he had laughed at me when I said I would not die a "sphincter." She informed me of my verbal blunder.

I had a bad experience within the corporation I had dedicated eighty-hour weeks to for five years of my life. I found out that my assistant manager was plotting with my senior manager against me, behind my back, to take my job. Even after I had fought with upper management to give him a raise, he obviously had no backbone. I found out about their plan, and I quickly fired him. He did not see that coming.

I had left on vacation for seven days, for the first time in five years, and I'd offered to pay my supervisors and my assistant operations manager bonuses if they kept the office running smoothly. They did a great job in my absence, and it cost me my job. Rumor had it that my boss was worried I would be starting a family soon, and he didn't want to have to deal with maternity leave. Four months later, I was downsized, given a severance package, and told of a plan that I would be opening up another office in another city for them. But the plan never came to fruition. I was now unemployed and five years had passed, so my teaching certificate was out of date.

After many interviews, job offers, and much contemplation, I plotted my dream to earn a Mary Kay career car and become a Mary Kay Sales Director in time to be trained by Mary Kay Ash herself, which I achieved.

My first husband was no help during this time and suggested I find a job fast to keep paying the bills we had. Two months later, I left for Dallas, Texas, for my first Mary Kay seminar.

I had, waiting for my soon to be ex-husband, a personally written letter and a letter from my lawyer requesting that our divorce be finalized upon my return. In my letter, I told him how much I loved him, loved him enough to let him go because we were no good together. The only phone call he made that I was able to see on my phone bill was a long-distance phone call to Sparks, Nevada, where his grandfather's gun shop was located. This frightened me, as I knew of his violent nature. I worked hard and fast and by October 1994, our divorce finalized.

Afterward, I felt so light, so happy, so relieved it was as if I had put off life! Now I was living again and feeling wonderful. I lost the twenty-five pounds I had gained in those last three years, and then investigated what I actually had lived through. I went and saw the police captain, and requested a printout of how often I had called them during my marriage. Seventeen times. I was disappointed, as I know now that will never happen again. One time is too many.

Me dancing in my favorite place to journal
after my divorce was final!

My marriage finally ended four months later. After I was out of the operation manager's position, more than half of my employees quit, including all my supervisors. The office I had run successfully for five years, failed six months later without my leadership.

While I was in line for unemployment, I chatted up the women who were also in line, and offered them free facials with makeovers so they would look good for their interviews. I committed myself to working my Mary Kay business and building a strong business. I earned a company car four months later, and four months after that, I was a Sales Director, registering in the top 2 percent of the company.

I earned the first of four diamond rings, and Mary Kay Inc. paid for the license, lease, title, and the 80 percent of the company car insurance. I drove the car with pride. I set a high pace for myself and learned through Mary Kay's Directorship Training how to work with others successfully. I am still a Mary Kay Sales Director today, as I tremendously enjoy being able to help others with their skincare needs, and take excellent care of my customers nationwide. By the time this book is in print I will have earned my 70th star on my ladder of success which represents quarterly work ethic that affords my selection of a high quality prize each month, working consistently with my customers. I help those who join my Mary Kay Unit grow personally, set goals for their businesses, teach them skills that they need to reach their goals, and applaud their every success. It's truly a very rewarding business.

My first husband was not willing to move out, even though the judge had issued an order that he was to leave the house I was paying for, once our divorce had been finalized. One day in November, thirty days after he was to leave my house, my cousin Andy Rosenbaum showed up at my door unannounced. He was a blessing and an angel.

He understood the situation I was in and quickly took immediate action. He took me to the grocery store, gathered all the empty boxes we could collect, returned to my house, looked my ex-husband in the face, and told him he expected him to use the boxes and be out of my house within the next three days. Andy was six-foot four and no less than 210 pounds of muscle. My first husband was six foot and about 175 pounds. It was no contest. Andy single-handedly came to my rescue, and my first husband was out of my house by the end of the weekend. I have never been able to thank him enough.

When I earned my first Mary Kay car, of the ten I've earned in the twenty-one years I've been affiliated, my father could not believe it. He drove from Cleveland to Bowling Green, Ohio, just to kick the tires and tell me not to sell the old one. He felt sure that the company would come back and pick it up in short order.

My father did attend my Sales Director debut, and it was there that he learned exactly how big a deal it was that I had reached this level of success in such a short time. Of the cars I've earned, four diamond rings, more than seventy quarterly prizes, and so much personal growth, I would state honestly that I would give it all back just to remain the person I grew to become today.

Chapter 13

My Fears Are Validated

My first husband committed suicide in March, five months after our divorce in October, two days before his birthday. I called the morgue and the doctor had to get his father's permission for me to view the body, and he gave it. It was such a sad moment for me to see a human's life lost due to mental illness, instability, and lack of involvement and support. I looked at his finger nails to see if he kept them long for his classical guitar playing, and they were in fact still long. I found out from my neighbors and my renters who lived above me, that he had come to the duplex yelling my name and waving a gun earlier in the day. I had been lucky.

I called my father as soon as I found out, around 4:30 p.m., and the secretary said he was on stage during rehearsal, but she would have him call me immediately. I waited while my friends came and went offering their support. It was lucky for me that day I had held a Mary Kay skincare class scheduled at someone else's house, when normally I held all my appointments in my own home. Thank you, God.

I called my father again after hours had passed. His secretary was surprised that I had yet to talk with him. I called three more locations during that day, leaving messages at each location that it was an emergency. He still did not call. My father finally called me at 7:30 p.m. and yelled at me, saying how dare I call him all over the city and what could be so important? I was so hurt. In twenty-nine years, this was only the second time I had ever called him with an actual emergency, and he had the gall to be angry with me for trying to rely on him. He obviously wasn't able to be there for me the last time, when I called from the woman's shelter, but I still reached out for his support.

I stated bluntly that my first husband had committed suicide today. Thanks for your concern, and then I hung up. My father took five minutes to process and called me back. I had friends with me at the time and I didn't stay on the phone long. He said he would arrange his schedule so that he could be with me for the Saturday morning funeral.

When my father arrived Saturday morning, he walked in just in time to see the man that my ex-husband's family sent to my home to warn me against coming to the funeral. The man said harm would come to me if I went to the funeral services. I couldn't blame my ex-husband's family for feeling angry with me. After all, I had told them for years that I felt their son was suicidal and needed mental support and help. They had told me

I was the crazy one, which I had become. The fact that he actually did commit suicide, five months after I divorced him, meant that I was correct in providing the family my concerns and warnings, and I was fortunate not to have been killed that same day.

He took his life with that gun at the special place I had shared with him shortly after we had met. It was my special place of peace and solitude. I went there often to journal. It was along the banks of the Maumee River, where I had danced in my freedom months earlier. He knew this was my special place, and that's where he killed himself. However, his suicide had nothing to do with me. Proof I had *not* been his problem.

The man, who the family had sent, said that I would be paid back the money that I had invested in my ex-husband's education. He looked right at my father and said that the loan my father had given him also would be repaid. So, the family knew about both financial arrangements and sacrifices, but neither happened.

I did not go to the funeral, but instead went with my father to brunch where all he could talk about was his work. He never asked how I was, no discussion of my feelings, or my next steps. At this time, I did not realize that I had not legally arranged for my co-signing of my first husband's multiple college student loans not to be my responsibility, now that the divorce was final. Within months, I began to receive the bills for those student loans. I was devastated. Again, my second-generation Holocaust survivor mentality stepped in. This was nothing compared to what my father went through, I know now comparisons are never fair or equal. Therefore I added to my work schedule two additional skincare workshops per month to pay on those student loans. In less than a year, I was debt free.

Chapter 14

Live Large Because You Are Here On Purpose!

I met my current husband, David S. Brass, while attending a Shabbat service at Temple Shomer Emunim, in Toledo, Ohio. We were both very active in our temple and it was surprising we hadn't run into each other yet. At the time we met, I was sitting next to one of my elderly friends who stated, "You really ought to meet this David Brass fellow. I hear he is nice, has a good job, and a car." It was about the twelfth time someone had mentioned to me that I ought to meet Mr. David Brass, but no one had taken the time to introduce us. On this night, he was sitting next to one of my good friends, Jodie Goldstein, one of my angels. I had met Jodie's husband on a few occasions, and the man I saw sitting next to her this night was not her husband. We were in the smaller sanctuary where the chairs were situated in a horseshoe shape. I looked at him, he looked at me, and we both smiled. After the services, in the social hall, still no one introduced us directly. However, I did have time to ask Jodie who he was, and she seemed excited to know that he and I were destined to meet that night.

When I made my way across the social hall to where I had last seen him standing, he was gone. I was disappointed, but it was time for me to go, so I went to the coatroom where I found he was waiting for me, holding my coat. He introduced himself and walked me to my car, which I just happened to park right next to his. Upon arrival that evening, I heard a voice tell me, "Park here." It was a deep voice, a male voice. But being who I am, I said aloud, "Why? I always park in the middle row?" Then the male voice said louder, "Park here." I don't know who it was speaking to me, one of my angels perhaps, but I believe I was meant to park in that second spot in the first row right next to the car David Brass drove.

For me it was love at first sight with fear. Beshert, they say when it is God ordained, or a match made in heaven. When he walked me out to my car at the end of the service, he saw that I had parked right next to him, which was a gift. He read the sticker on my car that said Mary Kay Sales Director, and he said he was impressed. We were lucky; we had mutual respect for each other. When he said his name was David, like my father's first name, and Brass, like the instrument my father played, I thought it was funny. I knew he was special, and I knew instantly that he was the one for me, my beshert.

David and I together at our temple's fundraiser
and 125th anniversary event.

We began dating and the whole congregation of Temple Shomer Emunim watched as our relationship grew. We continued to see each other every third day until the day we were engaged to be married. I shared with my father that I had met the man I was going to marry. Apparently, I sounded convincing enough that he drove all the way from Cleveland to my home in Bowling Green, Ohio, on a Sunday to eat my matzo ball soup and to meet him. David liked my soup so much that he ate six bowls the first time. He and my father ate in silence. My father acted as if he was in the Jewish mafia regarding his little girl. There is a first time for everything.

David and I began getting to know each other on a very intimate level, but not physically. We decided to wait to be physically intimate. On our third date, he asked me about my family's origin. I was very honest, probably brutally so. I talked with him about my mother and our relationship, which at the time was nonexistent, again. However, I talked of her in a much different way than I would have prior to therapy, Al-Anon, and my personal growth. At that time, my mother withheld her love due to her consistently unmet expectations. We had not spoken in three years. She has changed her mind since then regarding expectations, claiming that all expectations are unfair and unreasonable, unless you ask for them honestly and up front. She has grown too.

Regarding my father, even though it was all in my own head, I said that we were going through an emotional separation. I shared that I had chosen not to be his surrogate spouse. That sentence seemed to confuse David just a bit, but being on our third date, he decided to wait for more of an explanation. He knew my father was a Holocaust survivor, and he knew I considered myself a second-generation Holocaust survivor. Deeper meanings and explanations came later. David was supportive of my being both a Mary Kay Sales Director as well as a Holocaust education speaker as well as of my beginning a second-generation support group in 1995.

We were engaged in Estes Park, Colorado, on Rainbow Curve

We visited my father a few times during our six-month courtship prior to our engagement. David and my father got along well, and it was fun for me to go to the orchestra concert with David and share with him my father's love of music. Although David was a businessman, he also had an artistic side. He knew I volunteered at the temple, at an assisted living home, at Jewish Family Services, and in my community. He was impressed that I owned my own home, a duplex, which I both lived in managed and rented out. He too owned his home and was on a fast track at his corporation. The car I drove was my second earned Mary Kay career car, given as a bonus for high-quality work in helping other women to be successful in their Mary Kay businesses.

I began having nightmares when David and I began our wedding plans. They were regarding me and my dog,

Puma, being kicked out of our new home with David and walking in the deep winter snow with no coat or boots on. It was a reoccurring nightmare. I finally shared with David that I was having it and the next day he took a few hours off of work and added my name to the house deed, not the mortgage. I felt heard, loved, understood and cared for and now secure. David is an amazing man and we've been partners ever since.

The Bal Shem Tov Rabbi shared that our souls are each a bright light in the world, and when two souls destined to be together meet, their light joins to make an even brighter light than when the two are apart.

My father and me at our wedding

Our house together in Toledo, Ohio,
with my dog, Puma; all ours now.

David Brass and I were married in the fall at the temple in which we met. We had a beautiful wedding and a wonderful honeymoon in Greece, which had been a childhood dream of mine as well as David's. Greece in October is not what the travel agent promised, and I found myself needing to redefine my expectations of the honeymoon. Again, with the comparisons of expectations, I found a way to make what was wrong, right in my head. I had gotten sick with a sinus infection, obtained antibiotics, and everything that goes with that, on my one-week honeymoon. David was absolutely wonderful and we decided to change the event from our honeymoon to our adventure moon with a romantic honeymoon to come later.

In 1997, my father had played for the Cleveland Orchestra for thirty-nine years, one year without a contract. He is still the longest tenured trumpet player in the history of the Cleveland Orchestra.

The year my father retired from the Cleveland Orchestra, August of 1997, I traveled with him to Québec, Canada, to visit his brother, Solomon, who was sick with prostate cancer. My uncle Solomon lived with his daughter, Rosa, my first cousin, and her family. She is married to Michel, and together they had three children. Each of them is married now with children themselves. I love my Rosa! She was born much earlier than I was. My uncle Solomon is six years older than my father is, using their correct birth records, and he got married directly after the war in 1946.

My Uncle Solomon's family in Quebec, Canada

The trip from Cleveland to Canada by car was interesting to say the least. I didn't drink a thing for fear that my father's car would last longer between gasoline fill-ups than I would in needing a bathroom! The same rules applied; mind over matter. Suffer in silence. He complimented me for my ability to last as long as he did in withholding the urge to relieve ourselves. Yeah me!

When we got to the hotel and we were unpacking, literally at the same time, suitcase to drawer, suitcase to drawer, I stopped him and said, "We're not related or anything are we?" It shocked him to be shown how similar we were, but he enjoyed it, hugged me, and laughed.

My 1st Cousin Rosa!

Upon arrival, I felt fantastic among my real family! Rosa made me feel welcomed, loved, and immediately understood. As she was also a second-generation Holocaust survivor, we recognized each other as such. It was a wonderful visit for my father and I, and he and my uncle Solomon reconnected. It was awkward at times, but more beautiful at others. We sat at the dinner table together; a family of eight, and suddenly my uncle Solomon broke out whistling a tune from their childhood. Without discussion, my father joined him whistling the same tune. This was family, and I videotaped this event because I came prepared to be able to have proof that I had a family. I had never heard that tune before or since, but it was evident it was an important song for the two brothers.

Later that evening I overheard my father, while drinking heavily, sharing with his brother how the name Zauder was now well known throughout America as one of the top cornet players and trumpeters. My father was very proud that he had made a name for himself within the musical industry and had contributed something as their father had told them to do. My uncle Solomon was impressed and happy for my father, but it was evident to me that their father had not given him the same request, to contribute something, or he interpreted it differently than his younger brother did.

My uncle Solomon was a jovial, happy, musical man who had lived a happy life and was content within himself.

My father still was not most of the above. Language was difficult; my uncle Solomon knew little English, and my father refused to speak in Polish. My uncle Solomon spoke Polish, Yiddish, Portuguese, and French. My father refused to speak anything but English.

It was interesting to me to see these two men, brothers, who had lived the majority of their lives separately, trying to connect. Uncle Solomon had lived in Germany for two more years while waiting to get the visas before moving to Brazil with his new wife and son, Henry. Bella, had family in Brazil. My cousin, Rosa, being the second born child, moved her family to Québec, Canada, in the 1980s. Uncle Solomon's career was being an electrician, but he never stopped being a musician, even though the Nazis had destroyed and beaten his hands when they learned he was studying violin with Henry Rosner, yes, of *Schindler's List*.

My uncle's goal was to enjoy life. He was known for poor business management, sometimes not collecting for his electrical work from families who had little money. His first wife, Bella, had that as her main complaint.

My Uncle Solomon, I could not stop thanking
for saving my father's life!

My father married and then divorced the same woman three times and never remarried again. I know he had a number of important women in his life, one in particular with whom he was close, but he rarely shared her with me. So I never had a stepmother or a relationship that resembled such. My father was much more a loner, and my uncle Solomon was very social. I would have enjoyed being in his life very much.

My father and I were in Quebec twice. Once for the wedding of Rosa's son in February of 1997, which was a glorious celebration, whereby my husband, David, joined us. My father and I went back a second time together to say good-bye to Solomon, who was dying of prostate cancer. My father went again by himself in the spring of 1998. My only uncle passed in February of 1998.

David Zauder with his brother Solomon
before he died of prostate cancer.

During the wedding reception of Rosa's son in 1997, while eating dinner, I watched my father emotionally disappear while holding a piece of bread. It was odd because I knew exactly what was happening. My father was there representing himself as an uncle to Rosa. Holding that piece of bread, among all those people who were blood relatives, was overwhelming for my father. He held the bread and was gone. My husband saw my father's face and began to interrupt him to ask if he was all right, but I stopped him from doing so. I told my husband that my father was experiencing something very precious, a memory that had included both bitterness and sweetness. He needed to feel it. He needed to experience the memories and remember them while being in a safe place. Being a second-generation Holocaust survivor comes with the responsibility of bearing witness to the child survivor's pain and memories, as well as parenting and validating that child survivor in their moments of memory.

Rosa and her husband visited us after my father was diagnosed with the same. Here she is with her uncle, my father!

In mid-1999, when David and I became pregnant after three years of infertility and treatment, my father became much more involved in our lives. It was as if a light switch turned on. I am grateful that it was after he retired, for he would have been torn, I believe, between his love of his commitment to his work and his love of our first child. My father lived two-and-a-half hours away by car, and yet when I called him at 4:00 a.m. on our way to the hospital to give birth to our first child, Shannah Rose Brass, {named after my father's mother who was murdered in the Holocaust}, he arrived at the hospital in one hour and forty-five minutes. It was the beginning of his consistent arrival in my life. It was a true gift to me.

When my father walked me up and down the hallways during labor, bearing witness to my natural childbirth, which ended in an emergency C-section, and he did not leave my side for all twenty-six hours, I felt all the years of our distance melt away.

My husband, David, also did not leave my side, nor did my midwife, my doula, and the hospital staff. It was a difficult birth—Shannah was breach, upside down and backward, as I had been. After a necessary caesarian section, even following such a long natural labor, I was pleased. I had kissed each of her ten toes, and she breast-fed like a pro. I felt everything was right with the world. I had a family, my family, and I had dreams of a commune.

All seemed perfect until the nurse from our pediatricians office visited the next day. She said, "Your daughter's Apgar scores look great, and she even had her eyes open and looked right at your husband and held his pinkie. She's amazing! Except for her cone head from being stuck for so long, but that will go away in a few months. She does have a port wine stain tumor on her right leg, and her feet and toes bilaterally will need some surgery, other than that, she's in perfect health! Congratulations, and we'll see you in the clinic for your first week checkup next week."

I cried on and off for the remainder of our two days in the hospital. When I got home, I immediately went to work making appointments with specialists to confirm what the nurse had said. We did have work to do to avoid Shannah from becoming lame.

Within months, my husband had received an opportunity for another promotion. He accepted and moved us to the state of Colorado. My father was involved in the move. He drove my daughter and me ahead of my husband and the moving van. As we were coming up to the mountains on the southwest side of Denver, he said, "You know we Zauders are city people, we are not country people! Why would you want to live surrounded by Christmas trees?" He was referring to the pine trees on the sides of the mountains. He was happy for us and sad at the same time because we were now three thousand miles away, round trip, from him. However, moving somewhere warmer was apparently on his radar. My commune was becoming a reality in my mind.

When my father visited my family in Colorado, which he did on a quarterly basis since the birth of our daughter in 2000, I began to see glimpses of how he was dealing with his past, and how his past was affecting and invading his present.

Shannah was not the first grandchild he held. My brother and his wife had given birth to a baby girl named Kaylee. But by the year 2000, they had divorced, and the child had been moved with her mother back to California from Hawaii where they had lived together. I stayed in touch; my love for my niece and her mother continued, as Kaylee was family. Kaylee has visited us twice in the past few years, and we have had lovely times together. She even had a reunion with her father during one of her visits and spent valuable time with her granddad.

Cousin Kaylee with Shannah and Adam

Karl with his daughter when they were still together when she was young.

Valuable time spent with my niece Kaylee, and her with her paternal Grandfather, and cousins.

Kaylee with Shannah and Adam in my new MK
premier-level, car I picked up during her visit.

*We had a family reunion with Karl and his daughter Kaylee
in 2010. It was wonderful time and lasted for days. We were
truly grateful for the time together.*

We moved with our five-month-old daughter and began
to make a new life. Because of the no territories rule

within the Mary Kay organization, I maintained all my customers and my consultants on the East Coast while I lived in Colorado. I grew my clientele on both coasts and kept my priorities in order: faith first, family second, and career third.

My father made a "forced march," his words he said often to make a point of what he was pushing himself to accomplish, and that was to drive out every quarter and spend a week or two with us because he had a second granddaughter now. I loved his visits. We reacquainted ourselves with each other, as he really did not know who I was, what I did with my time, and how David and I had such a functional marriage.

We began Shannah's white pulse laser treatments for her port wine stain tumor every six weeks. I advocated that I hold her while she got the treatments, versus the staff holding her down with her eyes covered with gauze. Her tumor began to show signs of improvement. After our daughter was eighteen months old, I gave birth to our son.

It took a lot for me to get pregnant with Shannah. I had to use fertility drugs, and it took three years of constant medication changes, a trip to Israel, many prayers, and a few notes written in the Wailing Wall by both David and me.

With our son, Adam Gabriel, it just happened. Both births were early, our daughter by four weeks and our son by five-and-a-half weeks. I had hired a part-time nanny, Coleen Nieman, who helped me ten hours per week. She had two grown wonderful children of her own, and she had been a director at a childcare center, but had retired. Shannah adored her and called her K. K. even though she could say Coleen. My daughter showed Coleen how smart she was by showing her all the shapes she had memorized on the training board I had made for her, even a crescent shape! Coleen was one of my angels! When my water broke at 11:00 p.m., I called Coleen and she came right away. She cared for Shannah for the two days we were gone.

Our ride down the mountain to the hospital was fast, and Adam came in one hour and fourteen minutes of my water breaking! When Adam was being delivered, the doctor said, "Uh oh!" two words you don't want to hear when you're birthing a child. The next thing he told me was, "Push now, the cord is wrapped around his neck and he'll die if you don't push now!" So, like so many things in my life, I overdid it. I pushed my son out with one big thrust, and my personal parts prolapsed. I needed surgery to do the repairs, but refused at the time because every surgeon I saw wanted me to stop nursing Adam to have the surgery. I knew nursing him was the best thing to meet all his needs. Therefore, I waited three years to have the surgery, which made my situation much worse.

We could tell right away that something was wrong with our son. I had breast-fed my daughter until she was two and a half years old when she weaned herself, when the weaning milk came in during my eighth month of pregnancy with Adam. I continued to pump and give her breast milk by bottle for an additional year. My infant son could not hold up his head, he had no core strength; he could not handle bright lights, he screamed from loud noises, and he needed to be nursed in his room in the dark without a sound, but my quiet humming. He had difficulty latching on properly and was seemingly starving at all times. He slept for twenty minutes at a time day and night and tried eating for more than forty minutes at a time but failed to be satisfied. I had to employ two lactation specialists to help me, as I assumed I must have been doing something wrong. Both shared he had weak mouth muscles and low tongue stamina for the job.

The diagnosis we received later was cerebral palsy, reactive airway disease, and dysarthria, which is a condition in which you have a weakness or a difficulty controlling or coordinating the muscles you use when you speak. Additional diagnosis like apraxia, among others that appeared later included coordination disorder, sensory processing disorder, spina bifida occulta, auditory processing disorder, and autism.

By the time I had my much-needed surgery in May of 2003, I had pumped enough breast milk to last two months so that both my babies could have breast milk untainted by medications. Though my surgery appeared to go well initially, it was soon clear there were serious problems. One of which was that they left something inside me, which they looked for while I was in the hospital during my eight-day stay there, but because there was no metal marker on it, they could not find it. I found it myself twelve days later when I had become toxic and almost died.

It was during my recovery of this near-disaster that I found out what it actually would take to knock me out of commission. I remained in bed for six months and had to hire a full-time nanny, and an after school nanny in addition to Coleen, for my two toddlers who were now three years and five years old. I did most of my phone calls from bed working with my consultants closely, from eight in the morning to eleven in the morning, which was when I had energy. The rest of the day, I slept. A couple of times I had my husband carry me to my office to hold my weekly meetings, but everyone could tell how sick I was, even with good makeup applications. After that, my loyal and well-versed-in-customer-service-selling husband took over my weekly evening meetings for the majority of the next four months.

I never said it aloud to those women who worked their Mary Kay businesses with me in the past, back in Ohio, when I was disappointed that they let, what I believed was a little problem, stop them from attending a meeting or a training session they had scheduled with me. I believe now that they could tell I was disappointed in what they let stop them, as if I had the right to judge what it took and that they hadn't arranged for a plan B. I have apologized to each and every one of them for my unspoken disappointment. They all have forgiven me, and even a few said they did not blame me, because in the end they took longer to learn how to set up for a plan B than I did, but they learned the skill and were grateful.

During my bed rest, I helped one of my consultants, Dawn Carr, earn a company car and become a Sales Director herself, promoting myself to Senior Sales Director. When I went out to visit with her, offer her additional training, and give additional training to her people, I was so very proud of what she and they had accomplished together! She is beautiful, I still work with her today, and she is a "God first, family second, and career third" woman of high integrity! It took me four days of being in bed to recover, when I returned, but it was worth witnessing her work ethic! I attended our company Seminar in Dallas, Texas, in a wheelchair that year. Unnecessarily. No one would have judged if I had stayed home and continued to recover. But I pushed myself, always doing a forced march.

I finally found out what it took to stop me, and I'm so grateful that I learned everyone has his or her breaking point, and it is okay. I thank God for this lesson, as an unstoppable type AAA personality like me needed to be humbled, and I was.

After our son, Adam Gabriel Brass, was born on September 4, 2001, according to Jewish custom, we had his bris scheduled seven days later on September 11, 2001. It was a horrible day. My father's friend called early that day and told him to turn on the news. David and I were preparing our home for our friends who were coming to celebrate with us. A bris is performed on the seventh day following his birth, and it is a time when a boy accepts joining his Jewish heritage and becomes a part of Abraham's covenant. He is also given his Hebrew name. As it was for all Americans, it was an extremely emotional day for us.

Adam's bris 9/11/01

However, for my father, it was doomsday all over again. We all watched the TV screen in horror as the towers fell. My father began running around the house yelling, "We are under siege!" He wanted to drive to the nearest army post and reenlist. It was a very horrible, scary time for all Americans. Our hearts went out to those in New York, who were personally affected by this tragedy, as well as their families located around the world, and our souls were pained while watching my father's post-traumatic stress disorder in full distress.

I called our mohel, who happened to be a pediatrician as well, and asked if we should cancel our son's bris and reschedule due to the tragedy unfolding in New York City. He said, "I know of nowhere else I would rather be than celebrating a new life on this terrible day; I will be there." Even though we had some friends and family who originally had called stating they could not attend earlier in the week, everyone was present at our son's bris.

Our daughter, sensing the heightened emotional state of my father as well as the rest of us, could not stop sobbing. Our good friend and still part-time nanny, Coleen, took her outdoors until the ceremony was completed. We held our son's bris on time, and the mixture of fear, anger, tears and sadness, love and blessings washed over us all.

David Zauder with baby Adam, limp with his cerebral palsy

Shannah and Adam eighteen months apart

David Zauder visits came more frequently.
Photo of my father with Shannah and Adam

David Zauder with Shannah doing math homework.

My father began to visit us more frequently. One day during one of these visits, Shannah, now five and Adam three and a half were sitting on a blanket outside playing. My father was standing on the porch looking at them from above. I told the children I would be right back with their snack and my father lost it! He began yelling at me, "What do you mean you're getting them a snack, they're surrounded by food . . . food is on the bark of the trees . . . on the ground under the leaves. The grass . . . no one has touched it. Why are you bothering them?"

I knew immediately, because of what he was suggesting, his emotions, anger, and overreaction caused this post-traumatic stress disorder memory. I stayed calm and said, "Dad, there is fresh food in the refrigerator that I purchased yesterday. If they don't eat it today, the food will go bad. My children are young and need healthy, fresh snacks."

Speaking about purchased food in the refrigerator was enough to shock him back to reality, but it was evident that he had snapped. He shook his head and walked back into the house as I headed out to the children with their snacks. About an hour later, I asked him if he recalled what he had said to me. He said no. I retold the scenario to him. He said he did not remember it specifically, and yet he could not deny it either. Suggesting to me that my three-and-a-half and five-year-old eat bark was not going to go over very well with me, the biggest mama bear I know. However, I had compassion for my father and his

PTSD, and I knew his intention was good. I also knew that my husband and I were going to be in for one hell of a ride when he moved in with our family two years later, as was my plan, my commune. It took those two years to oversee and pay for renovating and adding onto our home to make room for my father.

Watching our children grow up and begin to reach the age at which his childhood ended was and is very difficult for him, and yet he could not look away for an instant.

Chapter 15

Our Commune, Forgiveness, and the Diagnosis

On my refrigerator there is a magnet that reads, "I didn't say it was your fault, I just said I was going to blame you for it." This is an honest statement, which after fifteen years of marriage; I can honestly say this phrase to my husband when it is necessary for me not to take responsibility for a moment. Just for a moment. For a Holocaust survivor, making a mistake could cost you your life and being blamed for mistakes could cost you everything, including your life. So I learned early to rarely accept responsibility for mistakes, it's a survival tactic, and I learned of this from my father. I worked very hard in the beginning of my marriage to overcome this sensitive issue, which made no sense in the day-to-day world we live in now.

In 2003, my father mailed me a photograph of his face beat up and bruised. It was in a plain envelope with no note attached, just a photograph of his face, which looked like he had been beaten by five men. It astounded me. I had no idea what could have happened because we spoke by telephone regularly now, and he had said nothing.

I called him and said, "What the hell happened?"

He replied, "I don't know what you're talking about."

I said, "The photograph. You mailed me a photograph of your face all bruised up. What happened?"

"Oh that," he said. "That was nothing, a bad day, that's all."

"What do you mean a bad day? How did your face get like that, all black and blue? What happened to you?"

My father said in a very calm voice, "You know the Zauder rule; "Don't catastrophize."

He shared with me how he had fallen on the stone steps of the capital building in downtown Cleveland. He said he bled all the way home, and used a rag from his car to clean up and attempt to stop the bleeding. He was surprised the bleeding did not stop and that it continued for two days. But he was all better now.

I couldn't believe it! I was horrified. I knew he was on blood thinners from his heart attack back in the late 1980s, and that being on blood thinners would make it hard for his blood to clot. He was very lucky he didn't get an infection from a bleeding wound. I told him I was very disappointed that he did not drive himself to a doctor, and he proudly told me he could take care of himself.

First, why was he sharing with me a personal issue regarding weakness and fragility, and second, why was he setting me up to be his rescuer? Something had to be terribly wrong and I was set in motion immediately.

I had no choice. He is my father and I love him, and this is our life, and I have chosen to live my life with no regrets. This includes full forgiveness on my part so that I could accept this honor; give my father a home in his golden years without anger or resentment for his past failings with me. So my husband, David, and I had a conversation that evening regarding whether we could handle including him in our home, along with our two special-needs children and their consistent extra requirements. We discussed where he would live, we discussed where the addition would need to be, and we discussed how the last chapter of my father's life would most likely play out. My husband was very aware of the number of post-traumatic stress disorder situations that would rear their ugly head.

This was the first of our conversations in formalizing our decision to make room for him in our lives permanently. The best advice we had gotten from a multitude of professionals—thank you close family friend, Lee Green—was to convert the attached two-and-a-half-car garage into a living space for him.

My father had in his mind that his coming was a way in which he would be of service to me and to my husband, helping us with our two special-needs children. He wanted to be there for me, the way he hadn't in the past. He was making up for his absence in my life. He contributed by doing some cooking, helping collect eggs from our ten chickens, and being supportive of our various therapies for both children. Early on, he even helped from time to time with driving our daughter to the three-tiered, special-needs school, Havern, the angel in our daughter's life, which she needed to attend to gain her first through fourth grade education, after failing out of public school's first grade two years in a row. Shannah needed modifications, accommodations and scientifically based strategies to help her learn. Havern had them for her and she thrived. My father also assisted by being a Granddad to both of them. His presence in our home was a blessing to us all.

I give my husband, David, a lot of credit for being willing to embrace my father; someone he knew had not been there for me most of my life. However, David had respect for my father and felt a level of responsibility to support his wife and her need to support her Holocaust-surviving father. He also saw the growth that my father and I had developed since our daughter's birth in 2000. We both embraced the idea and began making plans. More forgiveness and healing were to come.

We had a builder, contractor, and an engineer as well as all the electrical, plumbing, and septic people out for their opinions. We live in a three-bedroom home, and we could not afford to build a full edition for my father's needs, so my father offered to contribute to our renovations after the sale of his home in Cleveland. My husband went to my father's house to help him clean it up. David Brass painted walls, pulled up old carpeting, and repaired kitchen issues. After all his hard work, the house was ready for inspection and to be added to the failing housing market in Cleveland, Ohio.

While my husband was there, he measured the three main rooms my father spent the most time. They were his master bedroom and bath, a portion of his kitchen, and the television den. Adding to the attached garage by just a bit was the answer. I was the general contractor on this job and without pay, organized all the workers and made sure people were on time and came to work in order. We were able to add on to the back of the attached, soon to be renovated garage, a four-hundred-square-foot master bedroom, which includes a space for his desk, trumpet, and music stand.

Later, when we could afford it, we began to make plans for another garage that would incorporate what we would need. It was a huge undertaking and took two-and-a-half years and thirty hours per week of my time to complete. Everyone who worked on this project knew what we were doing and had the greatest respect for me, my husband, and for my father—for who he was and for what he had lived through—and for their kindness and their respect, we are grateful. We are still in touch with every single one of these special hearted people today.

My father has lived with us since July 2007. The details of what we went through while living together and caring for him while he, in his way, cared for us, may need to go into a separate book about caring for the aging Holocaust survivor. My main source of help came from the only book I could find on the subject, *Caring for Aging Holocaust Survivors, A Practice Manual*. The Baycrest Centre for Geriatric Care out of North York, Ontario Canada, was the source for research for both Paula David and Sandi Pelly, the editors, and they did a fantastic job and gave both graphs as well as detailed suggestions for the caregivers. I also immediately signed up for two 12 week courses on caregivers, a half a year apart from one another, one through Mount Evans Home Health Care and Hospice, another set of angels for me there. In addition, I added attending my local Al-Anon group weekly rather than quarterly. It became a life line for me and our life.

Both of our children were born with physical and learning disabilities, and I've had to be an extreme advocate for both of them and support their educational opportunities. Actually, in some cases, I had to become a Standupster® with those professionals who were untrained, uneducated, or unwilling to do the right thing by our children's needs.

Never once have I forgotten how lucky we are to live in this decade, in America, for if we lived in 1939, both of our children, due to their disabilities would have been taken and murdered. I never forget that reality.

Due to our son's Airway Reactive Disease, and the number of times per month he had to be hospitalized for years, we incurred a deep financial debt in our family. Prior to my CNA training, he went to the hospital to be treated with oxygen, nebulized every 3-4 hours, given special medications for his consistent and double ear infections and held upright while he aspirated to avoid further choking incidents. There in the hospital, they never addressed his physical needs for his Hypotonic Spastic Cerebral Palsy and Apraxia or Dysarthria, or any of his other physical needs because he was too sick to do anything but sleep on and off. At home and with: Occupational Therapists, Speech Therapists and Physical Therapists, Pedorthic specialists, Massage Therapists, Visual Therapists and Chiropractors, Adam began to learn to walk and hold himself upright. And now add head gear and painful braces, a bite palate expander to his very deep palate and extreme cross-over bite to his mouth for both better speech recognition and improved health issues in his future. Being his CNA afforded me the opportunity to serve his continued needs at home rather than in a hospital setting, which has been more than a blessing. Thank you PASCO!

I chose to become exceptionally involved in relationship building with the people who were going to be closest to our children in helping them to reach their highest potentials. Our son has had speech therapists as early as two years of age as well as psychologists, family counselors and educational tutors beginning at five years old for reading, writing and math, and additional medical care including chiropractic care, SCERTS model of autism training, RDI—Relationship Development Intervention and Applied Behavior Analysis therapy and healers. We've also had massage therapists and Pilate's instructors individually working with both of our children.

At the schools they currently attend, Elk Creek Elementary and West Jefferson Middle School, the staff from top to bottom have been very helpful in following their IEPs and willing to work out the kinks when we find them. They are all angels to our children, accepting them for who they are and guiding and supporting them towards their best and therefore angels to us. To name them all would be nearly another book. Suffice it to say, we are blessed for each and every one of those special people who took the time to give and care for our children in every way they needed help! They ARE "Team Shannah" and "Team Adam", and they are our Angels!

Showing Adam in his way—protected. His sensory processing dysfunctions and his autism affected everything.

Adam didn't want a photo included of himself sick, {which he is often} due to his reactive airway disorder; he uses a lot of oxygen, but he said showing the o2 and wearing his AFOs was fine.

Adam's AFOs are used to support his ankles and keep his toes up, heels down, when he walks and stands due to his cerebral palsy. He also wears ankle braces and orthotics.

Adam's AmTryke, a gift for service he gave helping to teach PTs at Children's Hospital, so now he can ride a bike, even with his cerebral palsy. Thank you Ambucs!!!

*Adam and Rockies head coach, Jim Tracy, playing baseball with
special needs through the National Sports Center for the Disabled.*

In October 2012, I had the honor to be one of the final
three nominated to be given The Citizen of Distinction
Award by the Autism Society of Colorado for all the work
I do in education regarding special needs children in our
schools and discrimination elimination. Fighting against
my son being bullied for his many disabilities, including
his autism became a passion and focus of mine. I was very
humbled by being recognized for my work by such a great
organization. I was nominated by The Jewish Disability
Network, who has also supported us financially for years
of special programming, camps, skill based training, and
even Adam's Camp for Adam's special needs. What a gift!

Since he isn't good at sports, Adam focuses on special projects with his father. The Kids Wish Network bestowed the greenhouse to Adam, through the UCP, United Cerebral Palsy of Colorado.

Adam continues to grow, with the help of the National Sports Center for the Disabled. He skied for the first time in 2011, on a ski bike and two ski instructors holding onto him!! He is fearless.

David and Adam's Boy Scout cross over, a way to be certain Adam has surrounded himself with high quality friends who understand and protect him.

Our daughter has had three major surgeries to date for deformities to her feet, as well as continued laser surgery every six weeks over the last twelve years for her port wine stain tumor on her right leg. In addition, she too was diagnosed with dyslexia, nonverbal learning disorder, auditory processing disorder, a short working memory, executive dysfunction, and most recently, severe adolescent onset idiopathic scoliosis. She currently is wearing a body back brace twenty-two out of twenty-four hours per day to both correct her scoliosis and avoid surgery in her future.

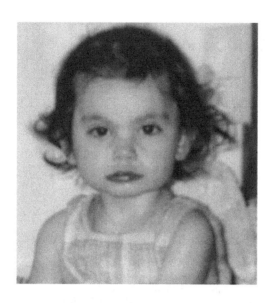

*Shannah looking lost and gazing as her processing was so
slow, she often checked out. Just like me on Santa's lap.*

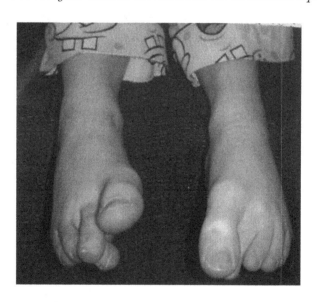

Shannah and her toes after her first of two bilateral surgery

Shannah after her bilateral second foot surgery, after the
wheel chair for two months, still in casts but walking!

Shannah's choir solo at Elk Creek Elementary in the fourth grade, succeeding in public school after she had received her 3 years at Havern, a three-tiered school and her continued accommodations and modifications worked at Elk Creek!

Team Shannah supporting her; behind Shannah:
Michele-Massage RMT and OT specialist and her husband
Mike, to her right: Courtney-PT and Pilates specialist and
Me, David Zauder, and Adam at her first winter concert
with the Evergreen Children's Chorale.

How our children have become so successful with the help of so many people who care about and for them, will have to be another book. We affectionately call the many people who have provided mental, emotional and physical support to our children "Team Adam" and "Team Shannah," and we know they all love our children. We adore them!

David Zauder practices daily, when he feels up to it.
McBoat photo

Due to my father's influences, both kids are musically inclined.

The children are very close and understand each other's disabilities and strengths.

GrandDad David Zauder and the kids in perfect harmony-McBoat photo

*Granddad David Zauder and Shannah have a special
bond–McBoat photo*

GrandDad David Zauder and Adam New Years 2012

Both Shannah and Adam know they are the third-generation holocaust survivors, not just because we've told them they are, but because they have watched and grown up with their Holocaust-surviving granddad daily. They've watched his perseverance though his prostate cancer metastases to his spine and bones.

*Shannah wanted to learn more about her granddad's tattoo
and history, so he shared with her, age appropriately.*

*The Brass family after he lived with us as GrandDad David
Zauder, surviving his Metastasized prostate cancer longer
then they predicted. McBoat photo*

When my daughter got her spinal brace, and I was upset for her, she shared that she was, in fact, grateful it wasn't cancer. She said that "this too would pass", like GrandDad says, she would be healed, and be okay in her future. She is painfully paying up front now, while she works hard daily to rehabilitate her body to be pain free in the future. She is strong and perseveres like me, like her GrandDad, like a third-generation survivor with pride in her heritage.

When our son shared that he knew he'd have to work all his life to compensate for his cerebral palsy, sensory processing disorder, his auditory processing disorder, his reactive airway disorder, asthma, and his autism, he said it was his greatest gift because now he had great work ethic.

These children are strong, resilient people with whom we are finding it a blessing to be bearing witness to what they are overcoming themselves without complaint, because their frame of reference is through third-generation eyes. We couldn't be more proud of them!

Az doz hartz iz ful, gai'en di oigen iber. When the heart is full, the eyes overflow. ~Yiddish Proverb

My father moved in with my family to assist us in raising two special-needs children, not because he is a Holocaust survivor dealing with aging issues and needing help himself. He did not accept knowing that he had any true illnesses at the time. The children were thrilled to have their Granddad moving in with our family. And I was hopeful that I would be getting my father in my life, moving in with us.

A Jewish meal together!

David and me; Adam's eyes closed . . . the kiss; Brass style!-McBoat photo

The day my father was to come, he arrived early by six hours. He was always early, so this was not a surprise.

The moving van was a few days behind him, and his car was filled with all of his most prized possessions.

When I ran out to meet him, and he got out of the car to hug me, his knees buckled. I quickly ascertained that he had not eaten and had not drunk anything other than coffee, on his drive from Cleveland to Colorado. He always pushed himself, but more than that, this time he pushed himself more than he should have.

He said to me with tears in his eyes, "Am I home now?"

I said yes knowing that my father had not arrived, but that I had just become a mother to another. He looked at me with childlike eyes, and I accepted him as such.

Even though he was pale, he refused to take a break, needing to empty his car completely before sitting down. I followed him around with a glass of water, begging him to drink and stay hydrated at our high elevation. Even though he had visited quarterly for seven years, I noticed that he had aged since our last visit and that complicated things. He, however, was not willing to acknowledge these changes.

He yelled at me and told me to leave him alone because he could take care of himself. Then he took out a brand-new bottle of some type of hard liquor and said we needed to toast his arrival. I said I would make a deal with him. I would toast with him if he would follow it with two glasses of water. He said okay, we toasted, but the water went untouched.

The kids were thrilled, and as we sat down to have dinner together, I put yet another glass of water by his place setting, which he refused to drink. He chose wine in celebration. Dinner was glorious, and we had a wonderful time together. Afterward I put the kids to bed.

My father decided he wanted to get into the hot tub that we had just installed two weeks earlier in his honor, and for which he paid one-third. I said I was not comfortable with him being in the hot tub after drinking so much and that tomorrow morning would be a better time. He told me that he was fine and that I was catastrophizing and over-thinking.

Two weeks earlier, I had completed my state board certification for becoming a certified nurse's aide. I did this as a parent to our son who has a multitude of special needs, as I've shared earlier. I did not expect to need to use my CNA services that night in support of my father's health. Upon entering the hot tub, however, my father began acting and looking strange and pale. My husband and I required that he got out immediately, as it was obvious his blood pressure was plummeting. We got him out and then had him sit down in a plastic chair, and again I handed him a glass with water, for the 8th time.

It was then, after he dropped the glass, that he threw his head back and his eyes rolled into the back of his head. He struggled to breathe and then lost consciousness. I used my CNA training immediately and sent my husband to dial 911 while I laid my 195-pound father backward onto the deck and straddled him. I couldn't find a pulse and began to give him CPR. In less than three minutes, he was conscious and telling me to get off him. A good sign.

The paramedics arrived a few minutes later, and they took the information I gave them and agreed with me that he was dehydrated and needed to go to the hospital. He was not happy with me, but he went because he was too weak to fight with them as well as me. My husband followed the ambulance down the mountain to the hospital.

I was furious and terrified. It wasn't enough that he was so self-disconnected, so unaware of his own physical issues, but I was a mother already to two special needs children, and I was actually mothering him now! How dare he be so selfish! Was he aware of his behavior, and how it affected my husband and me? What would our children think when they woke up to learn that Granddad had to be taken to the hospital on his first day moving in with us?

My father was no longer a loner now that he moved in with our family. He had some mind-set changing to do. I called and spoke Audrey, my really good friend, a psycho-therapist, for almost an hour that night. She shared with me that he needed to take responsibility for his actions and to apologize to me for unfairly jeopardizing his own life in my home. She had no extra empathy for his Holocaust background, which I kept referencing.

David and my father returned the following morning, and as I began to assert my rights to have boundaries with how he behaved in my home, his reaction was classic survivor. He was not going to listen to me, nor did he take into consideration my feelings, or my husband's or our children's. Had they been present and witnessed the event, it would have been a different experience for him because in our home children speak the truth and are not ignored.

He claimed it would never happen again. Period.

My father was ill, as evidenced by his fall when he sent me the photograph of his face two years earlier. But he was in complete denial. We dealt with a number of situations where he was not caring for his physical needs and refused our assistance and advice. I felt better prepared to handle my detachment with love from my father; however, with children in the house it becomes a higher standard of acceptance and responsibility. So with my husband's help, I began to research what was physically wrong with my father. We had many examples of physical issues to look into; however, the bottom line of the underlining cause we had not yet found.

Shortly after my father moved in with us, I held a mezuzah-raising event. Our friends, neighbors, and Jewish community, along with the rabbi of our temple, joined us. It was then, in front of everyone, with tears running down his face that my father shared about his father taking down their mezuzah on their doorpost in 1939. He explained that his father had asked him to get the hammer and take down the mezuzah. David Zauder had asked his father, Karl Zauder, my grandfather why. My grandfather answered, "So that we should not make it easy for them to find us."

My father continued and said that he did not know what was coming tonight, now that he had his first mezuzah since 1939 on his doorpost. He stated that he had lived a good life and was okay with what happened next, alluding to someone coming in the night again to take him away. That day my father shared his post-traumatic stress disorder with everyone present. There was not a dry eye in the house.

In 2008, a full year-and-a-half after my father moved in with us, we had another major incident. We were all sitting in the living room and my father got up from the couch and began to walk out of our part of the house and into his. While he was walking, his right foot was dragging, and he began to trip. Both David and I jumped up in an attempt to catch him, which only infuriated him because he didn't agree that there was a problem.

He never wanted to receive help because that equaled weakness in his mind. "I'm not an invalid!" he'd say.

By the time he reached my kitchen, he was yelling that it wasn't his right leg or his right foot that wasn't working, but the new slippers I had bought for him. He promptly took both of them off, and threw them in my garbage can, and stormed out.

David and I were both very concerned because it was evident that his leg was not working, and his foot was experiencing a lag that we later found out was called "drop-foot" caused by a nerve being pinched in his spine. He also was experiencing nerve pain and tingling in his feet, especially on his right leg. I did my normal due diligence, calling our family physician, and going one step farther by calling the VA hospital, the veteran's administration, and scheduling an appointment for him.

After that experience, he began having such pain in his back and in his hips that he began to slump over. This is not the normal stance of my father, who originally stood six-foot one. The pain on his face was so obvious I felt a stab in my stomach every morning he opened the door and we looked at each other. Knowing he did not admit pain to either our family physician or the VA physicians, I had had enough.

I must remind you that part of my father's history, as a survivor of the Holocaust, was that he needed to always be correct, and never found guilty of a mistake or found to be physically weak. If you made a mistake in the concentration camp, you were murdered. If you made a mistake while making horsehair brushes by not working fast enough, you were murdered. If you made a mistake on the death march, you were to be murdered. If you admitted to yourself a physical weakness you set yourself up to die. This was his history. Because he had spent years of emotional growth being stunted and developmental milestones being skipped while he spent time in the camps, he never comfortably managed to be able to take personal responsibility for errors in judgment or mistakes he made. It has sent him into a fight-or-flight mode each time. He had lived through atrocities, terror, mutilation, and witnessed countless murders. Genocide. He held himself to the highest level of standard of behavior never to have to "look down a barrel of the gun again."

By January of 2009, my father began looking worse and worse each day, and he was apparently feeling horrible as well. He finally agreed in February to allow me to get him in for an x-ray and MRI to find out what was causing his intense pain. While my husband was driving my father to the nearest image clinic, I was on the phone obtaining authorization from our primary care physician.

Before my father and my husband returned, I was in my kitchen, which is next to my father's kitchen, and I overheard our doctor leaving a message on my father's answering machine. She used the word oncologist, and I dropped to my knees and began to sob.

After I recovered, I knew that with my having my father's medical power of attorney, I could get the results of his test, so I called and had them faxed directly to me. I had to hold the paper up near the ceiling so that I could read it while tears fell like a river down my face. My father had terminal bone cancer metastasized from his prostate. Twelve to Fourteen years in the making according to the technician's report. The cancer was up and down his spine, in his ribs, sternum, and his arthritis lit him up like a Christmas tree as well.

When my husband arrived, I was still an emotional mess, and he did not know anything. He knew my father was upset because I made him go through this test, but he did not know why my father was so upset on the way home. The radiologist had called our family doctor while my father was dressing and asked how long her patient had metastasized bone cancer from his prostate. Since our family doctor did not know he had cancer, her response was one of shock. She said, "He never told me." So the radiologist told my father after he was dressed that he had metastasized bone cancer and needed to get help immediately. I'm certain the drive home with my husband was uncomfortable.

When he returned, I was aware that the radiologist had asked him how long he had had his bone cancer, and he had answered that he didn't have cancer. All he would tell me and my husband for two weeks was that he had an "imbalance in his bones." Our doctor told us that we needed to wait for him to wrap his brain around what he had just learned, and then we would investigate radiation and chemotherapy options together. He had little time left.

Back in 1997, my father called me and asked what I thought about him getting a prostate biopsy. He shared that he was having a little difficulty there, and he felt that the doctor was pushing him to get this biopsy and he was scared. I told him my opinion was that he should get the biopsy and if they found something, it would be early enough to cure it. Then I called the doctor's office directly, making certain he did have an appointment for the biopsy. I requested that they dispense Versed, a drug that would allow him to relax and perhaps not remember the experience. I informed them that he was a Holocaust survivor and it was most important for him to go through with the test. They assured me that they would take good care of him.

I called my father the morning of the test to be certain he was going. He replied that he was, and he would call me in the evening to let me know how it went. I waited, but he never called, so I called him. I asked him how it went, and he said he felt nothing. I assumed that the Versed had done its job, so I relaxed and asked when he would be getting the results of the biopsy. He responded in an aggravated tone and said that they would not find anything, and he would have nothing to tell me, and he hung up.

I should have called the doctor directly, because then I would have learned that the doctor who was to do his biopsy had died the night before of a massive heart attack. When my father arrived for his appointment, the nurse apologized and said it was canceled, and he would be rescheduled later.

I later learned that my father took this as a sign from God that he was not to get the biopsy. Many of his past signs from God had saved his life. This was no sign and his cancer grew for twelve years.

When we finally got my father into the oncologist's office, we learned that he was terminally ill. If his body accepted the therapy that they were proposing, at best he would live three more years. At the time this book is out, we will be at the end of 2012, and he has survived four more years and counting.

At the first appointment, the doctors told us privately in the hallway, that my father had two, maybe three, months to live. It was excruciating. My grandfather, Ben Ribiat, whom I took care of during his last summer of life, died of bone cancer three months from learning of his stage 4 cancer.

By the time my father told us the truth, we had been to three different doctors' offices, and they had a plan for radiation, chemotherapy, and hormone therapy. My father was exceptionally lucky; all three of the therapies worked, and his cancer went into remission and stopped growing for a while.

As I write this book now, and although I saved his life twice with CPR and David once, it has not been easy to watch a loved one deteriorate, one who is in denial of losing any of his faculties. David also saved my father's life once. He gave him mouth-to-mouth after my father received a head injury. He was getting out of the car, passed out and fell backward after standing up on the driveway. My husband and I took turns in the hospital so that my father would never be alone for the two weeks until the brain stopped bleeding and his dementia reduced enough that we could bring them home. He remained on oxygen for two months upon his return until he could get back to his elevation regulation.

Part of my reason for completing this book quickly is so that my father can read it, which he has, and see that I too have contributed something to this world. We are grateful for each day, forgiveness abounds, and we do live in the "here and now" in my home. We took photos at the time, as we were not certain how long we were to have with him.

If it weren't for the importance of supporting my father, all of this would've been considered a major inconvenience. But because we are family, we are supportive of one another. Many things have taken a backseat in importance in our lives during this time. As my father always says, "This too shall pass."

Chapter 16

How I Grew In My
Second-Generation Identity

In 1982, after witnessing Mary Neufeld, a Holocaust survivor, giving a speech at Bowling Green State University, I knew what my next step would be. After her speech, I introduced myself and spoke with her at length. We became friends, and she tutored me on how to share the lessons of the Holocaust through my father's personal story. She was one of my angels. I feel honored and privileged to have been able to be groomed by her, such an amazing, kind, and sensitive woman—a survivor.

In 1995, I was moved to search for others like myself, second-generation Holocaust survivors. My goal was to find emotional support from those who might have had similar family experiences as I did growing up. I was engaged to be married, knew I wanted to start a family, and wanted to do it with the safety of a village, not as an orphan. I've held these relationships with great regard and have been close to many second-generation survivors ever since, as part of my innermost village. My children know that they are third-generation Holocaust survivors, and they are exceptionally proud of, as well as close, to my second-generation friends.

I have always been a very involved community volunteer. I had the distinction and honor of being asked to chair the Raoul Wallenberg Scholarship Award at the University of Toledo in Ohio. Mr. Robert Karp had arranged for the scholarship to be set up in honor of Wallenberg's impressive sacrifices to help the Jewish people during the Holocaust. I was to gather a group of seven important community members to help me to decide who would be each semester's award recipient of the scholarship. I asked Mary Neufeld to join me on this committee, and was exceptionally grateful that she did, because I had a lot more valuable time with her before she passed. I held this honorable position for three years before I had to resign when my family moved to Colorado in 2000. I stay in touch with Mr. Karp regularly, as I see him as a visionary, and a man who has provided great community service by keeping Raoul Wallenberg's impressive life choices alive through this scholarship.

By 2009, I had joined many Denver groups, including the Rocky Mountain Dyslexia Association. Prior to my joining, however, they fought for developing a bill, SB #1234, in the state of Colorado. The bill was to ensure every teacher would be properly educated by 2010 in the understanding and treatment of students with dyslexia, now that more than 25 percent of students were affected by learning disabilities, which included dyslexia.

I felt united with them when I spoke, as an independent, to the panel of senators, and shared that I had attended college my first semester, on probation, due to a lack of understanding of my disabilities, and the modifications and accommodations that were lawfully mine. My daughter attended with me and took photographs of me speaking to Colorado's political leaders. SB #1234 is now a law.

On January 22, 2004, I spoke at a hearing at the Colorado State Capital building concerning Senate Bill #88, which involved the rights of mothers who breast-fed to do so in public. The bill stated, "Concerning the encouragement of breast-feeding, and, in connection therewith, recognizing the benefits of breastfeeding and providing for breastfeeding in public."

I was the last to speak, and I shared from a professional standpoint that if one would breast-feed **discreetly**, there should be a law allowing women to do so wherever one needs to feed their child. After five years of many organizations fighting, the bill finally became a law that year. The word "discreetly" was added into the vocabulary of the bill.

In April of 2004, I was able to attend the discussions and voting process by the State of Colorado, which resulted in the unanimous passage of House Joint Resolution

04-1053, declaring April 19-25 "Holocaust Awareness Week." I may be dyslexic, and have many disabilities, but it does not stop me from reaching my goals, or addressing my passions. I never give up in the face of possibility. I am fearless, grateful, and humble.

In 2003, I heard there was a conference being held in Denver. It was the Sixteenth Annual World Federation of Jewish Child Holocaust Survivors and Their Descendents Conference. I attended with great hopes that I would be finding more second-generation people with whom to be family, my mishpocha. Out of the twenty-four, second-generation Holocaust survivors who currently belonged to my support group, seven of them attended this conference with me.

We stayed in a hotel together in Denver and escaped our current life, abandoning it for a familial reunion most of us had yet to experience. The first night, following our amazing Shabbat dinner, we met in a conference room. It was after 9:00 p.m., and we simply went around the room introducing ourselves by name, the parent who was the survivor, sharing specifically what they survived, and why we felt we came to this conference. We completed that simple assignment by 12:15 a.m.

The next morning after breakfast, and after listening intently to our morning speakers, we headed into a room again to share our feelings. As we again, with a facilitator, went around the room sharing our thoughts of how we were different because of our upbringing, I felt an intense amount of emotion regarding the fact that my sisters and brothers now surrounded me for the first time.

There was a moment, following many adult children of Holocaust survivors sharing very intense emotions, and one in particular spoke up. She said she felt we were all using our parent Holocaust survivor experiences as a crutch for how we were handling our own current lives. I was incensed. I was so upset that this second-generation survivor would be accusatory during such a sensitive and in-depth look into each of our hearts that I could not keep quiet.

Each of the breakout sessions were supported by trained facilitators who often were psychologists, psychiatrists, and in social work services. For some reason, our facilitator this morning remained quiet. I felt violated. I felt that I needed validation for all that I had put down deep inside my heart and soul. Until she began speaking, I had been feeling validated. So, with my heart beating loudly, I began to share from my soul that all my life I have chosen to hold myself together, to be strong even when I wanted to be weak, to overcome each adversity that was given to me, and be my own survivor of my own life circumstances. I shared that I had never been more proud to be a second-generation survivor as I was at this very minute, while hearing others' feelings. I said that if not in this room, where we could be so honest about the burden we bared as second-generation

Holocaust survivors. Most of whom that had shared that day at that conference as well as all of those who I had the honor of being the facilitator for who attended my second-generation support groups over the years had shared that they too had not been properly parented.

Afterward people from the room rushed to my side. They applauded and supported me, and again I felt lucky enough to find more brothers and sisters whom I am still close with today.

The three-day conference included distinguished speakers Dr. Robert Krell, Agota Kuperman, Michael Berenbaum PhD, and Rabbi Zalman Schachter-Shalomi, PhD.

I felt healed at the end of the experience. When I returned home from that first conference in 2003, I found my father in my kitchen. He was visiting from Cleveland. He had planned to be at my home upon my return from the conference because he was concerned about what I was going to learn about him and his past. Actually, I had invited him to join me, but he refused.

When I walked into my kitchen following the Denver World Federation Jewish Child Holocaust Survivor and Their Descendents Conference, and I looked into his eyes, and I saw a child in him again. I felt so strong that I hugged him and told him he had done a terrific job.

Not only did he hold himself together upon entry into America, he dedicated himself to community involvement, volunteerism, and he developed expertise and recognition within his musical field. He still kept me in his life, albeit at a distance. I thanked him for being so strong, and tears rolled down both of our faces. He was so afraid that I would come back angry for his weaknesses and his failure to support me in all things emotional.

What I learned was he did not fail me on purpose.

It was never intentional for my father to abandon me; it was his intention to continue surviving the situations he put himself in to remain true to his father given legacy, to contribute to the world. In his failure to be there for me emotionally, I learned to strengthen my own will, grow, and increase my own vision for my personal success and for my purpose and personal contributions—being an American. We had a wonderful visit that day, and his fears were relieved.

However, the following day while eating dinner at the dining room table, my father stopped while holding a piece of bread. He was having one of his emotional disconnects when he is lost deep in thought and memory. My daughter, now five-and-a-half years old, tapped on his tattooed arm and said, "I know Granddad that you died many times when you were a child, but you're here now and you're safe. Eat the bread."

We were all flabbergasted, my husband, my father, and me. I had never discussed the Holocaust with my daughter before. How could she have knowledge of this magnitude? Her intuition and her sensitivity toward her granddad are still with her today as a twelve-year-old, third-generation Holocaust survivor. The information, the emotional knowledge, is passed down via osmosis and in the DNA. This has been documented as Trauma Transmission, by Dr. Eva Metzger Brown in her research.

I've spent a lot of time with other child survivors of the Holocaust and second-generation Holocaust survivors. There are two ways to play this life experience out with your legacy and your progeny—tell all or tell nothing. My father chose to tell nothing until I begged for more when I was in high school. Prior to that, I heard it all through his silence, and my brother heard nothing.

We each respond and react to our life situations based upon who we are, our personalities, our experiences, and what we're made of, our character. I am proud to share that as I write this book, my brother has reached his best now.

My father and my brother were not speaking regularly, and there was another World Federation Child Holocaust Survivor and Their Descendents Conference coming to Detroit, Michigan. I began advocating that my brother and my father attend this conference along with my husband and me. My goal was to continue to get my needs met with my second-generation brothers and sisters, introduce my husband to my other life, and to give my father a look into his daughter's life while supporting his son's eyes being opened for the first time to how David Zauder's history affected his only son.

I was excited that upon arrival, Eileen and Marty Rosenbaum, my cousins, met David and I, and we had a lovely dinner together. A great way to start the conference. Despite multiple e-mails to my brother reminding him to register, he actually failed to do so online. When he arrived, they did not have him on any list, and my father needed to pay for his registration and rescue him. It was obviously an emotional experience for my brother surrounded by second-generation survivors like him.

The food at these conferences is always wonderfully Jewish and surrounded by people who are going through the same experiences is supportive. My husband attended the spouses' classes, and Karl came with me on only a couple of occasions to workshops; the rest of the time, he went to workshops by himself. He sat next to me in one seminar where we were sharing how we were adult children having not gotten our emotional needs met with our Holocaust surviving parent. This is the first time Karl heard that I, in fact, had grown up alone. He reached out and touched my shoulder in an act of support, understanding, and sadness. We grew closer during that weekend; however, most importantly he and our father gained a relationship based on a more understanding of each other. They have spoken regularly since attending the weekend conference and I am grateful.

Afterward, David and I flew home, and my father took my brother on a tour of Detroit, Michigan, sharing with him where he had lived, attended school, and worked. Karl grew in accepting his second-generation Holocaust survivorship.

David Zauder, me, and Karl at the Shabbat dinner in Detroit during the WFCHSD Conference.

I feel a strong urge to share that the many second-generation experiences stemming from the impact of WWII that I've written about already, may also be part of the impact on children of veterans of other wars. I acknowledge the affects on those people, by referring to them as the second-generation veterans of our country's best. For the veterans who have served in World War I, World War II, the Vietnam War, and all of the wars our country has been in, I feel a huge amount of gratitude for their service and sacrifice, for that they gave of themselves and those sacrifices made by their families. I am humbled by their sacrifices and gifted by their dedication.

Post-traumatic stress disorder is real. It has continued to impact our servicemen and women when they return from active duty. Therefore, I'm not unaware that I am not alone in seeing these behaviors exhibited by my father after his war experience. The Holocaust is defined by Genocide and anti-Semitism. War is still about human beings fighting against other human beings regarding issues such as; beliefs, values, religion, and global resources. It has been said, war is hell, and I know I have brothers and sisters who are second-generation veteran survivors as well.

As my father began to have more bad days than good days each week, due to his growing and metastasized cancer, I decided it was important to my children to dedicate a Friday night service in his honor. An event that would be family remembered as a positive experience, one that my father could still enjoy. I met with two wonderful women who own the company called Mitzvah Magic, Cyndi Silver and Pat Stevens, and they decided to help me make this a celebration to build significant memories with my father. It was their idea to call it "L'dor V'Dor", which means from generation to generation. I had many angels watching over me during the planning of this event. Photographer Greg McBoat, whose pictures you have seen throughout this book, had gifted us with an amazing three-hour photo session documenting our family with my father. We used these pictures on a changing screen picture frame to share with our community during our service. My husband, David, and our children, both Shannah and Adam, were very excited in planning this event. We had special out-of-town guests, my father's God daughter Marion Green, and very close family friend and wife of Ray, who was one of my father's lifelong friends, Cecilia Benner. Our Rabbi Jamie Arnold at Congregation Beth Evergreen in Evergreen, Colorado met with us and assisted in our scheduled event. The children ran the service alongside the Rabbi, each taking their turn in leading the service and song as well as each sharing a speech they had written directly to my father.

I could not come up with anything to write. Every time I did I began to cry, so I decided music would be my best option. I chose to sing, "Holy Ground" written by Craig Taubman. I gave my father a copy of the song in font 20 so he would know what I was singing. I managed to get through most of the song without getting choked up and crying, however I don't believe that there was a dry eye in the audience. We had parts of Team Adam and Team Shannah present as well as our dear and close friend Tiffany Monat, one of my angels who had babysat our children since she was in 10th grade, and now she was a college graduate. Ryan Anthony also came into town and he played on his trumpet "Dreams of Karen" in honor of my father. My father did not say a word during the entire ceremony, but he smiled the whole way through. For all of us it was passing on the living legacy of love, family, forgiveness and unending commitment to one another. We all knew that this would be the last public event my father would agree to attend. For the three days following the service, he was so tired; he struggled to be energetic around our company.

Rabbi Jaime Arnold and Shannah and Adam at the Pulpit at Congregation Beth Evergreen.

*David Zauder sitting in the front row
with Ryan and Tiffany*

*Ryan playing the trumpet, Dreams of Karen ballad. This was
the song my father played for me when I was born, for all
important occasions, sometimes as encores at Blossom Music
Center 4ᵗʰ of July Concerts and at my wedding to David as I
walked myself down the aisle.*

David Zauder and Nancy holding the original photo of his teacher, mentor and friend, Leonard B. Smith, given by good friend, Nancy Mack.

Three generations of teachers, mentors and friends, together, David Zauder and Ryan Anthony.

Part of what I believe we are each trying to discover is who are we? I was fortunate because many local and distant friends financially supported me, and community members who found out I had this opportunity to go to Poland wanted to share in my educational successes. Without their financial support, it would have been impossible for my family to spare me for that short time because of all my responsibilities. With two children, who have special needs, and therapies they need to be taken to, as well as the care of my father, and the love I share with my husband, I was intensely aware of the gift to travel to my father's homeland and learn more about who I am.

I am grateful I met some of my mishpocha, my second-generation family, there in Poland. Each of us willing to set aside our fears, with great hopes for growth, acceptance of our parent's homeland, and the freedom they earned for each of us. To experience each of our religions, rituals, and praises to God, together, it felt so good to know I was not alone.

Upon arrival in Warsaw, Poland, it hit me first while standing in line to hand over my passport. I quickly, though knowing it was illegal to use a cell phone during this time, texted my husband the following, "I am here, and I'm about to give my passport to 'them.' I hope I will be let back out."

My husband wrote back, "What?"

I instantly knew he was not thinking from a second-generation Holocaust survivors' point of view. Then I texted a second-generation friend the same message, and her answer was, "I know! Right? Me too!"

There was fear, but I was calculatingly sharing it only with those who would understand, because I did not want to live in that fear anymore. I used a lot of sarcasm. I got my passport back and went to the baggage claim. The first billboard I saw was a "Love Kraków!" an advertisement for travel to my father's hometown. I had mixed emotions when I saw this.

On the plane, I had met a man who asked me why I was going to Warsaw. After I surveyed the plane and saw that there were empty seats in case I needed to move, I took a risk and told him the truth. He broke down and cried when I answered his question honestly. After he recovered emotionally, he gave me his business card with his cell phone number and told me to call him should I need anything. He gave me a very long list of Jewish monuments that he believed I must go and see. The list was so long, I knew there was no way I would have time to accomplish seeing half of his suggestions. He apologized to me on behalf of his family. This was my first experience coming to Poland. I was changed, and I no longer had hints of whispers of my own bigotry.

During the twenty-third annual WFCHS and Their Descendants Conference, I found old friends and made many new ones. We stayed at a lovely hotel and three days went by in a flash. I am exceptionally proud of the speech I gave while serving on the educational panel. It was truly a gratifying experience, and I look forward to Poland's continued education of their youth on the truth of what befell their country during the Holocaust and the rise of it.

I have attended every WFCHS and Their Descendants conference, except for one, since 2003. In fact, I was greatly honored to be an invited educational panel participant at the Warsaw, Poland conference in August 2011. I shared how I teach Holocaust awareness through my father's story of survival, as well as my anti-bullying Standupster® presentation. I was grateful that I was able to share what I have done in my Standupster® presentations, and I made a difference. When I completed sharing my presentation, a Holocaust survivor who regularly is a docent in the camp he survived, stood up and stated that he too was a proud Standupster®!

*My second-generation friends with me
at the Poland conference*

My adopted young mothers

While in Warsaw, I met and spoke with Jacek Michalowski, the head of the chancellery of the president of the Republic of Poland, as well as Marcin Chumiecki, the director of Polish Mission, and the female mayor of Warsaw, Hanna Gronkiewicz-Waltz. I also spoke with Rabbi Michael Shudrich, the chief rabbi of Poland, who was born in Queens, New York.

Being on the education panel at this conference, sharing my presentation on how I teach the lessons of the Holocaust, was a great honor. I shared alongside Charles Silow, PhD, and Program Director for Holocaust Survivors and Families/Jewish Senior Life of Metropolitan Detroit, Sanja Zoricic Tabakovic. Also the judge in the Republic of Croatia, and Norm Conrad, executive director of Lowell Milken Center, and Kaja Zalewska, principal coordinator of liaison officers of the Polish Presidency of the Council of the European Union.

Me with the mayor of Warsaw, Hanna Gronkiewicz-Waltz

The director of the Polish mission, Marcin Chumiecki and me

I had the honor and privilege to be recognized on the Educational Panel at the 23rd WFCHSD Conference. My work as a Holocaust educator and having started an Anti-bully program, which I have called Standupster®. I shared why my program is so successful in schools. I spoke amongst many great educators on my panel while at the conference in Warsaw, Poland.

Maps were everywhere showing respect for the Jewish culture.

Pensive, reflective, and caught thinking, my father was a slave here

My second-generation friends and I walked through Auschwitz here

Getting our photos taken by high school students as Second-Generation.

I walked where he walked, touched what he touched

The crematorium where my father . . .

I am here for a reason!

*In touring Kraków, we found Jewish festivals are held
annually, enjoying the Jewish culture*

My friend Isaac Kot agreed to attend my personal pilgrimage as I searched out locations in Poland that affected my father's childhood, and allowed me to take steps where he had once walked. We found everything that my father was willing to share. I even was able to go to the New Kraków Miodowa Jewish Cemetery, to see where my family's memorial bronze plaque had been placed, thanks to Rabbi Boaz and the Jewish community's president. I had hand delivered the plaque to a Polish, non-English speaking gentleman two days earlier. It was a complete success for me, and I was grateful to have my second-generation brother, Isaac Kot, with me to help document my every footstep.

Me touching the last remaining Kraków Ghetto wall

The New Miodowa Jewish Cemetery in Kraków

*Me with our Zauder plaque, which I brought from America
to be placed in the Jewish Miodowa Cemetery*

We found David Zauder's apartment!

*His apartment is three hundred meters
from the Vistula River, just as he said.*

I brought flowers, for the tenant, or someone at my father's apartment Complex, hoping someone would know.

She helped me know which was my father's actual apartment and where the Jewish Theater was next door.

My father's apartment in Kraków, Poland

*Me looking over the Vistula River down from my father's
apartment-thank you Issac!*

The president of the Jewish community helped me look for
the sister of my father's last name who died. The only list we
found—there was the question mark—common for the times
when a child died.

We toured everywhere, including Kraków, my father's
hometown. Most important; *St. Mary's Basilica, in Kraków,*
Poland, trumpeters' play "Hey Now" on the hour.

The Heynal (Polish: Hejnał Mariacki, "St. Mary's dawn",
pronounced hey-now mah-ryah-tskee), also known as the
Cracovian Hymn, is a traditional five-note Polish tune closely
tied to the history and traditions of the city of Krakow. It
is played by a trumpeter four times consecutively each hour
from the highest tower of St. Mary's Church (in Polish,
*Kościół mariacki) in Krakow. **Found on Internet regarding*
Krakow's History.

I was able to travel with my friend Charlie Silow to Lodz, Poland, to bear witness to his search for his grandfather and namesake's burial place. A new friend and second-generation Holocaust survivor, newly learning of her Jewish heritage who attended the conference with us, and who lived in Lodz also accompanied us, as well as a very well educated tour guide named Jerzey, who I've mentioned earlier. It was not an easy trip, as it was my first Polish train that I climbed onto; I got on as a free American, and I stepped off and learned of a rich Jewish heritage in Lodz, Poland, that I did not know existed.

We found only this as a sign of past anti-Semitism . . . In Lodz, Poland. The football teams were name-calling. Photo of Lodz Jewish star used as European football team graffiti.

I found one example of graffiti that looked anti-Semitic. My friend and I were very disappointed to see it but when we asked our new friends from Lodz what it actually meant, it took a little while to explain.

In the mid-to-late 1800s, a Jewish man named Kalmanowicz Pozananski opened and successfully ran a textile business there, making Lodz a very wealthy city. They had a hospital, school, day care, extracurricular activities, and housing for its employees, all in the area where this textile company was located. Pozananski paid for and promoted the two football teams there. In today's Lodz, only those two football teams still exist, and when they are teasing one another, they draw the letters with the Jewish star on top, which means, "You are owned by Jews." This could appear as anti-Semitic, but the Polish people in Lodz I discussed it, and they did not view it this way. We must keep an open mind toward their continued growth, while we continue to educate everyone on the importance of our use of language, communication, and their meanings. Today, the manufacturing plant and its surrounding buildings are now restaurants, a famous hotel, stores, and malls.

Helping my friend, Charlie Silow PhD. find his grandfather
and namesake's cemetery plot in Lodz, with the Auschwitz
memorial behind us. With friends Mirka and Jerzy. Jerzy
who found the document found on page 434.

My friend Jerzey, from Lodz, Poland, did research on my behalf, and located the man who was given the same tattoo number on his arm that my father turned his into. The real number three who survived the Holocaust was in Birkenau Concentration Camp last during the war and was liberated and then moved to Israel and raised a family. This was such a huge relief to me to learn, because I always wondered if my father's action of changing his number eight to the number three had caused harm to the real number three in any way. No, it did not hurt him, the Nazis had the two of them separated far enough that no list had been cross-referenced. Thank you so much, Jerzey!

U. IV- 8521 /3813 | | 84 | B - 14593
a/a

1 Nazwisko i imię / Surname and forename SZMULEWICZ LOLEK

a/ Nazwisko i imię w okresie deportacji do obozu / Surname and forename while being deported to the camp
SZMULEWICZ LOLEK

b/ Obecne nazwisko i imię / Present surname and forename SHALEV ELIEZER

c/ Inne używane nazwiska i imiona (lub pseudonimy) / Other used surnames and forenames (or pseudonyms)

2. Imiona rodziców / Names of parents CYWIA and JAKOB

3. Data, miejsce, kraj urodzenia / Date, place, country of birth 18. MARCH 1939
LODZ / or PABIANICE , POLAND

4. Narodowość / Nationality ISRAELI

5. Obywatelstwo przed aresztowaniem / Citizenship before arrest POLAND

6. Wyznanie (religia) / Religion JEWISH

7. Płeć / Sex MALE

8. Data, miejsce i powód aresztowania / Date, place and reason of arrest Mid August 1944
till 18 January 1945

9. Pobyt w więzieniach, gettach, obozach przed przybyciem do KL Auschwitz / Stay in prisons, ghettos, camps, before arrival
to KL Auschwitz PABIANICE GETTO(40-42) LODZ GETTO (42-44)

10. Data przybycia do KL Auschwitz / Date of arrival to KL Auschwitz Mid. August 1944

11. Numer otrzymany w obozie / Camp number B - 14593

*Jerzy found me Proof that my father changing his last
number from an 8 to a 3 DID NOT hurt anyone else! The
real #3 is alive and living in Israel and has grandchildren!!*

It was not an easy trip, as it was my first Polish train that I climbed onto; I got on as a free American, and I stepped off and learned of a rich Jewish heritage in Lodz, Poland, that I did not know existed.

I found one example of graffiti that looked anti-Semitic. My friend and I were very disappointed to see it but when we asked our new friends from Lodz what it actually meant, it took a little while to explain.

In the mid-to-late 1800s, a Jewish man named Kalmanowicz Pozananski opened and successfully ran a textile business there, making Lodz a very wealthy city. They had a hospital, school, day care, extracurricular activities, and housing for its employees, all in the area where this textile company was located. Pozananski paid for and promoted the two football teams there. In today's Lodz, only those two football teams still exist, and when they are teasing one another, they draw the letters with the Jewish star on top, which means, "You are owned by Jews." This could appear as anti-Semitic, but the Polish people in Lodz I discussed it, and they did not view it this way. We must keep an open mind toward their continued growth, while we continue to educate everyone on the importance of our use of language, communication, and their meanings. Today, the manufacturing plant and its surrounding buildings are now restaurants, a famous hotel, stores, and malls.

The Warsaw Jewish Museum under construction, due to be complete in 2013! Right across from the Warsaw Memorial monument.

Who are we? I ask again. I do not support making the Polish government teach of all the atrocities that took place, directly to the grandchildren, either second or third-generation, and outing the bystanders or the soldiers who actively took part during the Holocaust. Just as I am choosing today not to share with my children how their Granddad, while staring down the barrel of a machine gun, was forced to participate in lighting the match that lit the gasoline that was poured on half-dead and deceased Jewish bodies in Auschwitz, instead of being murdered himself. This is not just because it is not age-appropriate at this time, but because my father, their Granddad, currently lives with us and is beloved by them. They deserve to love him for who he is today, and not begrudge that love due to decisions and actions he was forced to take under those circumstances. Nor should the Polish people and their families suffer this now.

After he is gone, and they are older, I will tell them the entire truth. The actions that their granddad had to take in order to stay alive, so that I could be born, and therefore they could be born here in America as third-generation Holocaust survivors were necessary. You can forgive those you love for horrible things they've been forced to do in the past, <u>if</u> they are in fact regretful, which my father is daily.

After the convention, I participated in a Polish documentary. I was interviewed for thirty minutes regarding how I felt to be in Poland as a second-generation survivor. The documentary aired on public broadcasting in January 2012. One of my friends who lives in Lodz, Poland, e-mailed me and shared that it was a phenomenal documentary. She said she and her husband were proud to share with her family that she knew me, as she pointed me out during the program.

I ask again, who are we? I am a Jew, but that is not all I am. I am moral, and I am conscious of how I apply my words, my actions, my beliefs, and how they affect others. I do not wish to add to the disappointment, loss, anger, and certainly not to the anti-Semitic currents still flowing and affecting our world. I support the educators in Poland who are working steadfast on Holocaust education in their country now and in the future.

Within our own Jewish culture, we have diversity, but not all of the different affiliations within the Jewish faith accept all of it. With this kind of separation, we do not have a right to point fingers at what other religions are or are not achieving.

I ask again, who are we? The Jewish population in Poland is revitalized even though it is still small. Those who are Jews are dedicated to their culture and their rituals, as well as their Jewish heritage. The Polish people I met who are not of Jewish descent are fascinated by and supportive of the Jewish culture that they now lack. There were so many Jewish monuments and art installations that depicted the Jewish culture. Posters speaking the truth of what occurred to the Jewish people made it obvious that the people of Poland were sensitive, and I felt quite honored to be of Jewish heritage! I now understand why many Jews have returned to Poland in recent years, because the richness of the Jewish past is well documented with memorials everywhere you look. The experience of visiting Poland is not just about seeing the place where the Jews of the Warsaw ghetto rose up against their Nazi occupiers. It's not just seeing the stone-built wall that is left of the Kraków Ghetto or in coming to Auschwitz or Majdanek concentration camps to see first-hand evidence of the murderous Nazi network of concentration camps and death camps. Right now, in Warsaw, there is a museum being dedicated to Jewish history, Jewish culture, and all things Jewish that were lost during the Holocaust. Most urban areas in Poland are philosemitic, and yes, in some rural areas some people still hold hostilities against the Jewish population, and for World War II, as well as the Holocaust, because their families lost so much during that time.

I looked everywhere for anti-Semitism, and I found only those who were willing to help me locate my father's apartment, as well as helping me trace my families past steps. Thank you, Lucy!

I met and became friends with Polish people who are now learning of their Jewish past. Some of them have been raised Catholic by their Jewish parents who hid their true Jewish identities until recently. I felt incredibly Jewish while in Poland, and I felt surrounded by authentic people who wanted me there. My personal experience in Poland was very positive and encouraging.

The constant transition between witnessing places that celebrated Polish Jewry and the jarring difference of seeing the concentration camps was surreal to me. I did not get the feeling that Poland is in denial at all.

Who are we? As Americans, we must take more action to fight our hatred and intolerance of one another due to differences of skin color, race, religion, as well as political affiliation. There is so much to do. I am counting on you to help make the difference. This is why I speak. This is why I have such a vast message to share. I want the world that my children grow up in to be kinder, more accepting, and educated in the richness that diversity provides. We are a global world economy and a socially connected world. Will you help me to foster this change?

Once, when I was traveling with my father through the airport to pick up my niece, Kaylee, for her visit, we had to go through security to meet her at the gate. As we approached the security line, I saw my father become more and more anxious. I realized that the line itself was a reminder of those lines in his Holocaust experience. The security was heightened at the time and to my father, they were like guards all over. The rules are shoes off, pockets emptied, and belts like the one he was wearing needed removed and put through the scanner. He began to voice his frustration, stating that America was under siege at all times, and it was horrible that we, ordinary people, need to be put through such personal interrogation just to go into the airport. He went on so much so, working his blood pressure up that I felt compelled to go to the security guard, ahead of him, and say quickly and quietly, "My father is behind me in line. He has the gray hair and he is a Holocaust survivor. If he is put in a position to have to remove his belt, in addition to handing over his other personal items while we are just retrieving his granddaughter from her gate to take home, he will most likely lose it. Is there anything you can do to ease his pain and high anxiety?"

The security guard was in his fifties, knew what I meant when I shared my father was a Holocaust survivor, and he saw my father's tattooed arm was showing. He smiled at me, looked at my ticket for retrieving my niece, and quickly turned off the alarm system so my father's belt would not set it off. My father walked through, retrieved his personal belongings, put his shoes back on, and we headed toward the gate. As we were walking, he stated in a much calmer demeanor that the security in this airport stunk because they didn't even make him take off his belt!

Chapter 17

On Becoming a Standupster!

It took me quite a while to share with my father that I was speaking on Holocaust awareness and sharing our family's history. I started in 1982, speaking to local public schools. This included middle and high schools, temples, churches, and social groups. I had not told my father about my public speaking until after I had been involved with the Anne Frank Exhibit in Toledo, Ohio, in 1995. I continued to speak when asked, and I had a good reputation as a second-generation Holocaust survivor speaker, providing my audiences with a dramatic and honest explanation of my father's story.

I spoke at the Anne Frank Exhibition as a docent

In 1995, I also began a second-generation Holocaust survivors' support group in Toledo, Ohio, in an effort to gain support for the feelings I was having at that time. Over the years, I have met and maintained excellent friendships with other second-generation Holocaust survivors, most of whom have become my family. Unfortunately, I have met a number of them whose family members emotionally traumatized them, and who are affected by the Holocaust directly. Many count on their congregations to support their deepest needs for assistance.

In my experience, congregations, both Jewish and non-Jewish, treat Holocaust education differently, and there is no one methodology or programming for what they teach. There are so many opportunities for those who are interested in teaching about Holocaust studies, from Yad Vashem to the Holocaust Memorial Museum in Washington, DC, to groups like the Paperclip Project, whose shared experiences changed the world. It depends on who is in leadership at the time, and the educational staff and their knowledge on how Holocaust education can be used to support today's youth and educates them on humanitarian behaviors as well as choice behaviors.

I have been asked to be involved in third—generational discussion groups of Holocaust survivors. I have also been invited to join second-generation discussions with those from Nazi descent. Recently, I was invited to join the Netzwerk Gruppe and speak with teenagers from

Bünde, Germany, during their visit here in Colorado. The founder of the Netzwerk Gruppe is Christina Whitelaw. This group of high school students impressed me with their deep feelings, thoughtful questions, and willingness to share the vision of each of them being a **Standupster®!**

These German teenagers, who study about and do research on the Holocaust that happened in their town of origin, were being hosted by Temple Sinai and the Temple Sinai Youth Group as part of an ongoing exchange between the two groups. Their teachers and mentors who traveled with them were very proud of their willingness to add this group into their high school requirements, as it is seen as an extracurricular activity. They had a full week of programming, including doing a moving and inspirational presentation during Temple Sinai's Shabbat Service on Friday, July 15, 2011.

I had the opportunity, through Audrey Friedman Marcus, to speak to these students on Monday, July 11, 2011, serving on a panel of esteemed Holocaust survivors. Eric Cahn, Lea Schreiber, and Oscar Singer served on the panel representing the Holocaust survivors, while I served on the panel as the only second-generation Holocaust survivor present. The students asked many questions regarding what it was like growing up with a survivor and how it felt being of the second-generation. The students were exceptionally educated on Holocaust history, especially that of their city of Bünde, Germany, with fifty thousand citizens. They have done research and have studied what has happened to the Jews from Bünde during the Holocaust and hold to the belief that it should never happen again, both in their actions and in their hearts.

The Bünde group and Jewish youth members of Temple Sinai visit one another's countries biannually and try to heal the wounds from the Holocaust. The youth were very welcoming to me, their first encounter with a second-generation Holocaust survivor while in Colorado. It was a very rewarding experience, and I have stayed in touch with the leaders of this group in Germany. There are talks of getting more involved with the second and third—generation from each group and hearing one another out as well as supporting each other's healing process. Healing is one of the many goals this group has, and I am extremely grateful to have had such an opportunity.

When I asked my father once to share something for my next school speaking engagement, he wrote the following:

Written by my father, David Zauder, on 8-26-05

> *We are in the 21st Century. Atrocities against people have happened before. If you study history, culture, language, and customs, you will see the reason. Learn that crime*

445

and inhumane actions against other people have happened before and are happening now.

We are not that unique.

Uganda, the Irish people, Nigerians today, and then 6 million non-Jews perished in the Holocaust. We've learned [that] since 1945 [not] everyone is exclusive. Moslems and Jews and Arabs all have their roots in Abraham! And still no peace.

Just because I lost my family and was incarcerated doesn't mean I was the only one.

The Jewish Holocaust was a horrible example of man's inhumanity to man . . . it is not ethnic anymore.

The current situation between the Kurds and Sheeites in Iraq has been going on for years and it is over differing views on their Koran—their bible.

We must teach not to take advantage of others mentally, physically and sexually or emotionally. Without education and exposure of man's hatred to man, this will not change. Nowhere but in the United States of America has a better chance to change history of inhumanity to each other. The American concept of a free society is the best out there today.

For those second and third generations who are ill-affected by the Holocaust legacy passed down to them, I believe a scientific-based therapy is necessary. A support group that is at the same level of understanding is equally as important to provide understanding, and a safe environment to share deep feelings and their losses, without being judged. We are unique in our shared experiences. It would be helpful if each synagogue supported us in a unique way, instead of focusing only on the tragedy. Focus on the survivors who rose up and became modern day heroes, worldwide!

I realize Holocaust education can be of such great benefit to all communities, because it helps to teach humanity, human rights, and the ability to rise above oppression. Standupster® presentations support positive change leading to hope and driving community awareness. This can provide for improved quality of life, and teaches tenacity, mental toughness, and never settling for situational ethics.

In some Jewish communities, the Holocaust is still viewed as only a tragedy. Those who have survived and contributed to this world, can be considered as triumphant, just as the Jews involved in the Jewish exodus from Egypt were viewed in history. We celebrate Passover each year as part of our Jewish history and culture, and yet the Holocaust has not been assimilated as such everywhere. It is still more a day of mourning, which many want to avoid. We have much work to do, as people, to accept and support the great feat of survival by Jews and non-Jews alike, who have made something of themselves and overcome their obstacles and post-traumatic stress disorders, to offer their gifts of strength to us as a community.

> *It is inevitable that some defeat will enter even the most victorious life. The human spirit is never finished when it is defeated . . . it is finished when it surrenders.* ~Ben Stein

I feel like I am here for a reason when I speak to audiences about my father's Holocaust survival, when teaching Holocaust awareness, as well as my anti-bullying campaign, Standupster®. I coined the word Standupster® in the early 1990s, but it wasn't until 2011 that I had it trademarked and registered.

My father survived atrocities done from one man to another. Through his determination to survive, I feel I must protect the image, the expectation of a better life that he had in his mind when he survived. I, like my father, live with exceptional high personal standards and expectations. I believe that students today not only have not been tested or pushed to find out what they're really made out of, but they are also, in many of their own words, unaware how great and truly important their own lives are.

As I experimented with ways in which I could share my father's story, I sought out those who were doing it well already. Many people, some willingly, some unknowingly, participated in shaping how I share teaching Holocaust awareness today. Throughout my presentations, I ask questions of those in the audience to keep the communications fluid and open. Part of my hope is that through group discussions, education deepens, and it's not just about the facts and statistics of the Holocaust as much as it is about the effects of it on the psyche and hearts of those who were traumatized.

I am eternally grateful to all the schools, principals, history teachers, literacy teachers, temple, church, and mosque religious leaders, and our esteemed branches of the military, who have invited me in to share my Standupster® program.

Bell Middle school; one eighth grade class at a time!

Whole School Assembly at Bell Middle School

Left side of assembly at Bell Middle School

Compass High School

Platt Canyon High School right side

Platt Canyon HS 2

Left side of full PCHH school assembly

Platt Canyon High School—Parents and their teenagers were equally touched like Krista Hines and her daughter, Mackenzie.

West Jeff Middle students standing while pledging to be a Standupster® 1/3

After my Standupster presentation, David Zauder answered student questions.

West Jefferson Middle School Library supported continued
reminders by allowing students to place their thoughts on
Hearts which stated "I Promise to . . ."

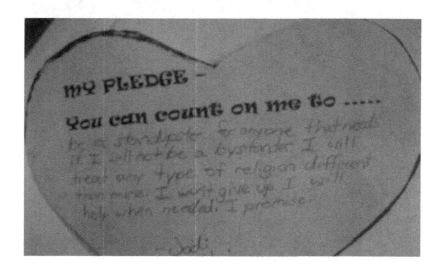

Heart1

Heart2

West Jeff Library!

Conifer High School legacy continues

Students, parents, and teachers line up to thank us

Shannah attended my speaking at Conifer High School and heard David Zauder, her GrandDad, answering student questions at the end. Photo by Karen Bennett, photographer and friend.

Shannah is now a proud third-generation and has started a Standupster® group at her Middle School, West Jefferson Middle School!

After my speaking at Peterson's Air Force base, then
NORAD, Cheyenne Mountain

My husband David and I were honored with going into
Cheyenne Mountain for a tour.

I was able to obtain special clearance the following
year to bring my father with me back to NORAD
for a special tour on his birthday!

National Days of Remembrance
"Choosing to Act: Stories of Rescue"

15 - 22 April 2012

Less than 70 years ago, witnesses to the atrocities of Nazi-occupied Europe were faced with the choice of stopping the persecution of their neighbors and fellow countrymen or standing by in acquiescent silence. Unfortunately, fearing for their own lives, many people opted for the latter. However, some remarkable individuals chose action over fear, courageously standing up to tyranny and hatred. This week we remember not only the millions of victims and survivors of the Holocaust, but also the heroes whose actions saved incalculable lives.

We remember heroes such as the villagers of Le Chambon-sur-Ligon, France, who hid 5,000 Jews and guided many of them across the Swiss border to safety. We remember the Danish resistance fighters who ferried almost all of Denmark's Jews out of harm's way and into Sweden. We remember the American Soldiers who liberated the Nazi concentration camps, and bore witness to horrors that many would try to deny. Many stories of rescue belong to individuals whose names were never recorded by history – the government official who forged identity papers; the families who hid Jewish friends in their attics and basements; the nuns who offered a safe haven to Jewish children.

Today, we can honor the courage of those individuals who chose to take a stand against persecution by rejecting all forms of prejudice and bigotry. During these National Days of Remembrance, let us pay tribute to both those who perished and those who quietly triumphed over oppression by ensuring our actions illustrate tolerance and respect for all people.

Raymond F. Chandler III
Sergeant Major of the Army

Raymond T. Odierno
General, United States Army
Chief of Staff

John M. McHugh
Secretary of the Army

HOLOCAUST
Days of Remembrance

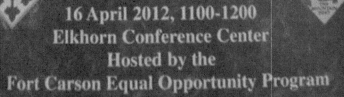

Choosing to Act:
Stories of
Rescue

Theme: *Choosing to Act: Stories of Rescue*

16 April 2012, 1100-1200
Elkhorn Conference Center
Hosted by the
Fort Carson Equal Opportunity Program

Mrs. Karen Z. Brass - Second Generation Holocaust Educator and Speaker.

Mrs. Karen Brass is the daughter of Mr. David Zauder, a Holocaust Survivor and detainee in 5 concentration camps, one being Auschwitz Death Camp. Mrs. Brass has provided her father's personal account concerning the atrocities that befell his family and other victims of the Holocaust. Since 1982 she has spoken at more than 300 public and private schools; synagogues, churches and to many educational and community groups.

Her story centers on her father's account as a Polish born citizen who was taken into slavery for 5 years by the Nazis, as well as his survival and impressive life accomplishments, in spite of his horrific past. Many details of her father's experiences parallel the movie Schindler's List, although he did not get on the list, and remained in Auschwitz for two years before being forced on the death march and into two additional concentration camps. Mrs. Brass shares the lessons of the Holocaust as shared through her Second Generation eyes.

Mrs. Brass believes no one should ever stand silent in the face of hatred. While sharing her father's story of survival, Mrs. Brass weaves in her thoughts concerning what it means to be a by-stander, and how to eliminate discrimination, as it is cruel, irrational, and only flourishes when by-standers are present and do not act. She promotes **Standupsters TM** and their inherent ability to rarify bullying in today's school environments, work environments and other community centers. She began her web site, www.standupsters.com to make what she teaches more accessible to teachers, parents and students and communities alike. Hatred of others' differences must be stopped, and together we are stronger because of our uniqueness's. She also teaches why it is important to put an end to stereotyping, selecting scapegoats, and the proliferation of racism and prejudice.

She has been a professional speaker for 30 years in over 300 venues. She was a Docent and speaker to over 5,000 adults and students at the Anne Frank Exhibit during its month long tour in Toledo, Ohio. She has organized and met regularly with other Children of Holocaust Survivors since 1995. Mrs. Brass was honored to be an invited Holocaust speaker to the military brass at Cheyenne Mountain's Norad facility and to the Peterson Air Force Base military personnel in Colorado Springs in 2006. Mrs. Brass has attended 7 World Federation of Child Holocaust Survivors and Their Descendants Conferences, including one in Amsterdam, Netherlands and most recently she attended the 2013 Conference in Warsaw, Poland where she was an invited speaker on the Educational Panel speaking to the Polish consulate.

Fort Carson, David Zauder applause

It is an honor and of great significance and a service for
me to give back to my country in this way. I am in the
far corner addressing the officers, to the right of the
slide, behind the podium.

Fort Carson; Me with Major General Joseph Anderson
and my Certificate of Honor

Fort Carson; Me, my father and my husband with Major
General Joseph Anderson

Certificate of Appreciation from Major General Anderson

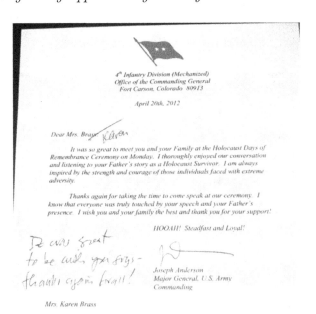

Fort Carson letter from Major Anderson

When you visit my website at www.standupsters.com, you can view a broad definition of what my program goals are and how I tie my father's story and the concepts of anti-bullying together to create a program that inspires and develops real change.

My Standupster® presentations provide an educational opportunity that calls on each of us to take responsibility for our actions and change our communities. As individuals, we make decisions based on our value systems and personal perspectives. I believe when we openly discuss the importance of value systems and the power of tolerance and understanding, we create a healthy, realistic perspective that can enrich life for each of us.

I believe education, understanding, and commitment are the keys to working together to achieve a deeper, more meaningful existence. No more situational justice.

One of the issues that many of us deal with while growing up is bullying harassment. Bullying harassment is common, but it should not be acceptable or tolerated. It is a good idea to teach our children ways to avoid bullies, and to teach them to treat others with respect.

A bully is someone who is overbearing or cruel. The aim of bullying is to cause embarrassment and humiliation toward the subject of the abuse. Often, a bully is someone who is bigger or stronger in some way, and who harasses those who are smaller or weaker. Harassment is systematically bothering someone to the point where the environment becomes dangerous in some way. Bullying harassment is aimed at intimidation and a desire to dominate. When there is a trained, educated Standupster® present, this behavior is interrupted. Sometimes that's all it takes to stop the path of the bullies behavior and interrupt the flow of negative intent.

It is important to note that bullying is not just physically aggressive behavior. While many people think of bullying in terms of physical harm and danger, this is not the only type of bullying harassment out there. It is also possible to bully people emotionally, verbally, sexually, or even electronically, without ever laying a finger on the victims. Nonphysical forms of bullying harassment can be just as traumatizing as physical bullying. The physical signs of bullying often disappear before the psychological effects of emotional, verbal, sexual, or electronic bullying disappear, if they ever do.

Even in its nonphysical forms, bullying harassment is meant to intimidate and terrorize the victim. Saying rude and hurtful things habitually, turning friends, classmates and coworkers against someone, or harassing someone online or via text message, are all forms of bullying. These types of bullying can inflict heavy emotional damage. When someone sees this behavior and decides to speak up against it, by being a Standupster®, more good can come from grouping students together to form a barrier against the violator. The violator's intent in bullying is to raise oneself up by tearing someone down and ruining his or her reputation. This can drive victims into depression, anti-social behavior, and even substance abuse.

It can be difficult to deal with bullying harassment. However, since bullying is a behavior aimed at choosing someone who appears weak and then intimidating him or her further, some techniques can help stave off bullies:

- Make eye contact so that you communicate you are not vulnerable.

- Show good posture to indicate confidence, and it may reduce someone's likelihood of being a target.

- Avoid isolated areas. Try to stay in public areas where there are likely to be witnesses, especially authority figures and others who are choosing to be a Standupster® to the bullying behavior.

- Keep friends around. Many bullies are not interested in picking on someone who has a support system. Try to go places with friends, so that you are not alone. Engage in making each of your friends a Standupster® so they can assist in providing support.

- Remove yourself from the situation. This can be difficult, especially for children. However, it is better to leave the situation than to comply with a bully's demands.

- Tell an authority figure. Children should learn to notify authority figures of bullying behavior. This can be a good move, since it will bring the bully to the attention of those who can keep an eye on things.

- Ensure that school professionals make it very clear to the bully and the parents or caregivers of the bully that they are being watched closely, and the behavior will not be tolerated. Make sure the professionals are checking in with the victim frequently to ensure the behavior does not continue in the shadows.

You will need to show that you are willing to listen to your child, and that you will take him or her seriously. Try not to judge, and teach your child tactics and strategies that will help him or her avoid becoming a target. The old adage "Sticks and stones may break my bones but words can never hurt me," is false information, and computer-based attacks online are written words, which start rumors that cannot easily be stopped or easily erased from the Internet. If your child is a target, let someone (teachers, etc.,) know about the problem. Have school officials approach the parents or caregivers of the bully to take rapid action.

The most effective approach toward anti-bullying is an environment in which principals, teachers, parents, and students are involved in a school-wide meeting in which a zero-tolerance environment is communicated to all.

When I share my father's Holocaust experiences as well as his early American experiences during my Standupster® presentations, I am very cautious and careful about making sure I can draw lines between the students' situation to what my father was going through during his situations. It's important to me that the students feel a connection, a kinship to my father. In many of the students' letters I have received over the years, I have been successful in doing so, making the program a great success.

> *We must always take sides. Neutrality helps the oppressor, never the victim. Silence encourages the tormentor, never the tormented.*
>
> ~Elie Wiesel

Thank you for your willingness to be open, to listen, and perhaps grow from hearing about the life that my father and I have shared.

I have always asked the students I work with to share with me their thoughts following my presentations. I provide teachers a list of questions they can use to help the students form their thoughts related to what I presented, and how students interpreted and utilized what they heard.

Here are some of the questions that I have provided and have used in the past. When asking your students to write their letter of thanks, be certain they have personally connected with the Standupster® presentation.

1. What do you think is the most important new fact you've learned from the Standupster® presentation regarding the Holocaust, and her father's experience?

2. Who were affected by the political climate in Germany and why?

3. What percentage of the population did the Jewish people represent in Europe at the time of Hitler's final solution?

4. Would you have escaped from the ghetto and returned with food for your family, or would you have just kept running?

5. How would it feel to be given a number, stripping you of your name?

6. How could a human being treat another person so horribly?

7. Are children inherently born with hatred or are they taught whom to hate?

8. What will you do differently now that you have heard the Standupster® presentation?

9. How do you view your culture, religion, and community now?

10. Are human being's differences what help to make America a stronger nation?

11. How have you been affected by bullying?

12. Have you been a scapegoat?

13. Have you been a bystander in the past? Will you continue to be now?

14. Has the presentation given you another perspective on the effects of bullying, scapegoating, and prejudice?

15. How do you see yourself as part of the solution?

16. What made David Zauder so strong to survive five concentration camps?

17. What were the four lessons for living life that David Zauder shared with his daughter?

18. What characteristics do David Zauder and his daughter possess that you would like to have as well?

19. Are you a good person?

20. How do you know?

21. Do you act your best through your actions when others don't?

22. Can I count on you to be a Standupster®?

I actually ask the audience to thank my father for being brave enough to share his story with me, giving me additional and personal details throughout the years that have made my presentation what it is today.

Chapter 18

The Message and Legacy is Passed On—Be a Standupster®!

I never teach my pupils. I only attempt to provide the conditions in which they can learn. ~Albert Einstein

I would like to share as small number of the letters that I have received, following my Standupster® Presentations here. They serve as their own testimony of lives being touched.

At my website you can find these presentation materials:

My middle school DVD

My high school DVD

DAVID ZAUDER plays "JUST FOR FUN"

Accompanied by Joela Jones

inside   outside

My father's CD cover

"The Music on this CD is a collection of favorite solos of trumpet and cornet players everywhere, and will speak for itself. But for me it was *"Just For Fun"*
- *David Zauder*

All Rights Reserved, 2012

DAVID ZAUDER PLAYS "JUST FOR FUN"
1. Carnival of Venice, "Fantasia Brillante" (Saint-Saens, arr. by Del Staiger) 3:31
2. Dreams of Karen (Roy Milligan) 2:26
3. La Mandolinata (Herman Bellstedt) 5:05
4. Ecstasy (Leonard Smith) 4:48
5. Prelude 1:50
6. Allemande 1:15
7. Gigue 1:37
8. Trumpeters Lullaby (Leroy Anderson) 2:30
9. Aria Con Variazioni (G.F. Handel) 5:01
10. Stabat Mater (G. Rossini) 5:06
11. Concert Etude (Alexander Goedicke) 3:17
12. Concertino (E. Porrino) 6:37
13. La Virgen de la Macarena 2:52
    (arr. by R. Mendez)

My father's CD—photo by McBoat

All endorsements

Diplomat in Clinical Psychology Author
American Board of Professional Psychology Mediator
Eva Metzger Brown, Ph.D., A.B.P.P. (retired)
Child Survivor of the Holocaust

It has been my pleasure to read the moving, honest and inspiring Book of Ms. Karen Z. Brass' life story. Ms. Brass is a member of the Second Generation of the Holocaust (her father is a Holocaust survivor). She is also a founder of a company called "Can I Count On You" llc and she conducts Standupster® Presentations Nationally and internationally. (www.Standupsters.com). These group presentations confronts bullying, using Holocaust education through her father's story, with the courage to find one's own voice—if one is the victim, and willingness to support the victim—if one is the bystander.

Ms. Brass describes her life's efforts in the context of being learning disabled and raising, with her husband, two learning disabled children. Ms. Brass teaches by showing that personal efforts and personal courage help make lives worthwhile—no matter what the personal challenges that confront an individual. Ms. Brass relates her life story growing up in a Holocaust family, in a way that encourages the reader to identify with her energy, her positive attitude and her willingness to learn and teach along the way. This is her story.

In *"I Am A Standupster" A Second Generation Holocaust Survivor's Account by The Daughter Of David Zauder" Written by Karen Zauder Brass,* Ms. Brass moves through her Holocaust life history in a way that teaches the reader about what she has lived through, and encourages them to identify with her energy, kindness and unwillingness and not to give up in the face of personal and historical challenges. Therefore, it is a book not limited to one slice of the reader population—the Holocaust survivor population or those challenged by learning disabilities. It is a book that I believe will have a universal appeal and will be seen as presenting a model for dealing with personal challenges, of which everyone has some. In truth and in my experience, all people live lives that require courage. In Ms. Brass' case, she has related a narrative of one woman's unwillingness to say, "I give up . . ." yet her story is more than this too: It is a story that invites the reader to examine what is important to them and to harness their "true grit" as they find what is most significant in their lives.

I encourage readers to check out Ms. Brass' Website and, to get a copy of her book from the bookstore and to order it for their own school and town's library.

Best wishes, Karen, and thank you for asking me to be one of your early readers.

Eva
(www.EvaMetzgerBrown.org)

Eva Metzger Brown, Ph.D., ABPP Child Survivor of the Holocaust—Author—Clinical Psychologist

People who have been through powerful and traumatic events don't talk about them. When they do, you can feel the emotional intensity as if you were right there with them witnessing the event unfold in front of you. When they do, a part of you shifts inside and is changed forever, as were their lives when they lived through the horrific event. There are moments in the human experience that are so powerful and sublime that nothing in language can describe them. For those who have experienced the event, nothing in their lives may have prepared them or given them words to do so. The cruelty or ugliness that they have witnessed or been through may have been so powerful and horrendous that they may think no one could understand or believe them. Or they do not want those they love to know about it for fear that somehow it may too damage them. So, they keep it in check and keep it from and try not to let it impact their lives. It is not that they do not share because they don't love; it is that they do not share because they do love and are trying to protect others from knowing their pain or the horror. But as it is with those we love, these experiences, their power and pain, can be felt without words, and be passed down unspoken through generations.

I met Karen back in her Bowling Green days. I had no idea of the extent of the abuse she was living in at the time until I read this book. Karen has been a good friend for many years, and as such, for years it has always been a challenge to get her to tell me how she is doing and not report on everyone else and everything else she has to care for. I have also asked her for years what it has been like for her to have a father who survived the Holocaust. Not only being interested in its impact on him, but its impact on her. So, when I finally heard she was writing this book I was both amazed and thrilled for I know she rarely talks about her own story, especially those parts of it that were painful to her. I also know she, for many years now, has stood as a voice and a witness to the direct impact of the holocaust on her extended family, her father and her own life and the lives of hundreds of others. What she shares in this book, as intimate and painful as her stories are, will help countless other lives of those who are second generation to parents who have lived through trauma.

There are no words that can embrace the horror of the Holocaust or the countless other forms of genocide that happened in human history. It is at the same time both overwhelming, and yet incredibly and painfully intimate, as is all trauma and all grief. By both Karen and her father sharing their personal story, they give voice to not only their own journey but to the journey millions of other people have lived through. And as such, offer both a witness to the atrocities for those who lost their voice in death, and a hope that there is life after that is more than the very real pain endured.

My son visited Auschwitz. He walked into the shower and said he could not take any photos, that all he could do was feel, that he could not find words for those feelings and knew that those feelings would never leave him. I could tell he had been changed by being there. I have a picture on my screen saver at work of Karen's grandmother, Rose Zauder. It is not the handkerchief that she passed on to her son, but it is my way of keeping her memory, strength, courage, life and love alive. It helps keep the petty things I deal with in perspective and reminds me that when it is all said and done, there is nothing more eternal on this earth than love.

Karen's book is ultimately a love story of the truest and purest kind. That despite the most indescribable evil ever imagined, and its very intimate impact on the human heart, in the end, the love shared in her family was the music that endured. That music has transcended generations in her family. Through the music her father shared for years through his instrument and the compassion in his heart. And now through Karen in both the way she advocates and cares for others. What they have given to others is some of the most beautiful I have ever known and certainly some of the most courageous. It has always been a gift to be Karen's friend. It is an honor to have had her open up her family's sacred memories to me and to include me as part of her extended family. I trust that her love story for her father will inspire you as both of their stories continue to inspire mine.

Douglas Hahn, M. Div., MA, MRC
LPCC-Supv., LICDC-Supv., LSW
Mental Counselor/Training Academy Instructor
Franklin County Sheriff's Office

September 25, 2012

RE: Ms. Karen Zauder Brass

To Whom It May Concern:

I am writing this letter on behalf of Ms. Karen Zauder Brass with whom I had the privilege of meeting in my capacity as principal at Conifer High School. As an Administrator at Conifer High School in Jefferson County Public Schools, I can attest we are always looking for strategies to assist kids in making the right choices. Having viewed and experienced the Standupster presentation at our school the past three years I can honestly state that this presentation has aided our students in being leaders not followers.

Bullying has life-long impacts on victims, friends and their families. By providing our students a resource for alternative thought (Standupster Program), we hope to see great gains in appropriate behaviors within our student body population.

I am confident that there are a number of our students who would say she has been influential in their lives. When Mr. David Zauder was present, his story impacted the kids in a very personal way. The kids said they were touched personally by the stories about Mr. Zauder and the Holocaust. The story of Karen's father's survival made a lasting impact on the students of Conifer. They were amazed at how a man could go through so much yet never give up, and still care about others after witnessing such a tragedy. The fact that Mr. Zauder was able to overcome this tragedy and become such a successful and world renowned musician is a testament to us all. Mr. Zauder's story is one that none of us will ever forget and we are truly thankful to Karen for sharing it with us.

Ms. Brass is dedicated. Her deep caring for students and her dedication to telling "A Second Generation Holocaust Survivor's" story motivates her. She is highly organized and truly enjoys talking to the students, parents and staff about her family's story. We thank Karen for her time and wish her good luck with her endeavors.

Respectfully,

Dr. Michael P. Musick, principal
Conifer High School

Endorsement for Karen Z. Brass' book;

"I Am A Standupster"

"A Second Generation Holocaust Survivors' Account by the Daughter of David Zauder"

Written by Karen Zauder Brass

After reading Karen's book, it took me back to when I first met Karen and saw someone who was broken and dispirited. As she began to heal from the emotional wounds that she had endured, I began to see a person who had numerous strengths that were hidden by years of despair and hopelessness. As Karen began her personal journey on the road to recovery, I saw her developing the strength and character that was always there but was masked by fears, apprehensions, and a variety of negative emotions that keeps us all from growing spiritually and emotionally. In looking at where she is today, I see someone who is passing along to others what she has learned, as they go through their different journeys in life, and how she is able to put into terms that are easily understood and able to be used in a variety of different ways. This book she has written shows her strengths and shows how one can once again gain hope to overcome any obstacles in their life. This book should be read not only by lay people but professionals who could gain a better understanding of how the issues that Karen described in this book can be dealt with in a caring and compassionate manner.

David Lewandowski, Med., LPCC-S, LICDC

MIZEL MUSEUM
ENGAGE HONOR INSPIRE

September 21, 2012

We are pleased to provide this letter of endorsement for Karen Z. Brass.

Karen has been sponsored by and spoken at the Mizel Museum, to hundreds of students from inner city middle and high schools, as well as to our esteemed military since 2001. She worked as a Holocaust museum educator, sharing her *Standupster Presentation* to many schools.

Karen received many thank you letters from teachers and students alike. She has been professional, reliable, but most importantly age appropriate, and has no racial, cultural or ethnic bias within her presentations. Karen's speaking style engages her audience and allows her to connect with students and hold them accountable for their actions and abilities to choose to not be bystanders. She focuses them to make choices that have a positive and strong impact in reducing bullying within school environments by sharing her father's intimate details of being held for 5 years as a Holocaust victim, choosing to act with morality despite his situation and then she shares more about his life as a survivor.

Karen has demonstrated that she is fully capable of speaking to all minorities with a spirit of full inclusivity and we would recommend her highly to speak to your school. If you have questions, we would be glad to speak to you. Our phone number is 303-394-9993.

Respectfully,

Ellen Premack
Executive Director
Mizel Museum

Jan Nadav
Director of Education
Mizel Museum

400 South Kearney Street ☐ Denver, CO 80224 ☎ 303.394.9993 ■ mizelmuseum.org

485

Dear Mrs. Karen Brass,   3/2010

Thank you so much for coming to this school and giving your Standupster presentation. You can count on me now and for the rest of my life to be a Standupster instead of a bystander. You don't know this, but I am a German foreign exchange student here and I was afraid of your speech today. I was afraid you were going to blame all German people and I wasn't sure how I was going to feel. But you didn't. In fact you made the distinction between German people caught during an insane time and the Nazis and the SS officers. You made it clear to me, and everyone else who was in the room, that you felt that there were more good people than bad involved in the Holocaust. I am so grateful to you because I have carried such guilt for what my people did.

I know you asked us to all write thank you letters to your father but I feel since you're the one that is doing the speaking and you're the one who is a second-generation who is sharing with us students how to be better people, you deserved the thank you note. In case you're wondering who I was, I was the blonde girl with the glasses who stood in line waiting to thank you like so many others did at the end of your presentation. I was the one who couldn't speak because I was crying so much. You hug me and told me you knew I was very strong and you thanked me for feeling so deeply about what you had shared.

In Germany they teach us about the Holocaust but they don't go into personal details like you did. We are forced to study it and many of us feel very very guilty. My parents were born after the war but my grandparents were not. They do not talk of what happened. They do not talk of what they did, but we all know it was bad. I was not raised to hate anybody, and I do not feel that I am an anti-Semitic person. But it is confusing because it feels like somebody should be blamed for what was allowed to happen to so many people. Like you taught us all the Gypsies, the mentally disabled, the physically disabled, the homosexuals, the political prisoners, and so many more. Not just the Jews. When you shared that your son has physical disabilities and that your daughter has learning disabilities and that you also have learning disabilities and had you all lived back then you might have been killed for that, it was shocking to think of it that way. When I get back to Germany I plan on sharing with my class my experiences here in Colorado and I will tell them about you and your standupsters presentation. You need to know you've changed my life just knowing that you don't blame all of us. I wish you could come and teach where I live.

Thank you so much and keep doing what you're doing. It is so important!

Anneliese

"Whether we admit or not, we each bear the burdens of our parents. Sometimes these are light and easily carried. Sometimes they are heavy and threaten to crush us under their weight. The burdens Karen Z. Brass carries could have been the latter, but she has transformed them into something else. The daughter of a Holocaust survivor she drew on her dad's strength to strengthen herself and others; she drew on his horror to give hope to many. This is a book about transforming horror into hope, of learning how to use our burdens to burnish our spirit and the spirits of others. Karen's story is rich and enriching, and I encourage you to read it."

Rabbi Rami Shapiro, author of The Sacred Art of Lovingkindness (Skylight Paths)

Karen has been a dear friend for 20 years. I have watched her in awe as she always does the hard work it takes to grow continuously throughout this time. She is someone who you want to have on your team. She's a real "go getter" and has the ability to inspire and motivate all who are around her.

Faced with many adversities in her life, Karen educates herself and works hard to gain the insights and strength to cope and deal with all of them as effectively as possible.

Although I am a psychotherapist with many years of experience, I learn from her all the time.

Karen is the most passionate and caring, smart, energetic and committed woman I have ever had the pleasure of knowing and call one of my "besties". I am forever impressed with all that she works on and has mastered. There is no half-way for her. Her life reflects her determination and commitment. Karen is a no nonsense person who never compromises her warmth and devotion which is beyond inspiring and helps elevate everyone she touches to a higher level.

Audrey Friedman

"Karen's riveting book brings you to the edge of your seat while making you think about what principles YOU want to live by, such as the ones that little David Zauder had to formulate when his parents were murdered by the Nazi's. Of course, he was sad and angry, but as he grew into a young man, he decided that each day he would be determined to do something spiritual, something physical, something mental, but most important of all, to bestow a kindness towards another human being.

David was a little boy when he saw his mother taken away, people killed, atrocities, starvation and other awful things. He managed to stay alive, by living by his wits. His life was miraculously spared, and he grew up to make a life, and he made it a good one. These simple tenets of David Zauder's life have created victory out of despair and are now shared with us by his now grown daughter, Standupster founder, Karen Z Brass. Today we have this book, so we can stand on David Zauder's shoulders and see how the world should be, and go forward, living his example. It is a pleasure to endorse this book. I have read every word and think you should too. And, congratulations to Karen Z Brass for her courage in starting the anti-bullying school program called Standupter®."

Anita Garrett-Roe
Elite Senior National Sales Director with Mary Kay Cosmetics

Isaac A. Kot, CPA, MST, PFS
Certified Public Accountant

One Burlington Business Center
67 South Bedford Street, Suite 400W
Burlington, MA 01803

Phone: (781) 229-5816
Fax: (781) 359-1832
Email: Isaac@isaackot.com

September 3, 2012

Dear Karen:

First I really loved your book, once I started reading I couldn't put your book down, I finished reading your book in three days (since I did have to work etc.).

Your life has been an emotional rollercoaster. As a friend and child of a Holocaust Survivor, I wish that I had known you during the early years, not just the last 10 years. Marcy and I would have been there for you in your times of need. That being said, until reading your book, I realized that I previously knew very little about you, other than how nice a person and how dedicated you are to your family, husband, children, father; as well as your dedication to the Holocaust cause. Aside from all the time you spend with your family and your work, your commitment to teaching the Holocaust and getting people to get involved is also amazing.

Although, our father's had very different experiences during the Holocaust, when I read about your relationship with your father, and because our backgrounds are similar, we come from mixed marriages (one parent is a Holocaust Survivor and one is an American), I compare your relationship with your father with my relationship with my father. Where your father didn't speak about his life before, during or after the Holocaust until very late in your life, my father told us at an early age. He probably had no choice. He had physical scars, in addition to the psychological scars that all Survivors had. My father lost his right hand, left eye, had shrapnel scars on the backs of both legs and mangled feet. Of course, a child will ask questions at an early age. I often think, what if my dad had not been physically injured, would he have been so forthcoming with information at an early age? I'll never know. Also, like you I was a sponge to absorb as much information as possible from my father, where also like you my sibling never wanted to hear it while we were growing up.

Even with all the differences our father's each lived through, there are still special connections that Survivors, Children of Survivors and grandchildren of Survivors have with each other. I have been proud to call you a friend and a "sister" before knowing your full story. Now after learning more about who you are and what you lived through, I feel even closer to you as my "super sister" and more proud of your accomplishments.

My involvement in Holocaust issues has guided me from attending annual Holocaust Memorials and Yizkor (Remembrance) Services, as a child, with my father and the community; too becoming involved with my local Generations After, Inc. (GA) (a Descendants of the Holocaust Survivors) organization. In GA, I became a Board Member in 1999, Treasurer in 2007 and since 2010, President and Treasurer. In 2008, I was the Treasurer of the World Federation of Child Survivors of the Holocaust's (WFJCSH) Boston Conference and in 2009 I was added to the executive committee and made the Treasurer of the WFJCSH. I have been on the executive committee of the American Association of Jewish Holocaust Survivors of Greater Boston, Inc. since 2008. In addition, I am a member of the New England Holocaust Memorial Advisory Committee (previously Friends of the New England Holocaust Memorial, Inc.) since 2010. Additionally, like you, I promote Holocaust education by telling my father's history.

I know your life is on better track now than ever and it is probably based on everything that you lived through to get here.

Love,
Your 2G Brother,

491

~Extermination of Jews. Studies and Materials, Vol. 5, 2009, s. 7-8

In Memoriam—Marek Edelman

"One Should Remember . . . First of all, we have to remember one thing: what the Holocaust was. It is not true that it was a matter of just Jews. It is not true it was a matter of a few extortionists, or a dozen or so. It is not true it was a matter of just one hundred or two hundred thousand Germans who personally took part in the murders. No, it was a matter of Europe and a matter for the European civilization which established factories of death. The Holocaust was a failure of civilization. Unfortunately this failure did not end in 1945. This is a fact that one should remember. We all should remember it." [Excerpt from Polish conference that took part in Krakow 10-11 June 1995.]

"While watching Karen Zauder Brass on her Standupster DVD, teaching in an American school, I see hope. Karen tells a story of her family. By showing the archive photographs of her family she brings us closer to the history of her father, a man who survived the Holocaust. We meet a man whom other people wanted to deprive of dignity by replacing his name with numbers: B-14598. Meeting of her three generations is so warm, that it encourages those young students not only to ask questions, but to stand up and become a Standupster. To stand and shake the hands of the survivor and his daughter. To touch living history. The Zauder family is filled with love. One should hope that a piece of this love will stay in ones heart and mind. To remember, we have to listen. Listen to Karen Zauder Brass and her presentation of her father's life. Listen to David Zauder and his daughter Karen, Second and next generation of the Holocaust. To remember, we have to see. See the DVD, "Can I Count On You?" David Zauder's Story of Survival and Success" To remember, David and Karen, father and daughter—who shared a story, who gave the testimony. Mrs. Karen Zauder Brass asks the question; "Do you want to be branded with a tattoo on your forearm and be just another number in a slave camp?" Dear reader, children of the holocaust, expect your answer.

~Jerzy Obinski-Holocaust Educator and Personal Guide to find family loved ones, Lodz, Poland

"It will come as no surprise to those that know her or have seen her in action that Karen Z. Brass has an incredible story to tell -- one that weaves together generations of family and centuries of wisdom. And she has done far more than share her story. It has been taught that the whole of a religious life comes down to two simple words, "bear witness." As a daughter, as a mother, as a teacher, as a friend, as a 'Standupster,' and now as an author, Karen Brass has done just that, born witness to a journey that is both hers and her father's and from which each of us can draw on-going inspiration and compassion, and a commitment to learn and implement the lessons of the past. Sit and read, then join a growing circle of Standupsters bearing witness."

Rabbi Jamie Arnold
Congregation Beth Evergreen

Over the years, I have had the privelege of filming many presentations given by Karen Z. Brass. I consider her to be a living National Treasure! Her insight into the history of the Holocaust is unparalleled. Mrs. Brass is not only an accomplished speaker, but as a Second Generation Holocaust Survivor, her message is both historical and compassionate. Aside from being a devoted daughter, wife and mother, Mrs. Brass is also a business owner, an activist, a volunteer, and a leader in her community.

Jim Floyd
Altitude Media Productions

Strength. Resilience. Love. These are some of the words running through my mind as I read this book. Karen's story, woven together with that of her father, is inspiring. While most people have some basic knowledge about the Holocaust, fewer have been exposed to the personal experience of those held prisoner and tortured by the Nazis. Far fewer have heard how survivors moved on to create new lives after being liberated from the camps. And very few of us are familiar with the personal experiences of the children of these survivors, the "Second Generation Holocaust Survivors". Karen shares her deepest thoughts and fears with us, and we are with her as she makes sense of her world and faces her fears with determination, courage, and grace. This book is deeply compelling, and at the same time, written in a familiar style that leaves readers feeling as though they are having a personal conversation with Karen. Karen's journey from a child struggling to have her emotional needs met to an advocate and speaker against bullying makes this book a critical read, not just for those interested in Holocaust survivors or working in schools, but for all of us. I feel honored to have read Karen's story.

Karen Fay, Ph.D.
Psychologist specializing in Trauma and Abuse

Karen Brass has written an absorbing book about her life growing up in a Holocaust survivor family. Karen has been very open and revealing as she talks about her often very difficult personal journey and her emotional growth. I am a psychologist and a child of survivors who works with survivors and the second generation; I found Karen's book to be honest, powerful, insightful, and engaging.

Karen is dedicated to teaching about the lessons of the Holocaust and in so doing, has helped to protect those who are victimized. As someone in the field in Holocaust education myself, I find Karen's educational work to be powerful and engaging. Her work is an important resource for Holocaust education as well as for *Tikkun Olam*, a work that tries to repair the world, to make the world a better place.

Dr. Charles Silow
Charlessilow@gmail.com

Letter of recommendation for Karen Brass and her book

I Am a Standupster: A Second Generation Holocaust Survivor's Account,
by the Daughter of David Zauder

Karen Brass is one of those second generation Holocaust survivors who openly and honestly broach this issue. Having thoroughly reflected on her personal biography and her relationship with her father, David Zauder, that was influenced by his experiences during the Second World War and National Socialism, she makes a point of standing up against discrimination and speaking about past and present day atrocities.

Karen Brass is an eloquent speaker who knows how to teach her heterogeneous audience not to be a bystander but to commit themselves to fight racism and any other form of discrimination. Having heard her give a lively and engaging presentation in Denver in July 2011 was deeply moving both for me personally and for the group of students that I was accompanying. Many of the atrocities during the Nazi time were only possible because many people closed their eyes and were bystanders. This is one of the reasons why Karen Brass strongly believes that everybody ought to be a so-called 'standupster' and assume responsibility in their everyday lives in order to fight discrimination.

Karen gradually learnt about the shattering experiences her father underwent as a victim of the Nazi terror. This made her analyse the impact that the biography of her father has had on her and her relationship with him. I am convinced that her biography of her father is not only an account of his life but also an honest and detailed examination of the implications that his traumatic experiences have had for Karen. In providing her father's personal account of his life story to the reader she honours him and his perseverance in life. While the book can be considered an appraisal of her father's energy and achievements in life, it is also a very important contribution to contemporary attempts to pass on eye witness accounts and their messages to younger generations. Personal stories about experiences during National Socialism often have a far greater impact on the audience than the mere presentation of facts. Especially at a time when only few Holocaust survivors are still among us, written accounts are getting more and more significant. At the same time the book is a timely and valuable contribution to the voices of second generation survivors many of whom have long kept silent about their personal experiences of having been born after the Second World War and yet having been greatly affected by the traumas the Shoah has caused.

I am convinced that Karen Brass' book will not only be relevant for the US-American market but also for contemporary discussions about racism and discrimination in Germany. In the country of the former perpetrators the focus is still largely on the first generation of perpetrators and victims. Only recently has some greater understanding for the situation of the second and third generation of survivors been shown. Nevertheless attempts at working through and understanding the legacy that the distressing experiences of persecution, hardship, destruction and death have had on survivors and their descendants have mainly been made on a local level. However, understanding the past—be it one's family background or the larger history of the country one lives in—constitutes the basis for assuming responsibility in the present. This means that Karen Brass' educational programme, her DVD as well as her latest book are important contributions to raising awareness for social commitment and against discrimination.

Dr. Angela Brüning
Leader of the group Netzwerk ('Network')
Bünde, Germany

September 16, 2012

Dear Karen,

I wish I had a more effective word other than WOW! I read your book "I am a Standupster: A Second Generation Survivor's Account" in two days. The book was one that could not be put down. I look forward to re-reading it again and again to learn and remember the messages that you send to your readers.

As a second generation Holocaust Survivor myself the book was intense, sad, invigorating and mesmerizing. There were so many parts that were similar to my own life and experiences, that there were times I would have to remind myself that this was your story. There were several statements that made a light bulb come on. I always had feelings that I could never live up to my father's expectations, but could not put the feelings into words. David, your father's statement: "Now I survived what are you going to do?" really hit home. I didn't realize that this comment from my father: "Why are you always defending the underdogs?" really meant he wanted me to be in a position of power so that the Holocaust would never happen to me.

Professionally I am a school social worker for grades K-12. The Standupster is a powerful program that every student including higher level education should be a participant. Bullying is the number one reason so many students don't want to attend school and/or their grades are low. Bullying, as with the Holocaust, can cause trauma to students with no one "standing" up against the bully. With the publishing of this book anyone can find a connection to Karen's biography of her father and Karen's experiences. In each chapter there are bullies, by standers and the effect it has on a parent and their children.

Thank you Karen for sharing the experiences you encountered and your Father's horrific experience of the Holocaust. Second Generation children of parents with trauma from all over the world will be able to relate and have a better understanding of their parent. As well as understand why the "child" inside all of us continues to affect our life.

Sincerely Your Second Generation Friend,

Pitou (Behr) Ireland
MSW, LCSW

Dear Karen,

I have watched your DVD presentation several times. Each time, I learn more. Each time I am inspired. I read the whole website. I think it is more than well organized. It is user friendly. It is also touching, humbling, and inspiring. The pictures of your grandparents and their stories always touch me, and move me. Knowing they are two of millions even more so. It makes it intimate, thus disturbing, provocative and life changing. I think so often we distance ourselves from how powerfully intimate violence is. I love how you are advocating and teaching others for what is right against all that is wrong. Your father's advice to never let anyone intimidate you, to learn something new daily, to not lose your sense of wonder, to do something kind to others echoes inside me and serves as an inspiration in my daily work and life. Your courage to advocate for your father, to be a witness to the intimate impact of the power of human suffering not only for his generation but for ours and our children's is awe inspiring. I know how much work this takes, and what an emotional toll it can play on being an advocate. Human cruelty is real and tangible. I see its impact every day of my life. I love what you have done and are doing, not just for the second generation, but how you honor those who lived through and died at the hands of such horrible atrocities.

Douglas Hahn LPCC, LICDC, LSW.

"Dear Mrs. Brass,

Your presentation I found wonderful and quite touching. Your father's story was very amazing, the fact that he could survive that long without his family, without friends, without barely any food and sometimes without shoes. Now that I have heard your amazing speech, I will do some things different, that I've never done before. I will no longer be a bystander. Your amazing speech taught me a lot. I hope you continue to go to many other different schools and teach a lot more people about this heart-breaking, heart-stopping story. It would be an amazing book! I wish you and your father and the rest of your family good luck through the rest of your lives.~Theresa

"After watching your Standupter DVD, I was so moved afterwards that I could not write any feedback to you then. I watched the film with my husband and both of us were very, very impressed. Firstly, with the whole story of your father's family. Secondly, with the professionalism you did this lecture and the whole meeting with the pupils. You are amazing! We were also admiring your father's attitude and his answers to the questions.

I hope that one day you come back to Poland to give the speeches to students here! I think that's one of the best places to speak about tolerance and anti-semitism. And I could not imagine a better person than you to do this job."

*** *Written by Mirka Gluck, a Second Generation Holocaust Survivor in Lodz, Poland who discovered she is of Jewish Heritage only two years ago, in 2009, when her mother finally shared her hidden secret.*

Dear Karen,

I had to put into writing how your presentation on your father's life impacted my 8th grader. I have never heard her react to something so passionately. She retells it to anyone who will listen. She shared with me how she reacted with a combination of goosebumps, tears and awe. She tells me many of her friends had similar reactions, though I suspect my daughter was especially moved. She doesn't impress easily, so it caught me off guard that she was so intrigued. You must be one heck of a speaker! You kept the interest of a whole lot of kids who are by their very age, so far removed from the events of WWII. Thank you so much for coming to West Jeff. Middle School and sharing your training on The Holocaust. WE ALL MUST NEVER FORGET. Sincerely, Cathy D. Parent

Selected letters from students, parents and teachers

Elizabeth Milligan
Conifer High School
February 3, 2010

Dear Mr. Zauder and Mrs. Brass,

I can't thank you enough for coming to Conifer to talk to the kids again (I'd heard amazing things about years past). I am Jewish, so have always learned about the Holocaust in a setting where people have background knowledge and personal connections. I became involved in Darfur activism in college (this is my first year teaching) and worked with high school students who had chosen to take action on the genocide.

This was an entirely difference experience – to watch kids who barely have any knowledge about the Holocaust (and some who don't even know a Jew) learn from your story. After talking with the kids today in class and reading their thank you letters, I am floored. I was afraid that only the kids who already lived by your message took it to heart. That's not the case at all. My shyest, quietest student who gets taken advantage of often (and always has amazing things to say on paper) told you that she will try to stand up for herself. My kids who hate history class because it's "hard" and have trouble connecting to the past were the most touched, particularly by the lesson you shared with them about engaging brain, body, soul, and other people.

Some kids had endless questions for me about Darfur today. They were outraged in a new way and wanted an answer from me about the justification the Sudanese government has been using. There obviously isn't a good one, and they want to do something about it. The passion and emotion you have invigorated in these students is incredible to witness. Moreover, it has helped them connect to history in a way I cannot facilitate for them on my own.

Thank you both for teaching us. You've brought something incredible out in our students, and helped them connect to the past and the future.

Elizabeth L. Milligan

Dear David Zauder and Karen Zauder Brass,

    I almost don't know what to write. Your presentation and, Mr. Zauder, your story left me along with the majority of the sophomore class speechless. I can't imagine what it would be like to suffer through so much at such a young age and be forced to grow up so fast; I literally can't comprehend it. If I'd been in your position, I am very sure that I would not have made it.

    If you don't remember me, which I'm sure you don't, I was the girl that asked you, Mr. Zauder, why you came and spoke in front of us when it was such a difficult thing to do. You told me that you came because of your daughter and because she believed in sharing your story. So, Karen Brass, I would like to say that I am eternally grateful you are willing to share something so personal and emotional to a bunch of highschool children like us. I know I speak for more than one person when I say it affected me in a way that will stay with me for the rest of my life.

    What astounds me is that throughout the whole presentation, you retained your composure; you, the people who have first hand experience with some of the most horrible things ever to have happened and to happen. Meanwhile, I was bawling my eyes out feeling sorry for you, I believe you have enough strength for 10 people, probably more. I hope one day the world will, too.

Sincerely,
Samantha Pettus

504

Dear Mr. Zander,

Thank you so much for letting us hear your story; I know it must have been hard to recall such memories but it not only made an impact on my life but in all of the students and teachers that heard it. When we we heard the part about how you snuck out each night to get food from the butcher and return to your mother, I would hear some murmerings about how that would have been so hard to do. To me, it showed how much you loved your mother to do that each night for her - reminding me of my own mom and how we get along. Your story has helped me in many ways: to have more compassion towards people, forgive those who have wronged you, respect those you meet, and to love your friends and family.

I am tremendously sorry that you had to experience that, I truly am. However, your story has helped to shape us into better people. I wish and hope that someday I can meet you, it would be an honor to do so. Thank you again for sharing your story with us, we'll remember it always.

Yours truly,
Jessica Fisher

505

Dear David Zauder,

    I was sad to hear that you couldn't make it. But from the way your daughter told your story, I would imagine, had as much impact as if you yourself would of told it. (I hope that makes sense) I have been really intrested in the Holocaust for a long time. When I heard that you came in last year and you were a Holocaust survivor, I was thrilled. But I was a freshman so I couldn't go and listen.

    Anyways what I thought was the most intresting part about your story was that you learned 5 or 6 different languages at the end of your story. That is awesome! I love different languages, and being able to communicate with different cultures. Also the way you squeezed out the ink in your tattoo. So you could keep your identity, that is really brave. Also your belt. When my brother started wrestling about, a year ago, and he had gone WAY

506

Dear David Zauder

Your story touched my heart. My Grandfather was in the holocaust as well. He was at the same camp as you. I wished you were there so I could have talked to you about it. I'm so happy for your success in life, My mom has always taught me to earn life not to waste it. My Grandfather story was just like yours And I cry every time I hear your storyes. I hope I never let you down and live life to its fullest. Your a hero in my eyes. My Grandfather lived in Russia. And was in The red Army He was 18 when he Joined But then when he was captured he was around 20. He wont tell me most thing Just that he helped as many people as he could. He lived cause when they shot him it missed his lung but he almost died. He saved 12 others by running away and coming Back for each one. I am so humbuled that you are here with us. I keep asking my self if you may have even met my Grandfather of If he may have been one of the ones who held you up. I will never let you down And love you for your strenght.

love Josh O'Shea.

507

David Zauder,

Though you weren't able to share your story personally, your daughter did a wonderful job at portraying the life in which you endured during the rise of Hitler. Funny how one persons story can make another person change their outlook on life and only see the beauty. Your story, I think, was meant to be shared. From the words your mother left you, you truly fulfilling your destiny. For that I just wanted to say thanks. Thank you for telling your story so you daughter could come and share it with us and thank you for showing people that you're only as weak as your minds leads you to be. Your story has truly changes lives even if it was in the tiniest sense, you now have had an impact on may young people, and for that I have nothing but gratitude.

Best wishes,
Dakota Miller-Thomson.

Dear David Zauder,

Thank you so much for having your daughter come and talk to us, and share your amazing story. Studying the holocaust in school has changed my perspective on life. I've watched the movies Shinlers list, Anne Frank and Pearl Harbor, but after hearing your story, those movies mean so much more to me.

So many miracles happened in your life during the holocaust, and hearing of all of them has truly changed my perspective on life. Through all your struggles and obstacles that you've gone through, you're still willing to share your story and touch the lives of others. You truly are a blessed person, and it's an amazing opportunity hearing of your story. I will be a standupster.

Not only did your daughter, Karen, tell us of your story, but she's also made us realize that you don't know everyones personal stories, so we should always treat everyone with respect and never stereotype. My best friend has down Syndrome. When I'm with her a lot of people tease her, but after listening to your daughter speak, I truly will learn to stick up for her.

Thank you so much for sharing your story with us. I was changed and affected by your story, and I know you've touched the lives of many.

Thank you,
Kaitlyn Smith

509

Dear Mr. Zauder,

Your daugter, Karen Brass, came to our school to tell us our story of the holocaust. I was deeply moved. It is amazing, everything you went through. However it is more amazing that you've come to America and made a name for yourself.

I appreciate you wanting to come and speak to us. And I'm sorry I couldn't hear your story from you. Knowing that you came to the school and talked last year. I realise that this must be extremely difficult to talk about. I thank you so much for shareing your story with other people, and teaching them different life lessons that you've learned.

Thank You Again,
Alex Ader

P.S. I helped to teach Adam and Shuana at Peak Academy of Dance. I just want you to know they are some of the nicest kids I have ever met.

Dear David Zauder!

First i wanted to say thankyou for sharing your Amazing story with us. That was one of the most moving storie i have hurd! After listening to your daughter tell the story [she did a GREAT job] I went home and shared it with my Mom. She was Just as moved as i was and wants to come next year. My favorite part was when the death march was taking place and you feel after so many years of staying alive [and i admire your strength and will power.] and you fell. The one person who helped you was your brother who you hadn't seen in years!! A True miracle that was. I dont want to even start to say that was the only one that stuck in my head. The other one that had an great impact al me was your tatto. How you squezed the ink out! That Saved your life! I am absoluty going to go next year and i really hope to you feel better soon.

from - Katie Ellerman

511

Dear David Zauder,

    After hearing your daughter speak of your stories & life experiences, it gave me a whole new perspective on the meaning of life & life in general. Realising what you have done & the amount of courage that lies in your body amazed me. I am personally German & knowing how you treated those two kids gave me a whole new meaning to life. (on how when they were mean to you, you just gave kindness back) I personally dont know to many people that can do that. I'm really glad I was able to hear your story! If there were only more people in this world like you, it would be so much better!

A Standupster I am!

Thank you!!!

Ashtn Ch—

512

Dear Mr. Zauder,

Hey, I thought your story was unbelievable, it's crazy how much you went through. I've heard your story twice and it still hits me everytime. Your story would make an incredible movie. My favorite part of your story was when your brother saved you on the death march I actually started to cry. Your daughter, when she was telling the story said some things that really spoke to me i guess you could say. It was definately a memorable experience. Its really cool that you and your daughter take time to come and talk to us so Thank you!

~ Ashley

Dear Mr. Zander

When I went to your daughter's speech, I wasn't sure what to expect. The way your story was told, even from a second-hand witness, was truely amazing. I was surprised by the forgiveness you showed as well as the perserverance. Your daughter did an excellent job of passing your story on. Thank you for allowing us to hear and learn from what you went through.

February 7, 2008

Dear David Zander + Karen Brass,

Thank you so much for coming to speak to us about your past. It was wonderful hearing history first hand. I was amazed at your good luck, in the bad times. You expressed intrast in our past, so since you shared your story with us, I will return the favor. I was born in 1992 in Kansas, we moved to Denver when I was 2, and up to Conifer when I was 4. I have been greatly affected by Boy Scouts and that is why I love teaching, nothing is quite like seeing someone excited about doing something for the first time. I plan to go to School of Mines and Teach Highschool Science or History. I will always remember your story, and appriciate your bravery in speaking to us.

Sincerly,
Adam Maxwell

514

under his weight. He had lost so much weight, that I remeber, him putting notches/holes in his belt. He got so skinny that his cheeks sunkin. It was a really scary sight. So when your daughter talked about your belt, that reminded me of my brother. While I was sitting there listening to your daughter, it was hard for me to imagine what my brother looked like, not to imagine what the Holocaust survivors looked like.

So to end this letter, your story made an impact on me. I love how your daughter incorporated life lessons into the assembly. When I got home from school, thats all I could talk about with my family. I am very thankful that you are here with us now, to tell your tale or "Your Hero's Story", with Conifer High. Standupsters!

Sincerely,
Kiah Rudnicki

Dear   Mr. Zauder

The intensity of your miraculous story quickly
became an inspiration for me to work as hard as
 I possibly can to accomplish my goals.
Your tale is one of immense suffering and
unwavering courage. You fought even when deaths
 fingers reached out to grasp you.
The struggles of my life are menial in comparison to
the struggles that you have had to deal with.
However, I do believe that the same motive
can be drawn from each life story.
That, whatever it is that you wish to accomplish,
 you must throw yourself to the feat of hard work to
be able to accomplish it.
I would like to thank you for taking your time to come
and tell us your amazing story.

Yours truly,
Mark Mangelsdorf

Mr. Zauder #

Words can not show how your story made me feel.
Even though you were not able to make it, your daughter
gave an amazing presentation. I thank you for giving
us part of your life, sharing your past with us.
All that you went through... words can't explain it.
Your life was truely a blessing. I hope to be as
strong as you some day. God has granted you favor,
and may He always.

Lately, I have been trying to write a story.
WWII and the Holocaust have really hit me
hard. Your story has helped me a little bit more
in my writing. I want to honor the people that
had to go through all of that. I will try.
Someday, I hope to finish it and maybe more
people will understand.

Everyone does have a story and yours has
possibly changed mine just a little bit.

God Bless,

Ella Ahlers

517

Dear Mrs. Karen Z. Brass,

I know you asked us to write a thank you letter to your father, but since you are the one speaking to all these schools, I felt more compelled to write one to you.

You taught me so much more about the Holocaust than I have learned in the past three years of classes. It was horrible what your father had to endure, but he did. I liked the way you stressed that if he hadn't worked hard, showed good work ethic, and if he hadn't made compassionate friends, he wouldn't have made it and if he wasn't willing to take risks to live, he wouldn't be here today, and neither would you. That would be a great loss to the world to not have you, because your speech really touched my whole school.

It was important for me to write this because you stated that the Nazis took many kinds of people. Not just the Jews and the handicapped and the gypsies, but also the homosexuals. I am gay. It touched me when you shared your son has both physical disabilities and has autism and had you lived in 1939, he probably would have been murdered too. Thank you for sharing that, because I would have been murdered too back then. I know you said he is getting help and has gotten better with therapy, but I don't want therapy to change who I am. I just don't want to be bullied for it any more.

After your Standupster challenge to my school, I actually got knuckles from what I think are now former bullies in the hallway. I hope so. Like they decided not to be like the Nazis and pick on me because I'm different from them. Your speech changed my life and I can't thank you enough. I feel lucky to have someone teaching in our schools the way you do, making us more aware that our actions do affect others.

Thank you to your father for sharing his story with you so that you could teach us what we needed to know to be better.

You can count on me, Mrs. Brass, to be both a Standupster and to be strong. I have a lot to give and contribute to this world, and I won't give up!

Yours forever,

Chad

518

Date: May, 17, 2012

Dear Karen Brass,

I find it sad and immpressive
What your father went through.
He didn't deserve to go
through the holocaust but
he survived. What had a
large impact on me is that
your father never gave up
and never lost hope.

What I'll do to be a
standupster is to stand up
against bullying which is
a big problem. I will take
chances with new things.

Thank you for visiting
our school. It was a wonderful
experience having you here.
We got to learn things
about the holocaust we never
new before. The Holocaust is a
major part of history, it may
not be the best though. Again,
thank you. Sincerely, Sophia Pearcy

5-17-12

Dear Mrs. Brass,

I never thought that I would learn anything about the Holocaust. I guess I never really wanted to learn about it. Now that I do know about the Holocaust it impacted me because the thought of all those families dying or hurting was and still is almost impossible for me to think about.

I will definitely be a standupster because there are more and more bullies. I've always tried to be a standupster and when I have I think of three that you during the presentation. Courage, Hope, and Integrity.

Thank you for sharing this touching experience with our 5th and 6th graders. I will never forget that I was and am a standupster because we all need to stand up. Thank you for showing us the change that we can make.

Sincerly
Alyssa Garcia
Belmar Elm

Dear Mrs. Karen Brass,

There were many things that touched me. But the thing that touched me the most was that your dad didnt give up. I wish I had a work ethic like him.

When you talked about being a stand upster I learned somthing, I learned that if Im not a stand upster Im not helping. From now on Ill try to help stop bullying.

Thank you for coming and teaching us all a lesson. I think you changed a lot of people. I know you changed me. Thank you.

Sincerely,
Brian Lihor
Delmar Elementary

521

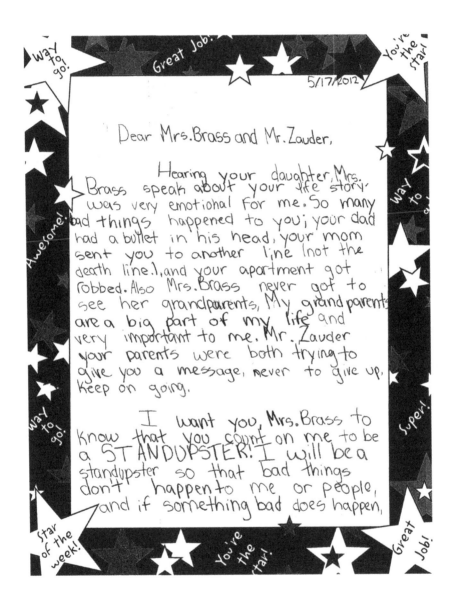

Great Job!

Way to go!

You're the star!

5/17/2012

Dear Mrs. Brass and Mr. Zauder,

Hearing your daughter, Mrs. Brass speak about your life story, was very emotional for me. So many bad things happened to you; your dad had a bullet in his head, your mom sent you to another line (not the death line.), and your apartment got robbed. Also Mrs. Brass never got to see her grandparents. My grandparents are a big part of my life and very important to me. Mr. Zauder your parents were both trying to give you a message, never to give up, keep on going.

I want you, Mrs. Brass to know that you count on me to be a STANDUPSTER! I will be a standupster so that bad things don't happen to me or people, and if something bad does happen,

Awesome!

Way to g...

Way to go!

Super!

Star of the week!

You're the star!

Great Job!

522

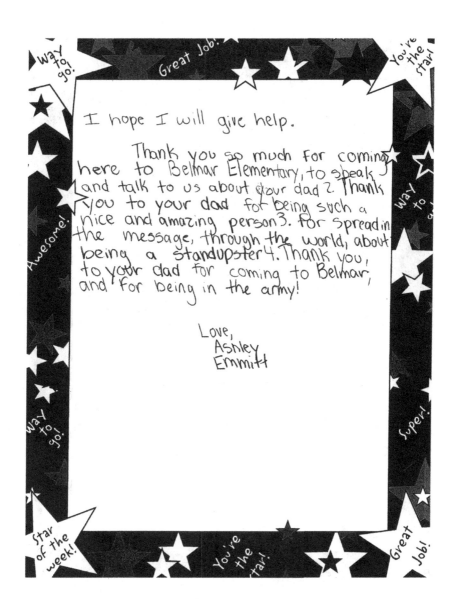

I hope I will give help.

Thank you so much for coming here to Belmar Elementary, to speak and talk to us about your dad 2. Thank you to your dad for being such a nice and amazing person 3. For spreading the message, through the world, about being a standupster 4. Thank you, to your dad for coming to Belmar, and for being in the army!

Love,
Ashley
Emmitt

May 17, 2012

Dear Mrs. Brass and Mr. Zauder,

Many things touched my heart. When I listened to your daughter Mrs. Brass, tell about your life, One thing that touched my heart was when you showed us your tattoo. I had heard about the Holocaust, but I never imagined it was that bad and teribble I could not belive that you could live through this and also that you could be alive after 5 years of being a slave and treated so brutally.

You can count on me to be a STANDUPSTER. Being a Standupster means helping others and not being a bystander, You can count on me to be a Standupster by helping others So they won't be bullied. Thank you for comming here to Belmar and telling the 5th and 6th grades about your life.

Sincerely,
Kargme R.

Great Job!

You're the star!

Star of the week!

Super!

Way to go!

Awesome!

Way to go!

You're the star!

Great Job!

Way to go!

Dear Mrs. Karen Brass,   3/2010

Thank you so much for coming to this school and giving your Standupster presentation. You can count on me now and for the rest of my life to be a Standupster instead of a bystander. You don't know this, but I am a German foreign exchange student here and I was afraid of your speech today. I was afraid you were going to blame all German people and I wasn't sure how I was going to feel. But you didn't. In fact you made the distinction between German people caught during an insane time and the Nazis and the SS officers. You made it clear to me, and everyone else who was in the room, that you felt that there were more good people than bad involved in the Holocaust. I am so grateful to you because I have carried such guilt for what my people did.

I know you asked us to all write thank you letters to your father but I feel since you're the one that is doing the speaking and you're the one who is a second-generation who is sharing with us students how to be better people, you deserved the thank you note. In case you're wondering who I was, I was the blonde girl with the glasses who stood in line waiting to thank you like so many others did at the end of your presentation. I was the one who couldn't speak because I was crying so much. You hug me and told me you knew I was very strong and you thanked me for feeling so deeply about what you had shared.

In Germany they teach us about the Holocaust but they don't go into personal details like you did. We are forced to study it and many of us feel very very guilty. My parents were born after the war but my grandparents were not. They do not talk of what happened. They do not talk of what they did, but we all know it was bad. I was not raised to hate anybody, and I do not feel that I am an anti-Semitic person. But it is confusing because it feels like somebody should be blamed for what was allowed to happen to so many people. Like you taught us all the Gypsies, the mentally disabled, the physically disabled, the homosexuals, the political prisoners, and so many more. Not just the Jews. When you shared that your son has physical disabilities and that your daughter has learning disabilities and that you also have learning disabilities and had you all lived back then you might have been killed for that, it was shocking to think of it that way. When I get back to Germany I plan on sharing with my class my experiences here in Colorado and I will tell them about you and your standupsters presentation. You need to know you've changed my life just knowing that you don't blame all of us. I wish you could come and teach where I live.

Thank you so much and keep doing what you're doing. It is so important!

Anneliese

525

November 18, 2009

Dear Mr. Zauder,

I was very touched by your story as well as astounded the amazing talent, and the extreme character your portrayed even at a young age. It was so incredible to me how even after the holocaust, being given the chance to fight back; you chose the higher path to be the bigger person. From that I know even in tough situations if I make a conscious effort, I can keep my cool and continue to maintain myself as a strong character. This is something we strive to do here at my school.

Our crew at odyssey is very lucky to hear from your daughter Karen about your experience in the holocaust. I was in awe at the hard time you endured but even more impressed with the proud life you led after your experience. You have showed my how I can make smart decisions and create my own goals even in bad situations. Your lesson is one I could not have learned anywhere else.

You and your daughter have clearly made a conscious effort to educate us as kids and for that I would like to thank you. You have clearly made a huge influence on our community and am very grateful.

Sincerely,

Lee Christensen

November 10, 2009

Dear Mr. Zauder,

The stories Karen told us today about your personal experiences were breathtaking. I've been reading the book *Night* by Elie Wiesel, but I feel like your stories made the Holocaust much more real. By having Karen speak to us everything felt so personal that I was able to grasp a really meaningful idea of what kind of life you were living at my age. I can't even begin to imagine how difficult it must be for you to have to remember all of these things. I really appreciate that you are so willing to share your experiences with us even though they are so private. I feel really privileged to get to hear your life story because I know it's the pure truth.

Before Karen came to share, I was very interested in how Jews and others kept faith and hope to survive. From your stories I was able to discover many different ways people kept their spirits up as best they could such as living to see family members again, playing instruments, having the constant thought that the world will see what horrible acts were being done to you... Overall, your stories helped me gain a much clearer understanding of what helped you personally as well as others to survive through the concentration camps.

The pictures that were incorporated were also very interesting. Learning about the history of your family was fascinating because it set the scene for the stories Karen told about you later. Also, we got a closer view of the friendships you had or came back to throughout your life. Your story of being reunited with your brother on the death march was incredible. Who would have guessed you would have had such luck? This story gave me a really vivid example of how important family members were during this time for you and others.

Mr. Zauder, I doubt I will ever forget some of the stories that were shared today. Once again, I'd like to thank you for letting your daughter carry on your legacy by sharing your amazing story.

Sincerely,

Poulami Wielga

Poulami Wielga
8th grader at The Odyssey School

November 18, 2009

Dear Mr. Zauder,

Thank you so much for letting us hear your story. It must be really hard to think about everything that happened. I had heard different stories about Holocaust survivors in books and movies before, but I had never been so amazed at the struggles faced. Before hearing the presentation, I mostly just thought f the Holocaust as something really horrible that happened a long time ago; now I see how personally that will affect oneself and others. I can hardly believe that this kind of thing actually happened. To have such an evil dominator who hurt and ruined so many lives, and for so long got away with it. I can't imagine what it was like for you, all of the struggles that you faced, yet you stayed strong and didn't give up hope. I greatly appreciate hearing your story; it has given me so much insight on what happened.

My own father died when I was three. It has always been hard thinking about it, and normally I just try not to. Hearing your whole story helped me to not just think about it in an absolutely tragic way, but to persevere.

I loved hearing your story about when the American soldiers told you to beat up the German boys, but you refused. I think it's amazing that even though they were part of the group that oppressed and hurt you, you refused to do the same to them.

Thank you again so, so much for letting us hear your story. I learned so much from it about what happened before, during, and after the Holocaust, but this way I was lucky enough to learn about it through a personal experience.

I hope that you soon get better. I now cancer is a horrible disease.

Sincerely,

Grace Crummett

Grace Crummett
The Odyssey School, 8th Grade

Dear Mr. Zauder and Mrs. Brass,

I would like to personally thank you both for coming to talk to our school about your incredible life story, and for your courage to delve into the harsh memories swimming through your mind. You are truly an amazing man, you've faced horrors beyond my dreams and still, after so much, conquered them. You have reminded me of how important it is to never give up and to never let myself or others turn their heads at the immoralities happening in the world today. Your story shall be one I will never forget and I am grateful for that fact. I do hope I am able to meet you in person one day, but if not, I hope you have long and joyful time ahead of you.

And also to Mrs. Karen Brass, I would also like to personally thank you for the wonderful presentation, without you I would probably never had heard such a story. And I am very thankful that I have.

P.S. I apologize for this being so rough, it was written off the top of my head!

- Thank you,

(Chris McLaughlin) Chris McLaughlin

529

David Zauder and Karen Brass,

Thank you so much for taking time out of your schedule to come and talk to us. The school is very honored to have heard your story. I found it extremely moving. I love the message you send out during the presentation about morals, integrity and compassion. Thank you for mentioning Darfur. I am personally very passionate about protecting human rights. I was able to see your presentation last year. I think it was very awesome for Mr. Zauder to come on stage and answer questions. I hope you start feeling well again.

Sincerely,
Jessie Zook

Dear Mr. Zauder,

I would like to thank you for letting me hear your story and past experiences even though it might be hard sometimes. I learned what it was really like to be in the holocaust, and at the camps. How it felt, and what you had to go through.

When I was listening to your story, I was inspired and had many thoughts that rushed in my head like, "Wow the Nazis really did this" and moments were I was just speechless. I had many different reactions to your story, some of shock others of sadness. One part that Karen told us was when you were on your knees in the coldness, trying to decide what language to speak. And you spoke polish right when your brother was walking. Then he came and carried you the rest of the way. That made me have a wave of emotion … it gave me hope.

I did not know that there was so much care, compassion and faith that people had for each other and for the people they loved. I noticed that when you had each other her, (like your brother and you) it made it easier to have hope and resilience. I felt that you would have been a lot more comfortable when you were in the arms of your brothers when you had to be swished in the cattle car.

Most of all I feel that it is so incredible that after all you went through, you are still an great person today and that you made it through, you survived. And I want to say that I will be an up stander in every situation I am in.

Again I want to thank you for sharing your breath-taking story with me. I hope you have a wonderful day. With all my respect.

Love,

Zoya

November 18, 2009

Dear David Zauder,

   I would like to thank you for sharing your story with the world. Your story made the Holocaust very personal and more real to me. It is still hard to believe human beings can torture, starve, kill, and enslave other human beings to the point that their eating the living person next to them. This happened to you on the train and it made me feel that humans can turn into beasts when put in the situation you where put in. Your story also inspired me to be a better person, to choose the high road, to stand up for myself and the people around me, to keep going, and to never give up. I feel that doing this could help keep the Holocaust from happening again, because if there had been a majority of people standing up for the people getting persecuted by the Nazis the Holocaust might not have happened.

   I feel that you will make it through this cancer and have more to contribute to this country as a cancer survivor. I hope you feel better soon. You are strong even if you hurt, so it's ok if you say you're hurt. People today will not kill you for that. Thank you for staying strong and sharing your story with us.

Sincerely,

Mikayla Patty-Fortner

Mikayla Patty-Fortner

P.S. You definitely contributed something to us. Thank you.

Dear Mr. David Zauder and Mrs. Karen Brass,

I can't thank you enough for coming to our school and sharing your touching and uplifting story of survival.

Karen, how you delivered your father's story was haunting. I felt about every emotion a person can experience during your presentation. I respect your dedication to making an impact in young people's lives. You have definately made an impact in my life. I will never forget your presentation — I'm sure it will stay in my memories for the rest of my life to come.

Mr. Zauder, when you made your appearance after your daughter had told your life story, I was absolutely riveted. You have an extremely strong presence that made me unable to look away. You are a hero, Mr. Zauder, and your story is one of hope, strength, and survival. I am honored to have met you. It has truly been a highlight of my life and I greatly thank you for giving my school this once-in-a-lifetime experience.

Sincerely,

Keira Sztukowski
—Sophmore
16 years old

November 19th, 2019

Dear Mr. Zauder,

I loved hearing your tragic story because you definately touched my heart. My name is Radiance Azura Bukari, and I am a thirteen year old African American girl. The Holocaust has always been a subject I desired to study. So far, I have not heard a true story of a Holocaust survivor make me feel so connected to that person just as yours did. My favorite part of your story was when you were told to attack those two German boys and you chose to refuse instead. Personally, that is what struck me the most because when I think about this cold, terrifying event, evilness comes to my mind; not kindness or humanity.

Although I am not Polish and don't know of any European history in my family, I can attempt to imagine what your life was like. Of course I will never truely know how your experience made you feel but I do have a clear idea from your daughter Mrs. Karen Z. Brass presenting it to us 7th and 8th graders. From that presentation, I have something important to take away; be greatful for the lives we have now in America because presently AND throughout history, there are/have been children in the midst of more harsh conditions. Today, our generation worries about not having a cell phone, not enjoying school, or disagreeing with their parents at home. But really, we are lucky to be able to communicate with people we know, to have the opportunity to gain an education, and even still be with our

534

parents at our age. That is one of the reasons that your story was so important to me; you contain a level of perseverance that I can't comprehend and I know that this is still true as your cancer struggle continues.

I am aware of the fact that sharing your story must have been a hard decision for you to make. But from my observation of the rest of my classmates, you have definitely made the right decision and I deeply thank you for that. I hope for the best for you & your family and pray that you will stay strong through cancer just as you did through the horrific torture of the Holocaust.

Best wishes,
Radhanee Bukari
Radhance Bukari
The Odyssey School, 8th grade

November 18, 2009

Dear Mr. Zauder,

     Thank you so much for all of the knowledge that I have gained to day. I have never heard something so touching and painful. I cannot in any way feel your pain. I never knew that prisoners had to walk from camp to camp. I can't believe that your brother came and got you when you could not walk any further. I can't imagine how bad you must feel now about what happened.

     The part that stood out to me the most was when you got told to go beat up the German boys but you told them to go study. That to me is the best role model, because you did the best thing possible. I will always keep that story in the back of my head. I never knew that someone could be so mature. I also never knew that the Jews got killed for praying when needed.

     I am also Jewish and through my nine years of Sunday school I have never found out more about the Holocaust than this. Almost all of my family got killed in the Holocaust and all that we have left is a pair of brass candlesticks. The only one that did survive was my grandpa and he passed away three years ago. So once again thank you so much for all of the knowledge you let me gain.

                 From,

                 Leo Lehrburger

Dear Mr. David Zauder,

Thank you so much for sharing your incredible story with us. It has forever changed me, and it completely amazed me how you survived. From now on, I will think twice about how lucky I am, and to always remember the 4 things to do everyday to be happy.

1. Activate your brain
2. Be good to your body
3. Honor your religon and family
4. Do something nice for someone else

Thank You Mr. Zauder,

Tina Giess

Dear Mr. David Zauder,

Thanks a lot for sharing your incredible story with us. You showed us how people should never quit fighting and should never quit hope. Miracles do happen and it seems that something more than luck helped you survive the hell on Earth. I also felt ashamed being human being as same as those Nazis that tortured all the jewish people (and killed them as well), I know that those memories will never go away but I hope that you will be able to recover from the shock. I would also like to ask if there were moment when you thought that you might not survive. And since I'm an exchange student from old Yugoslavia I would like to know if you knew anyone from that are and did you ever again saw any other Holocaust survivor. You can answer me on my e-mail kristijond@t-com.me or tell Ms Gill.

Thanks a lot
You are a survivor but more important
You are a fighter!

Yours faithfully,

Kristijan Dapčević

Ms. Karen Brass,

Thank you so much for coming in to my school on behalf of your father. your performance and story was incredible; It felt very real.
I also highly respect your father for living and surviving this.

I also respect that you added differences that everyone can create to build a better society and help everyone respect each other In order to avoid another occurrance like this from happening. Coming from a homosexual, I was flattered.

Thank you so much for visiting and Sharing your father's story as well as your morals.

2·4·2010

- Kevin

Dear David Zauder and Karen Brass,

Thank you so much for ~~the~~ time you took out of your day to come and talk to our class. The speech I heard yesterday from you was the most amazing speech I have ever heard. It is truly amazing what your whole family went through and how you stuck through it. I have been having some trouble in my life with stress and other things but your speech made me realize what the important things in life are. It taught me to not worry about the small things in life and to persist with whatever you do. I encourge you to share your families story with other schools because I know that they all will apreciate it and get a lot out of it. I want to thank you again for your time and what you have encouraged me to do.

        —Anthony Lederhos

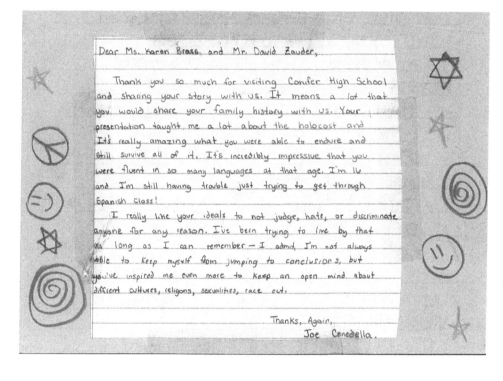

Dear Ms. Karen Brass and Mr. David Zauder,

Thank you so much for visiting Conifer High School and sharing your story with us. It means a lot that you would share your family history with us. Your presentation taught me a lot about the holocost and It's really amazing what you were able to endure and still survive all of it. It's incredibly impressive that you were fluent in so many languages at that age. I'm 16 and I'm still having trouble just trying to get through Spanish Class!

I really like your ideals to not judge, hate, or discriminate anyone for any reason. I've been trying to live by that as long as I can remember — I admit, I'm not always able to keep myself from jumping to conclusions, but you've inspired me even more to keep an open mind about different cultures, religons, sexualities, race ect.

Thanks, Again,
Joe Cenedella.

Dear Mr. Zauder, Mrs. Brass,
Thank you so much for coming to
talk to us. I have never heard a
story more inspiring▽ We hear about
the war and we know it was awful
but when we heard it first hand
tears flowed. As soon as I left
I called my mother I just wanted
to hear her voice, and eventually
she told me the stories my grandfather
had told her about the war. He was
a German immigrant turned U.S.
soldier (Army). Although nothing
compared to what you endured
it opened my eyes further.
I wish there had been more time
to ask you the plethera of questions
that still riddle my mind▽ Anyway
your story was a true gift to
hear and your 4 pieces of
advice will be taken to heart.

Thank You,
Rachel E Dyer
(Rachel E. Dyer)

Dear Mr. Zauder and Ms Brass,

Thank you both so much for coming to our school. I've been learning about the holocaust in almost every history and social studies class I've had since middle school, and it has never seemed so real to me till today. Hearing your life story, and then hearing you simply stand and speak seemed to shift the world's perspective for me. In some ways, I believe a part of me has changed. I've re-examined almost every aspect of my life, and realized things I may have never realized otherwise. In a way, it feels like my vision has grown wider and clearer, and I can see more of the world than ever before. I hope you continue to give this presentation for as long as you can.

Sincerely,

[signature] Parforce

Compass
Montessori SECONDARY SCHOOL

April 15, 2010

The administration,
teachers, and parents of
Compass Montessori High
School aim to nurture the
whole child, adapting to
meet each student's unique
intellectual, emotional,
social, physical, and
spiritual needs. Our goal is
to foster competent,
responsible, and innovate
problem solvers.
At Compass Montessori,
students will learn to
respect themselves, other
people, and the
environment. In addition,
we will strive to instill a lifelong love of learning in
every student using
genuine Montessori
methodologies and
Montessori trained
teachers.

4441 Salvia Street
Golden, CO 80403
Phone : (303) 271-1977
Fax   (303) 271-1984

Dear Mr. Zauder,

Compass Montessori High School students and teachers would like to offer our immense gratitude for allowing us to hear your history. Karen presented your stories of survival during the Holocaust with such candor and grace; we felt your presence and your message.

As a school of *peace education* and *social justice*, your story has changed our understanding of what those words mean. We were bluntly aware of our own by-standing capabilities, and were encouraged to look beyond ourselves. As educators, we need to have more of these moments in our classrooms. Your story had a greater impact than any of the Holocaust education work we have ever done.

Within the following pages, we hope you might see how sharing your experience will continue to educate and transform students who are longing to create peace and social justice for all of humanity. Thank you. We will never forget.

Respectfully yours,

Kristy Cash, Carrie Talcott, Eric Albright and Daniel Marsh
Compass Montessori High School Teachers

544

Compass Montessori High School Students

Dear Mr. Zauder,
I don't know how I can possibly fully express my gratitude; I am so thankful that you are willing to share your incredible story with the world. I am sure that it changes the lives of everyone who hears it, I know it changed mine. Your compassion and everlasting faith in humanity through one of the most horrible and devastating events in history is more than inspiring. There are so many powerful moments in your past and I was extremely moved by your strength and sacrifice. I loved when Karen made a point of showing how the Holocaust was an example of severe bystanding. I believe that this type of education is some of the most important for us to learn and I thank you for having the courage to share it with us. The part that touched me the most was the perfect unsuspected ending. I truly admire your ability to overcome something so terrible and continue to give back and contribute to this world. It is amazing to see how you got past this experience with such little hate and continue to have an optimistic attitude in life. I have always wanted to change this world for the better and you have proven to me that anyone has the ability to do so. It is difficult to hear about the trauma and brutality that you experienced, but I think it was the miracles that saved your life which finally brought tears to my eyes. I was amazed at how much good existed in people who were living in a world full of hate, it gives me hope. You have changed many lives and your story is one that I will never forget, it will continue to inspire me for the rest of my life. There is no doubt that you have made the contribution to this world that you worked so hard for, and so much more. Your determination and hard work have made a lasting impression that will never be forgotten. This story is more than a lesson, it is a gift to everyone you share it with. And it is gift that will stay in my heart forever. I cannot thank you enough. -Cheyenne Croy 18

Mr. Zuader,
Your experiences that your daughter shared with us were very upsetting by how you were treated, but were very inspirational on how you made it through the Holocaust. Hearing your experience has taught me that just being a bystander on something little can turn out to be a big problem. A part of the story that really got to me was how you were talking about the death march, and how when people fell, no one would help them, and how your brother was there for you when you fell. That was something I will never forget. It is amazing that you survived what you went through. It really makes me think of how I take daily life for granted. But after hearing your life story, and how traumatizing it must have been to grow up like that, I have learned to appreciate everything in my life, and to be thankful everyday that I wake up. Thank you so much Mr. Zauder, for allowing your daughter to share all of your life experiences from the Holocaust. -Tamara Thomas, 17

Dear Mr. Zauder,
This is actually the second time that I have heard your inspiring story. Your daughter spoke at my middle school up in Evergreen a few years ago. I have my own little struggles in my life, but stories like yours remind me to keep pushing myself and to never give up on myself. When Karen spoke about the death march and how your brother helped you nearly the entire way, it reminded me that when I am going through tough times, there are people out there that really want to help. If someone can get through all of the terror that you faced every day, and still become an amazing and accomplished person despite everything that happened, I can accomplish just about anything. Thank you and Karen for your work, and we at Compass will never forget. – Graham Stone, 16

Dear Mr. Zauder,
Your story has really changed how I look at life in the aspect of not acting like a victim. Also live each day to the fullest. Your story is truly a life changing one thank you for sharing it with the world. Thank you, ~Rachel Newton, 17

Dear Mr. Zauder,

Listening to this story, it really helped me get a better understanding of what happened. It made the horrors and disasters become very real. I knew that this happened but it seemed so outrageous that it in my mind it was not real. Hearing this personal story helped me understand. My family is Jewish and I could not imagine having the strength and courage to survive and live on.
Marc Fay age 17

Dear Mr. Zauder,

Words cannot describe how fortunate I feel to have heard your first hand account of the Holocaust and I'm so grateful for your contribution to our community and to the greater society. It's amazing that through miracles such as pinching the ink from your skin and encountering your brother on that fatal march you, like other survivors, endured so much torture without tears and hatred of your own. To have had so much forgiveness, so much compassion, is truly remarkable and to have heard your struggle through your daughter, and with such honesty and emotion reduced me to tears. Your have opened my eyes. I respect those like you who have gone on to educate other despite the pain it may bare and despite the misunderstandings many have regarding the Holocaust. You have inspired me to actively combat hatred within society and voice my opinion rather then shrinking in times of need. I sincerely thank you for your contributions to society through your music and your story.
-Gabii Burton, age 16

Dear Mr. Zauder,

I don't think that saying Thank You is nearly enough. You are a truly incredible man who has lived an incredible life, and thank you so much for letting us hear about it is quite powerful enough to describe the experience of hearing your life's journey. Everything your daughter told us last week has altered me. Whenever we feel inspired, I think that initial shock of Wow, this is something that I want to remember, imitate, or create sort of fades a little after the moment passes. After hearing your story on Thursday, I felt inspired to do something to help humanity, whether it is a great action that changes the world or small actions that change someone's world. I still feel that drive just as strongly today. The motivation comes entirely from your powerful personality. The thing that really struck me about your story was how you managed, through all the horrors surrounding you, to see the humanity in those people that were the subjects of such incomprehensible inhumanity. How you managed to look at the world around you and see an older man who was worse off than you, who had so little, and give him your only piece of bread. Thank you so much for sharing your remarkable life's journey with our school, I will never forget the things I heard April 8th, 2010.
-Meghan Marreel-Alley, 18

Dear Mr. Zauder

I appreciate so much that you have allowed and encouraged the sharing of your experiences during the Holocaust. When your daughter Karen came to speak to us, the whole time I had chills thinking about all that you experienced. During the entire presentation I was moved by every little miracle that happened, and by every horrid experience. One of the stories that moved me the most was when she told us how your brother helped carry you through a large portion of the Death March. Thinking about how amazing it was that you had your brother there made me think of my brother and how often I take him for granted. Your story has inspired me to spend as much time with my brother as I can. Furthermore I want you to know that your story has further strengthened my will for never forgetting the Holocaust. I will never let the Holocaust be forgotten and I will work tirelessly to help spread education because as of now it is up to my generation to continue reminding the world. Finally, thank you so much for allowing this opportunity to happen for us. I will never forget the presentation or your story, so thank you and bless you for everything you have done for this world. -Tyler Maydew (17)

546

Dear Mr. Zauder,

I greatly appreciate your eagerness to share your story with us. Although, we have studied many aspects of the Holocaust, hearing a personal account allows us to see the human beings among the numbers. Personally, I was deeply moved by your daughter's speech and it has encouraged me to know more of my own family history. Three of my great-grandparents were polish Jews during this time but did not survive the concentration camps. Hearing your daughter tell your story made me realize the responsibility I have to them. It was inspiring and I think it reminded us all how fortunate we really are. I sincerely thank you. Karla 17 ✓

Dr Mr. Zauder,

A thank you cannot completely encompass my gratitude to you for sharing your story with your daughter in order for her to share it with the world. Your personal strength and faith amazes me and inspires me. I believe that it is so important for the Holocaust to be talked about. In my family, all of my great grandfathers had served in WWII, and they never spoke about their experiences in the war. I think that the war and the Holocaust was swept under the rug in a sense, and the generations to follow WWII do not have a grasp on the horrors that so many innocents endured, because so many were ashamed or afraid of telling everyone about their experiences. I admire your courage to speak about your experiences, for I imagine it cannot be easy. The Holocaust needs to be remembered, and I believe that you and your daughter are doing a wonderful deed to humanity by sharing your story. I admire your strength to hold yourself proudly in the face of Nazi soldiers, and your work ethic is something I will strive to meet in my life. Your intuition and ability to learn astounds me, from changing the number in your tattoo to learning new languages. Every new story I heard about you was more empowering than the last. Although I didn't speak to you in person, I felt as if I got to know you, and I feel that your story has touched me, to the bottom of my soul. I wish now to strive to bring justice to humanity, and though I'm not sure how yet, I think stopping the genocide in Africa is a good start. I again cannot express how thankful I am to have learned your story. Your experiences have changed my perspective on compassion and life. I thank you.
Anastasia Abraham, 16 ✓

Dear Mr. Zauder,

For me, it was so important that your daughter came and shared your story with us. It really touched me because I can connect it so easily with my own experiences, visiting Sachsenhausen in Germany, and several Jewish cemeteries in Prague and Berlin, having visited the Holocaust Museum in D.C. and being both one of Jehovah's Witnesses and of German descent. It also opened up a discussion within our community that might not have happened otherwise. We talked about the Holocaust and our international trip to Czech, Germany and Russia last May. We talked about how unaware we sometimes are of tragedy in other parts of the world. We talked about Columbine, and the Oklahoma City bombing and the 9/11 terrorist attacks on the U.S. Karen's presentation really opened the channel for these discussions which are so so important. Not only that, but your story heightened my awareness of how unaware I am. Some of the things that stuck with me the most are how you treated those two German boys, while you were living with the American soldiers in Germany. The fact that Karen pointed out, no one is born hating anyone, that genocide and oppression are still happening in Sudan, Darfur, Rwanda, Uganda, Tibet. Especially striking are the definitions of Social Responsibility, Integrity, and Courage that we were presented with. How fitting they are. I love that you showed compassion throughout your experience. That provides such a great example to everyone who hears your story, to show compassion and humanity always, to contribute something to the world, to leave a legacy. So thank you, for your story, for surviving and having the courage to have your story told, and thank you to your daughter Karen, for working to make people aware and for sharing your story. It means the world. Thank you. ~Jessica, 18 ✓

Dear Mr. Zauder,

Thank you so much for sharing your story with our school. I think it helps a lot of people to realize that we are very lucky for everything that we have and to value those things. I just want to let you know that, at least for me, you are going to be an example how to confront the hard thing in life, and your story encouraged me to make myself be a better person. -Ana Sofia, 17 ✓

Dear Mr. Zauder,

Your inspirational story on your experiences in the Holocaust has changed the lives of so many people. I am so grateful that your daughter was able to change our lives as well. Your determination for life and your determination for success will always stay with me. Your story has made me realize to cherish everything and everyone in my life. You fought for your life, and stayed strong through the worst of times. Your life has changed mine, and I will remember your story for as long as I live. - Cami Moss, 17

Sydney K
2/10/99

Dear Mrs. Brass,
I thought your presentation was very inspirational. It showed me that I need to be more like mr. Zaunder in that helping people out is being more of a stand upster and not a bystander. But what really moved me was when mr. Zaunder found his brother and was reunited with him after he thought that all of his family was killed. After your speech you can definetly can count on me.

Dear Mrs. Karen Brass…

Your presentation I found wonderful, and quite touching. Your father's story was very amazing, the fact that he could survive that long without his family, without any friends, with barley any food, and sometimes even no shoes, and then finding his brother in the end, after being away from him for so long. Its pure luck that his own brother picked him up when he fell, and was about to be killed. I know you probably hear that a lot from others, or... Not... but I have to say that was the best part of your father's miraculous journey through the holocaust. Now that I have heard your amazing speech, I will do some tings different, that I never have done before. I will no longer be a by-stander. Your amazing speech has taught me a lot, and I'm not kidding about that, I swear. I hope you go to many other different schools and teach a lot more people about this heart-breaking, heart-stopping story. It would be an amazing book. But that's just my opinion. Wish you, and your father and the rest of your family good luck through the rest of your lives.
-Theresa

548

Feb. 14, 2♥11

Dear Karen,
     I had to put into writing how
your presentation on your father's
life impacted my 8th grader. I
have never heard her react to
something so passionately. She
re-tells it to anyone who will
listen. She shared with me how
she reacted with a combination
of goosebumps, tears and awe
at your father's experiences.

     Sophie tells me many of her
friends had similar reactions
to your words. I suspect, though,
that my daughter was especially
moved. She doesn't impress
easily, so it caught me off guard
that she was so intrigued.

     You must be one heck of a
speaker! You kept the interest
of a whole lot of kids who are
by their very age, so far removed
from the events of WWII. Thank
you so much for spreading the
story of your father. We all
MUST NEVER FORGET.

sincerely,
Cathy Didier

549

Jasper Davidson
Period 7th · Kelly
Feb· 14th · 2011

Dear Mrs. Brass

    I honestly have no words to describe how i feel, The feeling trapped inside me is indiscribable. I feel like crying. The words you spoke made it impossible to think normally afterwards, i feel trapped inside my own thoughts — unable to get out. Mr. David Zauder and Mrs. Karen Brass possess characterists such as, hopefullness bravery, strength, courage, trustworthiness, honesty and simply amazing. I would like to have all those. The presentation brought not only tears to my eyes, but gave me strength to stand up to bullies. I learned if you work as hard as you can you can acomplish anything you set your mind to. I loved the presentation very much. The tatoo made me very emontional because i remeber how you said it basically meant they took away their identies. To me that tattoo would show honer but im sure thats hard to think of it like that. Thank you so much for showing the story i learned alot, thank you.

~ Jasper Davidson
7th grade Mrs. Kelly
Febuary 14th · 2011

February 25, 2011

Dear Mrs. Brass,

Thank you so much for presenting your dad's story about the Holocost. It meant a lot that you shared with us, especially me because I am also Jewish. After your presentation I went home and talked to my grandma to see if we had any family connection with the Holocost. Turns out my great grandparents were about to be killed, because they have dark hair and eyes, so they escaped through the Soviet Union and took a boat to the U.S.

I remember you telling us about your dad's tatoo and how when they thought it was a 3 instead of an 8 and saved his life. Thanks again!

Sincerely,
Jodie Bluestein

5/24/2010

Dear Mister Zauder,

My name is Donavon Zerbest I go to bell. When your daughter came and presented your story I was speechless, the way that you persevered throughout the Holocaust was astonishing. Mister Zauder you are a brave man ,we have been studying the Holocaust for around 2 and a half months. We have heard a lot of stories but yours hands down was my favorite.

Things we have studied so far are ones like how the people of the Holocaust where oppressed, and how they where resisted against Nazis in the concentration camps. When the people of the Holocaust told us there stories you could here in the way they spoke the trauma that they had gotten from the experience that taught us about how true this was and that this should never happen again and that the reason the war started was because of discrimination and not being able to settle differences.

This country can learn a lot about the holocaust and noticing small things before it escalades into a full racial discrimination or worse another genocide. The holocaust was a genocide that could have been easily avoided by just making sure

552

that racism does not lead to things that can completely go out of proportion and hurt many minorities, religious groups, and different people. We shouldn't judge someone because they are Black, White, East coast, West coast, Christen, Jewish, because it all comes down to one thing the simple fact that all of us are humans and that we all are equal. Not one man is better than the other humans should have respect for each other no matter what.

In my community what I can do to make a difference is to stand up for myself or others when discriminated against. This simple plan has a big effect it tells people that its not alright just to pop off a racist remark at someone because of there beliefs, skin color, or individuelalities. People can slowly learn to except people for who they are and as you can see in our country today people have learned its ok to go to church with someone who's a different skin color, its alright if you play basket ball with a kid who has a different religious view than yours because once again we are all human.

Mr.Zauder I appreciate your time for reading my letter you are a courageous man thank you once a again for letting your daughter come in and telling your story. I hope you enjoyed the letters it was a way of showing how thankful we are for your story. Thank you Mr.Zauder I hope we can here back.

Dear Mr. Zauder,

My name is Jordan Walkup, and I'm an 8th grader at Bell Middle

School. I am writing you because as you probably know, your daughter,

Karen came and spoke on April 9th, and told us your story. Over the past

couple months; we've been studying the Holocaust in my Language Arts

class. We've watched several films, and read lots of literature. We have

also studied the ways of resistance many Jews and non-Jews used while

in the death camps.

So far over this unit I have learned many new things about the

Holocaust, this includes the 5 million other people who were killed

besides the Jews. The Holocaust is a fascinating, but terrible event in

history. So many different people and Jewish people were oppressed in

death camps, and so many were tricked with awful things such as; they

were told they would get nice warm showers, but then were dead

within a matter or 2 minutes because of the gas. The Nazis also had their "prisoners" write postcards to family members saying that they were okay when they were really being beaten and starved. Before this unit, I never knew how awfully tortured these Jewish, and non-Jewish people were in the death camps, and how many terrible things the Nazis did to make their stay even worse.

There are many things we as a society can do to never let the Holocaust happen again, such as; sticking up for people being mistreated. A major reason the Holocaust happened in the first place. No one stuck up for the Jews, or anyone else, they just let it happen. Also to treat others how you would like to be treated. So, if you don't want to be mistreated, then don't mistreat others. One more thing we as a society to can do to never let the Holocaust happen again is too be nice to others. If everyone was nice to everyone, there would be no problems.

The things that I can do to stop discrimination against others are; I need to start being nicer, because usually I'm not very friendly, so I need to work on that. Another thing is too not be racist, or discriminate against other religions. I never was racist, but I just need to keep it that way. One more thing I can do to make a difference is too stick up for others, when I see them being mistreated. When I'm walking around school, or wherever I am, at least once during the day, I hear or see something racist or mean. So next time I hear something like that, I need to stick up for that person. If I kept doing these things for the rest of my life, hopefully, there will be no trouble, or drama. Also these things could make a difference in the world.

Thank you so much for having your daughter come to our and share your story with our 8th grade class! It gave my insight a new outlook towards the Holocaust. I hope you and Karen are doing well! I promise I will do my best to stick up for others and make the world a better place, Have a great day.

Sincerely,

Jordan Walkup

May 24, 2010

Dear, Mr. Zauder,

My name is Breanna Lynn Trujillo and I am an 8th grade student here at Bell middle school. I would just like to say the way your daughter Karen Brass spoke to us about your story of surviving the Holocaust, really got me thinking, and since then I have been trying to make sure that I take a lot of pictures of all of my family for the future so that if anything happens I'll always have pictures. And that I make sure I know my family history. And from doing my research about my family I found out that a famous person from the Civil War I forget his full name, but his last name is McClellan he is my great, great, great, great, great grandpa. Any ways back to school, we have been studying what it is to resist, how the Holocaust could happen, and what happened before, during, and after the Holocaust.

From the Holocaust, we have learned that it had began very secretive, and as they got more and more people, then more and more people began to notice and ask questions.

And that the Nazi's tattooed ever one in the camps with different numbers, and when your number was called you would have to up to the smoke tower things, and you would be gassed and then burned to your death.

As a society, we have learned that we all need to pay more and closer attention to what's all going on in our communities, so that if this does try to start again, then we can try and stop it sooner so not so many people have to die. We also as a society need to not be prejudice and if we can't stop it as a whole, then we at least need to minimize the amount in specific places. Such as towns, cities, communities, even schools.

The question though that keeps running through my head though is what can I do to help make the change. And what can I do to make the difference. Well my answer I guess now would be to have more respect for people of other races, and if I see someone treating someone else different for a specific reason such as . . . they may be a different color or race, they might have a different religion, or they just might dress different than you, but now I know what I need to do, because usually I would just leave it be and not do anything, and I *would wait for the problem to get bigger and bigger and finally when something would affect me, then I would do something. But not anymore now I'm going to actually stand up for someone, even if them being made fun of or teased doesn't affect me, because maybe in the long run it might end up coming back to hurt me. (it's called KARMA!)*

Well anyways thank you very much Mr. Zauder for letting your daughter share your guy's story. I hope you feel much better and I hope that you all live very healthy lives to continue to tell you survival stories with the world and make sure they are aware of what had happened.

Sincerely,

Breanna Lynn Trujillo 8th grade

cause others to follow. Whenever I see someone getting picked I should do something about and not be a bystander like most people. There are a lot of things I can do to make a difference and I will try my best to do it and prevent more bad things to happen.

I want to thank you and your daughter for sharing your story it must be hard to hear it a lot. I hope you are doing well right now you have a sad story but I enjoyed it too. Thank you very much again for sharing your story.

Sincerely,

Will Taylor

November 18th, 2009

Dear Mr. Zauder,

Thank you for letting your daughter share your horrific experience in the Holocaust. Your daughter's presentation was so extraordinary. It especially struck me because the torture the Nazis did to everyone. Something from your story that really struck me was when your brother came and picked you up on the death march. He came and helped you up and I thought "Wow, I have never seen such a beautiful moment in my life!" This affected me so dearly because from what I know right now there has never been such a horrible event in our history, yet even today people still try to exterminate races like in Africa. I don't like this and I hope not many will repeat that mistake constantly.

For you Mr. Zauder and your daughter, I have learned that this mistake will show us how bad the world can get. I have learned to never let this mistake happen again, ever. I personally don't want the whole world full of hatred and murder. My family has the same reaction as I do because our whole family believes the world must be safer and not be overruled by a certain race. Again your daughter Karen did a magnificent job presenting and describing an unbelievably hard subject. I think she did a job/presentation that no one I knew could do. I am very proud of her.

Sincerely from,

Estela Marmolejo-Daher

Estela Marmolejo-Daher
Student of Odyssey

Mr. David Zauder and Mrs. Karen Brass,
   Thank you for coming to my school on Tuesday to
share your personal histories, story, and experience. I
appreciate the time you shared with us and
am grateful for the opportunity to learn about
the Holocaust, especially as it helps us to create
a better future. I will keep it in mind
and try to improve the world bit by bit
within my own sphere of influence. Once
again, thank you for your time.

                            Sincerely,
                            Kaden Powell

With Special

Thanks

Karen,
Thanks again for coming
to Belmar. Students are
still talking about being
"Standupsters!"

                    Ry

Karen —
I just wanted to say
Thank you for taking
the time to share with
us your father's amazing
story. He is blessed to
have you ... :) It's an honor
to serve customers like you
and your family in our
store.
Thanks again :) "Team"
Kelly Gay

Feb 2009

Dear Karen,

...just a huge Thanks for giving that awesome talk and answering questions at CHS. It was inspirational and I'm so glad I had the opportunity to attend this year.

    I so admire and appreciate you putting the immense energy it takes to do this into such a giving and educational experience for our youth. It is just the kind of example they need in today's world —

    I'm so glad we're part of the same "village" !
love & gratitude — Katie Joe.
Enjoy this meal with your family!

563

2008

Dear Karen,

    I just wanted to drop you a note and tell you how much I enjoyed your presentation at CHS on Thursday. Thank you so much for sharing your dad's story. I know it must be a very difficult and emotionally draining thing to do.

    It was so wonderful to see your dad and hear from him directly. What an amazing man, and how nice that he is able to share in the raising of your children.

    I was proud of our community's teenagers who sat respectfully, rapt in attention. You get a lot of credit for that though, because many of them would not have been able to do that if your presentation was not so compelling. Jenna told me that the boy who raised his hand at the end and thanked you for coming, had badly beaten up a freshman boy just last week. So maybe your message got through to him. That's pretty powerful.

    I spoke to my sister, and her oboe teacher's name was Souder, not Zouder. Sorry, I was a little girl at the time so it sounded similar to me.

    Congratulations and appreciation to you for your good work.

Sincerely,

564

March 27, 2003

Dear Karen,

Thank you so much for sharing the stories and such a wonderful message with our Religious School students. Your visit was both sobering and empowering for them and I know that your words are engraved on their memories. (I could tell by how attentively they were listening!) I was also impressed by the way you adjusted your presentation for two different age groups. And I noticed that the adults present, including me, were deeply moved by your words as well.

We all look forward to making your visits an annual event. Again, thank you for giving such an important gift so generously.

B'shalom,
Irene Clurman

565

Dear Karen,

I keep replaying in my head the events that brought you and your father into my life allowing me to bring your story to 400 people. It all seems so serendipitous! You were needed and supposed to speak with these students last week. Their reaction confirms that. Your father's story is inspiring, heroic and beyond our comprehension but your ability to share it brings his story alive. Without your passion and skills for public speaking your father's story would have remained lost. Instead, you have changed the lives of so many. You have given these students and anyone listening hope in the times of darkness and strength in the times of weakness. You opened their eyes to a world they thought they knew but had no idea.

In class after your presentation, we spent an hour talking about Darfur. They had so many questions. They repeated the same words over and over again in regards to Darfur: Respect, motivation, sympathy, understanding, caring, never again. How can I help? How can I make sure this never happens again? What can we do? These were all questions asked desperately by the students. These students were inspired by your father's actions and your ability to portray them in words. They discussed how people needed to treat each other. What its like to be bullied and put down for one reason or another. What its like to just stand by. They discussed what they need to change and they were truly motivated. For a lot of them, this passion will not end and they will go on to do courageous things. They are inspired and it is through your passion. This is an incredible gift and ability and I cannot express how thankful I am for sharing it with us. I hope that your presentation at Conifer High School will become an annual fixture in our school and our community. Your gift is something to look forward to when so often we lose hope and purpose. Thank you, thank you, and again thank you.

Sincerely,

Amanda Fuenzalida
CHS History Teacher
2008

566

To Karen Brass,

Thank you for your unselfish retelling of the personal journey that your Father had to take as a child to survive the Holocaust. No child should suffer what he has had to bear and live with these memories. I am so glad that he is able to enjoy and participate in your children's upbringing.

I love that you add the thought in the students minds to not tolerate the injustice of a bully. Also the way that you weave the small human kindnesses into the story shows that in the very worst of times some humanity and goodness shines through and offers a glimmer of hope for life.

I know that this is hard for you to retell and refine into words that can have a positive result in times of much freedom and relative peace for Jewish people in America, for injustice not to be tolerated, freedom not to be taken for granted, for bullying not to be just watched, and worldwide mans inhumanity to man not to be ignored in places like Croatia or Darfur or many other places.

You tell the story so beautifully with an emphasis on positive human values which are what we teachers at Beth Evergreen aspire to convey.

Thank you for all the kindness, respect, humanity, dignity that you bring to the students. It will not be forgotten as they grow into adults.

Sincerely,
Karen Bennett
Hebrew School Teacher
2005

"Be a Standupster®," is my motto. Early in my book, I shared a story that I feel a need to refer to again. I once saw at a bus stop an advertisement for Heineken beer. It had a picture of two people, one at the bar, and one about to leave with car keys in hand. The slogan read in capital letters, THERE ARE NO INNOCENT BYSTANDERS. That is my message, plainly and simply. We are all in this world together, and we are responsible for one another. We are truly our brother's keepers. We are each responsible for what we see happen and allow to happen on our watch. Are we willing to take action, is the question. With a deeper understanding of what happens to those who needed help and didn't receive it, I hope the answer, after reading this book, is a resounding yes.

My hope is that, in reading about parts and pieces of my life and my ability to pick myself up by my bootstraps, and carry on with a strong, positive willingness to grow and to heal, you will find yourself empowered, just as I have. If my father could get through what he survived, and develop into who he became, what is holding anyone back?

> *In everyone's life, at some time, our inner fire goes out. It is then burst into flame by an encounter with another human being. We should all be thankful for those people who rekindle the inner spirit.* ~ Albert Schweitzer

Our family in the mountains of Colorado

Biography of Karen Z. Brass

Second-Generation Holocaust Educator and Speaker

Karen Z. Brass is the daughter of David Zauder, a Holocaust survivor and detainee in the Kraków Ghetto, enslaved in the Płaszów work camp, the Auschwitz death camp, the Flossenbürg concentration camp, and the Sachsenhausen concentration camp, as well as being forced to take the death march from Auschwitz. Brass has provided her father's personal account concerning the atrocities that befell his family and other victims of the Holocaust since 1982.

Her father's story is impressive. A Polish-born citizen, his experiences of being taken into slavery for five years by the Nazi's, as well as losing both parents to murder, is powerful. His survival, liberation, and immigration to the United States, and his life accomplishments, in spite of his horrific past, are impressive.

Brass shares the lessons of the Holocaust through her second-generation eyes. She believes no one should ever stand silent in the face of hatred. While sharing her father's story of survival, she weaves in her thoughts concerning what it means to be a bystander, and how to eliminate discrimination, as it is cruel, irrational, and only flourishes when bystanders are present and do not act. She promotes being a **Standupster®** instead of being a bystander. She defines a **Standupster®** as any human being who chooses to take a stand and use their sense of personal responsibility and moral leadership to take action to stop bullying and discrimination in today's school environments as well as in the public domain.

She started her website www.standupsters.com, and Standupster® program as a nonprofit organization. She has as well her company, *Can I Count On You? LLC*, to make what she teaches more accessible to teachers, parents, and students. Hatred of people's differences must be stopped, and she promotes that together we are stronger because of our unique qualities. Brass also teaches why it is important to put an end to stereotyping, selecting scapegoats, and the proliferation of racism and prejudice.

Brass is happily married to David Seth Brass, and they live together in the mountains of Colorado with their two children, Shannah and Adam, and Karen's terminally ill father, David Zauder. She is the mother to their two children, each with learning and physical disabilities, including autism. She has seen firsthand what bullying does to self-esteem through her children's eyes, as well as through the eyes of their friends who didn't know what to do to help them. She enlisted their assistance by first educating them and their parents on her children's unique strengths as well as their disabilities. She then focused on building a stronger community, surrounding each child with friends who understand, care, and have learned the meaning of compassion and personal accountability for their own actions. Watching these other children rise to the occasion of not allowing bullying to occur in their presence, has been a great source of strength and hope for Brass and her children.